T0329917

HARVARD ECONOMIC STUDIES

Volume 160

The studies in this series are published under the direction of the Department of Economics of Harvard University. The department does not assume responsibility for the views expressed.

Economic Analysis of Product Innovation

The Case of CT Scanners

Manuel Trajtenberg

Harvard University Press
Cambridge, Massachusetts
London, England   1990

Library of Congress Cataloging-in-Publication Data

Trajtenberg, Manuel.
  Economic analysis of product innovation : the case of CT scanners
  / Manuel Trajtenberg.
    p. cm—(Harvard economic studies ; v. 160)
  Includes bibliographical references.
  ISBN 0-674-22540-6 (alk. paper)
  1. Medical imaging equipment industry.   2. Tomography, Emission—
Equipment and supplies.   3. New products—Management—Case studies.
  I. Title. II. Series.
  HD9995.I432T7   1990   89-19959
  338.4'7681761—dc20   CIP

To my beloved parents,
Sara and Julio

Acknowledgments

This book originates in work I did at Harvard University, where I benefited from the support and encouragement of many teachers and fellow students. I am particularly indebted to Richard Caves, Zvi Griliches, and Michael Spence, and to Daniel McFadden of MIT, for their guidance, patience, and generosity. I owe the most to Zvi Griliches, who nurtured my interest in technical change, imparted to me the highest standards in the conduct of empirical research, and lent me his support in so many ways. I feel privileged to have been in close contact with Zvi all these years, as admiring disciple, as respectful friend.

Morris Teubal ignited my interest in innovation during my studies at the Hebrew University in Jerusalem, and offered precious support and encouragement at that early stage. I carried out much of the research for the book at the National Bureau of Economic Research in Cambridge. I am most grateful for the institutional and material support provided by the Bureau, and to the many people there who contributed to my work. Summanth Addanki, John Bound, Rochelle Furman, Adam Jaffe, Ariel Pakes, Andrei Shleifer, and Alan Siu deserve special mention. I was also fortunate to work with Shlomo Yitzhaki, with whom I collaborated on related joint research. Several colleagues at Tel Aviv University offered helpful comments and suggestions at various stages of the writing, and Ezer Soref gave me invaluable research assistance.

Many people helped me gather data on CT scanners and contributed to my grasping the complexities of the technology; among them Philip Judy of the Harvard Medical School and Gerald Cohen of the Texas Medical School deserve special thanks. I am also grateful to the firms that provided me with most valuable information on their CT operations: Elscint, General Electric, Omnimedical, Technicare, Picker, Siemens, Toshiba, and Varian; I extend my thanks to Siemens Medical Systems for permission to reproduce figures 2.4 and 2.5.

My deepest gratitude goes to my dear wife, Nadine, not only for her unwavering emotional support, but also for her extensive contribution to the substance of this book. I am very fortunate to have had her by my side—friend, companion, and peer, all in one.

Contents

Economic Analysis of Product Innovation

Introduction

One of the most remarkable features of modern industrial economies is their relentless ability to expand and improve the universe of goods and services available to society. Indeed, if we look back in time and compare the economic world of our grandparents to ours, we are not likely to be most impressed by changes in, say, the relative prices of given goods, the extent of monopoly power, or the content of macro-policies prevalent then and now. Instead, we will quite certainly find the most striking differences in the number, variety, and quality of goods and services at their and our disposal. Of course, there are also great disparities in the sheer quantities consumed (which are primarily linked in turn to process innovations), but with few exceptions "more" is inextricably linked to "better."

Today's standard set of household appliances and devices is a microcosm embodying a great deal of this remarkable tale of dynamic performance: personal computers, "intelligent" telephones, video cassette recorders, sound systems of astonishing fidelity, programmable microwave ovens, all these and many more simply did not exist, and were not even dreamt of, just a few decades ago. Neither did ultrasound and Computed Tomography (CT) scanners, tiny pacemakers and hearing aids, and similar technological marvels that have contributed enormously to the quality of health care that we enjoy today. And even before we had time to grasp fully the extent of the revolution brought about by microelectronics, new synthetic materials, bioengineering, and now superconductivity promise to bring about new, sweeping "gales of creative destruction" (in Schumpeter's famous words). This is undoubtedly what the dynamic performance of the economy is mostly about, at least in this second half of the twentieth century, and probably what best characterizes today the comparative performance of economic systems, countries, and sectors.

The prolonged exposure to a steady flow of product innovations has affected our perceptions of things to come as much as our immediate well being. In fact, we have grown so accustomed to it that our overall welfare depends in no small way on the expectation that technical change will keep delivering indefinitely an ever improving menu of goods. Accordingly, our disappointments as consumers are often due to delays, real or imaginary, in the ability of the economy to turn the all-encompassing promise of technology into reality, rather than to failures to satisfy our appetite for things known. How can it be, we ask in disbelief, that we have not yet conquered cancer, built commercial aircraft that would fly at many times the speed of sound, or seen the spread of two-way television networks? Why do cellular phones still cost hundreds of dollars, video-phones thousands, sophisticated robots millions, and trips to the moon billions? Why has bioengineering failed to turn out more than just a handful of "wonder drugs" after more than a decade of intense efforts, rosy expectations, and high stock prices? Will that be the case also with superconductivity?

Of course, for most of humanity those questions are altogether incomprehensible and painfully irrelevant: the third world is still struggling for bread and shelter, not for yet another electronic gadget. And even the industrialized countries still exhibit vast disparities of riches, so that for many in our midst technology and technological expectations are also far removed. Important and unpleasant as those facts are, they do not invalidate the perception regarding the prominence of innovation in our lives. There is after all such a thing as a technological frontier, and yes, it is at least as important to know where society is gravitating, in the wake of sweeping technical advances, as where it stands now. Thus it should not offend anybody's sense of fairness if I articulate, perhaps a bit too stridently, a feeling of awe at the sight of that frontier relentlessly receding before our often incredulous eyes.

The range of new or dramatically improved products at our disposal is extraordinarily broad and comprises virtually every conceivable area of production and consumption. Such conspicuous abundance and diversity conceal, however, the fact that there is a key commonality to the great majority of items now figuring in the available menu of goods, namely, the ever growing power of electronics. In fact, there is probably as much in common today between, say, a jet fighter and a CT scanner, as between either of them and its corresponding predecessor of a generation ago: both pack enormous computer power, and virtually every one of their functions depends upon electronic systems and components in ways that would be impossible to replicate with any other existing technology. The crucial phenomenon, though, does not reside just in the ubiquitousness of the silicon wafer: the point is that electronics has proved to have the inherent potential for persistent and manifold technical progress along its main performance dimensions; and moreover, that those quantum advances impinge upon a wide range of applications, bringing about a reshaping of the universe of goods and services at our disposal, not their mere proliferation.

Take for example the number of individual components that can be put on a single chip. In the early sixties an integrated circuit comprised just a handful of them; in the early eighties there were over one hundred thousand; and as we approach the end of the decade the number of components has reached one million. The implications of those figures are mindboggling, considering that the amount of operations that a chip can perform (process, store, transmit, or otherwise transform information), and the speed at which those things can be done, are a function of the number of components on a chip. As a consequence of those momentous advances, a personal computer today is thousands of times more powerful, versatile, and efficient than the first mainframe computers were. A simple digital watch that can be bought today for a few dollars was a technological impossibility at the time when the Sputnik was launched. CT scanners, requiring the collection, processing, and visual display of millions of pieces of information in a few seconds, are almost as much a commonplace in hospitals today as X rays were a generation ago. These are the things that come to mind when the notion of product innovations is invoked, and this is why product innovations have become such a prominent feature of our economic landscape. To insist, progress in the leading technology of our time has been so dramatic that it has brought about, time and again, swift *qualitative* changes in the material world around us, changes that surely cannot be expressed simply as variations in prices or quantities.

Economics has come a long way from the days when technological progress was regarded by and large as "manna from heaven," feeding the residual of aggregate production functions and hence having little to do with economic phenomena proper (save for its consequences). Few will seriously dispute today the contention that innovation (not *invention*) is first and foremost an economic activity, governed by the same universal forces and motives that determine more conventional undertakings, such as production or physical investment.[1] By the same token, it is now widely recognized that the behavior of economic agents, producers and consumers alike, has to do with the design and choice of products and qualities as much as with the attaching and pondering of price tags. Yet many economists continue to regard prices as the paramount economic entity, and their formation and fluctuations as the prime, if not solely legitimate, object of study. This manifest bias is deeply rooted in the reigning paradigm, and hence reflects the associated system of professional incentives and rewards more than the underlying economic reality. More important, those perceptions have been molded by the very fact that innovations come about in dimensions other than prices and quantities, often far removed from the economist's turf, and hence cannot be easily apprehended in terms amenable to economic analysis. Therefore, the challenge lies in devising the conceptual and methodological tools that will help bring the formidable apparatus of economics to bear on those elusive dimensions. In particular, I believe that it is crucial to be able to quantify product innovation, in order to advance significantly our understanding of technological advance.

Indeed, many of the leaps in the study of technical change have occurred in the form of empirical breakthroughs, based on the gathering of new kinds of data or in the application of novel techniques to their analysis. That was certainly the case with the monumental work of Simon Kuznets, and with the pioneering studies of Abramovitz, Solow, Griliches, Schmookler, Denison, and Mansfield, to mention some of the most prominent. The realization that technical change has been the major force propelling modern economic growth (rather than capital accumulation) is perhaps one of the most important empirical findings in economics, and one that provided the drive for a great deal of theoretical pondering. Likewise, the econometric evidence to the effect that various aspects of technical advance are indeed endogenous to the economic system (such as diffusion, investment in R&D, the rate of patenting, and so on), has changed forever our perception of such phenomena.

Measurement is important not only for purely scientific purposes: we live in what may be called the "quantified society," that is, a human milieu where anything that counts is to be assigned a figure or, to put it

1. In contrast to innovation, *invention* refers to the creation of new knowledge (primarily scientific), regardless of whether or not such knowledge ends up having economic significance (the distinction between discovery and invention often found in older literature parallels the now accepted invention-innovation dichotomy).

more bluntly, where the relevance of things seems to depend upon our ability to quantify them. In our society numbers are not just a means to summarize certain aspects of reality so as to make it more comprehensible. Instead, they have become a part of reality itself, perhaps even an arbiter of reality: by signaling what is supposed to be important and what is not (that is, the quantifiable versus the merely qualitative), figures mold our perceptions, manipulate our sensitivities, and direct the focus of our attention.

There are probably as many dangers as there are advantages, moral and otherwise, to this self-imposed "tyranny of numbers," but that is not the concern here. The point is that our perceptions of economic performance and of economic well being might be seriously distorted because we have not yet succeeded in attaching numbers to the fruits of innovation. Yes, we do have fairly good measures of productivity growth, and yes, we do know how to correct prices so that economic aggregates would reflect real rather than nominal changes and even incorporate the effect of some moderate quality improvements. And yet the sweeping changes occurring in the universe of goods and services at our disposal do not leave much of an imprint in the statistics. We are as much in the dark with respect to the welfare consequences of product innovations as previous generations were with respect to the growth of product, in the days when national accounts were a far-fetched dream. The trouble lies not just in the ignorance of facts (and of underlying processes), but in the potential for misperceptions of the economic reality, and hence for gross errors of judgment in any attempt to manipulate such reality.

Responding to those concerns, the main objective here is, simply put, to seek an answer to the question "how much innovation there has been, in a certain field, over a certain period of time," and, in so doing, to illuminate some of the contours of the innovative process itself. The magnitude of innovations will be equated here with their value as this is understood by economists, that is, the money equivalent of the social benefits stemming from new goods and from improvements in the qualities of existing products. Drawing primarily from the "characteristics approach" to demand theory and from the econometrics of discrete choice, I put forward a practical methodology for the assessment of such benefits. The basic idea is as follows: in every period the market displays a set of different models of the product class under consideration, each offering the consumer a different bundle of attributes and price. Consumers choose one brand out of the available set, as they try to match the characteristics of products with their preferences. The econometric analysis of data on such choices may allow one to uncover the structure of preferences for the attributes of the product, which can then be used to evaluate changes in the set of goods. As the technology evolves, new products (that is, new vectors of attributes) are introduced, old products disappear, and the attributes of existing products are enhanced. By evaluating this continuous stream of product innovations with the method just outlined, one can obtain the social gains of innovation from one period to the next.

Since the acid test of any methodology lies in its actual implementation, I will apply the framework just outlined to a particular innovation, namely, CT scanners, one of the most remarkable innovations in medical technology of recent times. Much of the book centers on the detailed study of this innovation, the intention all along being not so much to learn about its particulars, as to use the case at hand to tackle issues of general interest. Indeed, I believe that one needs to submerge oneself into the details of specific cases in order to gain a better understanding of the intricacies of the innovative process: technical change has become an exceedingly complex phenomenon, far removed from the immediate spheres of personal experience, and hence introspection or pure reasoning alone will not suffice to grasp it. Neither will, for that matter, vast cross sections or panels (with their unavoidable "flatness"), made of data on what *can* be measured on a wide scope, and not necessarily on what *needs* to be measured.

This, then, is the answer given here to the perennial question, why a case study? We definitely need to know much more about the basic facts of technology at the microlevel before indulging in sweeping generalizations (or, worse still, before trying to rationalize the presumed "stylized facts" of this area—do we really know what they are?). The choice of CT scanners for this purpose responded to a variety of reasons, among them the well-defined nature of the product and its attributes, the suitable number of brands offered in the market, the fact that it commanded a great deal of public attention and hence generated much needed data, and so on. To be honest, I was also captivated by the sophistication and glamor of the technology of CT. As the story of this innovation unfolds throughout the book, I hope the reader will come to share my fascination and enthusiasm with the case: CT is one of those rare junctures where advanced technology, medicine, and economics meet, engendering some of the best of what our age has to offer.

Taking advantage of the uniqueness of estimates of the value of innovations obtained in this project, I proceed to address a number of outstanding issues in this area: the nature of the interaction between innovation and diffusion, the rate of return to research and development (R&D), the validity of quality-corrected price indices based on hedonic price regressions, and the significance and usefulness of patent-based indicators (including patent citations). One of the key findings has to do with the profile of gains from innovation over time: they are very large (and rising) early on, and then decline rapidly, carrying a low-level tail into the future. Thus it seems that the greatest benefits to society occur not at the very introduction of an innovation, nor in the wake of its refinement when the technology is already well established, however dazzling those later improvements might seem. Instead, the largest gains appear to come about with the—relatively early—advent of a model in which some key attributes (including price) are greatly improved, turning the new product from an ingenious into a practical device that can command wide appeal. Examples abound: the Ford Model T car, the DC-3 aircraft, the UNIVAC I computer. Such a pattern can be rationalized in terms of an initial phase of scale economies, promptly followed by sharply diminishing returns. What is peculiar in the context of innovation is that these "nonlinearities" take place simultaneously in three different dimensions: in the production of innovations, in the utility generated by them, and in determining the size of the market for the products embedding those innovations. An important implication of this finding, if typical, is that we may be missing a great deal if we concentrate our empirical efforts in the study of industries at the time when they have already reached maturity. A closely related point is that the reliance upon the hedonic method to create "quality-adjusted" price indices may be quite appropriate for sectors experiencing moderate rates of product innovation, but it might be seriously mistaken if applied to new, technologically dynamic product classes.

As already mentioned, I rely throughout on well-known theoretical building blocks and econometric models and techniques. The novelty is to be found, perhaps, in bringing together the various components of the methodological apparatus, and certainly in the actual execution of a project of this kind. Much of what there is to be learned in the coming chapters lies, I believe, in pondering the various anomalies and dilemmas that presented themselves quite unexpectedly in the course of the empirical work. Thus, for example, I had to contend with the rather

disturbing finding of upward-sloping demand curves, and of preferences that seemed to change over time, hence introducing a wedge
between earlier and later valuations of the same innovations. Close
examination of those issues led me to a better understanding of the role
of prices and of quality uncertainty in markets for rapidly advancing
products, as well as of the limitations of welfare comparisons when both
technology and tastes change over time. Of course, many of these
conundrums have not been satisfactorily solved here; I hope, however,
that the very attempts to tackle them with a blend of theory and com-
mon-sense empiricism will prove useful and stimulating.

One special feature of this project is that it calls for large amounts of
data, much of it rather unconventional for economists, such as data on
the performance of CT scanners. This feature reflects both objective
econometric requirements and the conviction that if we truly want to
grasp the phenomena of innovation, we have no choice but to seek data
that have a direct bearing on such phenomena. This is less obvious than
it sounds: first, economists are for the most part reluctant to engage in
raw data collection, trying instead to overcome the meagerness of available data with econometric ingenuity and sophistication (incentives in
the profession are set accordingly); and second, the prevailing conception of "legitimate economic data" is rather narrow and conservative.
This may be justifiable in other areas of economics, but it will not do in
the realm of innovation: the study of technology requires that we gather
and learn the facts of technology themselves, be it in the form of the
changing qualities of goods, the organization of research, or the contents
of patents. Data based on remote proxies can provide us only with a
blurred image of the phenomena, accompanied by a highly disturbing
feeling of uncertainty about having mastered the hard facts. I very much
hope that this book will contribute to enlarge the scope of empirical
material that economists will come to regard as legitimate, and perhaps
even routine, in applied research. I also hope, restating Chamberlin's
wishes of long ago, that "the product" (that is, its evolving attributes,
attached services, reputation, and so forth) will become as important and
prominent an economic variable as price and quantity are today.

As will become clear in the coming chapters, the actual gathering of
the data for this project turned into a major enterprise, requiring tena-
cious efforts, generous budgets, and institutional backing. This is the
bad news, for even if the admonition of the previous paragraph is well
received, the data difficulties encountered in the course of this work

might deter others from pursuing a similar line of research. The good news is that some things have changed dramatically for the better in the last few years: nowadays dozens of computerized data banks contain data relevant for the study of innovation, which can be easily accessed and searched from one's office. Likewise, the handling of large data sets and the econometric analysis of such sets with, say, discrete choice models, have become far easier and cheaper tasks today than they were in the early eighties. It remains only to take much greater advantage of the fruits of technology for the study of technology.

The book is organized as follows: Chapter 1 sets up the theoretical and methodological foundations for the measurement of product innovations. This consists primarily of the assessment of the social benefits from innovations, using the demand-for-characteristics approach in a discrete choice context. The chapter also deals with the problem of constructing price indices that would accurately reflect product innovations (based on those same social benefits), and inquires into the limitations of indices based instead on hedonic price regressions. Chapter 2 is an overview of CT scanners: their origin and development, the evolution of the market and the nature of competition in it, the diffusion process and the effects of regulation, and the detailed account of the attributes of CT and of the data gathered for this study. This is essentially a self-contained piece that can serve a wide range of interests in fields like business, the history of technology, the economics of health care, and others. The appendices with original data on CT scanners can be used to pursue further research in the area.

Chapters 3 and 4 are the core of the actual empirical work, taking us from the econometric estimation of preferences for the attributes of CT to the computation of the total gains from innovation and the calculation of quality-adjusted price indices. Chapter 3 contains most of the econometric analysis, and makes a closer examination of the dynamics of preferences and technology—that is, the fact that preferences for attributes seem to change over time in a pattern closely related to changes in the attributes themselves, suggesting a sort of inducement mechanism in characteristics space. Chapter 4 centers on the actual computation of the gains from innovation on the basis of the econometric results of the previous chapter, and examines some of the implications of those estimates. Much of the effort in the first half of the chapter is devoted to tackling a series of interesting issues that presented themselves in the course of the work: upward-sloping demand curves, welfare comparisons when preferences change over time, and the implications for those calculations of the distortions prevalent in the health-care sector. Following an analysis of the interaction between innovation and diffusion for the purposes of computing the total gains from innovation, the chapter concludes with the computation of a rate of return on R&D, a close examination of the time profile of benefits and costs, and the estimation of price indices.

Taking advantage of the availability of unique measures of innovation in CT together with the complete set of patents granted in that field, Chapter 5 probes the adequacy and significance of various patent-based statistics as indicators of innovation. The key finding is that patent counts weighted by citations appear to be a good indicator of the value of innovations in a given field over time. Beyond these and other more specific results, the chapter offers a close-up view of the informational content of patents, and some encouraging thoughts as to the potential usefulness of patent data in economic research.

1

The Measurement of Innovations

The main objective of this chapter is to lay down the theoretical and econometric building blocks for the measures of social gains from product innovation that constitute the core of the book. Building on the characteristics approach to demand theory on the one hand, and on models of discrete choice on the other, I draw a particular "social surplus" function that has highly desirable features for the valuation of innovations. A great deal of the discussion centers in fact on this surplus function, covering its formal derivation, properties, and limitations. The last section links the proposed measures of gains from innovation to the construction of price indices that would faithfully reflect the effects of quality change. In a closely related argument, the section also draws a clear distinction between product and process innovations on the basis of the nature of the observed characteristics of products.

1.1 The Magnitude of Innovations: A Preliminary View

How should one go about quantifying innovations? What is the meaning of the "amount" or the "magnitude" of innovations from the vantage point of the economist? How can we compare the extent of technical progress occurring, say, in personal computers to that in automobiles? Clearly, the difficulty in answering those questions has to do primarily with the problem of defining or visualizing the thing we are trying to gauge: the quest for the "how" should therefore be preceded by the clarification of the "what." Pressed for a definition, most economists would probably agree that innovation means the creation of new, economically valuable knowledge. In other words, innovations can be thought of as increments to the stock of knowledge available to society, which take the form of improvements in (or additions to) the set of available goods, services, or production processes, and hence have a direct bearing on our well being. Accordingly, it is clear that the magnitude of innovations ought to be related to the *economic value* of the additional knowledge generated by them, and probably be equated with it.

When one thinks, as economists do, of value as price times quantity, it would be nice if one could get one's hands on those "bits and pieces" of new knowledge and multiply them by some measure of the "shadow price of knowledge." The problem is that the output of innovative activities does not present itself in countable units of any sort: what we observe is a continuous stream of disparate improvements taking place in a multitude of technological dimensions, and defying any sort of partition into nonarbitrary segments. Of course, the use of units in any context presupposes some notion of homogeneity or equivalence, that is, it implies that each unit represents approximately the same quantum as any other in the relevant dimension. Thus the problem is not to come up with some segmentation of the innovational stream (that in itself is always possible, as with patents), but to have the units so defined uphold the said equivalence property. Unfortunately, innovations exhibit an enormous variance in their economic and technological significance, whatever the grid one uses to look at them. This is as true for simple counts of innovations as for important innovations (provided, say, by experts in each field),[1] rates of changes of attributes of products, or counts of scientific publications linked to particular innovations. More important, it is also the case with the one universal and supposedly standardized segmentation of technologically useful knowledge, namely patents (see Chapter 5 for an extensive discussion of this issue).

In the absence of meaningful units, the magnitude of innovations has thus to be defined directly in value terms, that is, in terms of their impact upon social welfare. In other words, the question of how much innovation was there in a certain field over a certain period of time, can only be interpreted as asking how much are those innovations worth; that is, how much consumer and producer surplus was generated by technical advance in that field and time. Concepts such as magnitude, extent, economic impact, or social benefits from innovations are therefore one and the same, and can be used interchangeably.

1. See Schmookler (1966) and Mansfield (1968) for examples of the use of counts of important innovations in specific fields as measures of the output of innovative activity in those fields.

It is important to stress what the above definition is meant to exclude, as much as what it comprises. First, it rules out any attempt to assess the magnitude of innovations from the input (or cost) side: simply put, a technical advance that costs more would not necessarily be worth more, and vice versa.[2] Second, and closely related, it does not allow one to infer the extent of innovation solely on the basis of technological variables, such as the rate of improvement in the quality dimensions of products. Thus, for example, a dramatic increase in the maximum speed of automobiles may render little benefit if the vehicles are used primarily for commuting in congested highways, and hence those improvements would amount to little innovation even though they might be associated with a technological leap.

Congruent with this conception of the magnitude of innovations, the view of the innovative process to which I adhere here sees it by and large as a continuous time process, as opposed to a sequence of discrete, well-compartmentalized, and sizable events.[3] The latter view still governs some of the research in the area, perhaps because of the influence of popular accounts of the history of technology, which dwell mostly on breakthroughs and emphasize the often dramatic role played by individual inventors. Thus it is not uncommon for the discussion of topics in this area of economics to be conducted as if innovation were in fact a well defined unit of analysis, and technical change a collection of such units.[4]

Quite clearly, the view of innovation as a continuous process does not negate the possibility of describing, in an interesting and informative way, the innovative stream as a sequence of distinct advances. The point

2. The distinction between costs and end-value is often clouded in the literature, precisely because of the difficulties of assessing independently the value of innovations. Some of that confusion is present even in the seminal article by Kuznets (1962) on the definition and measurement of innovations. Kuznets stipulates that innovations have to be, inter alia, the result of "a mental performance above the average". According to such a definition, the implementation of a novel idea resulting in sizable social benefits would not qualify as a significant innovation if it came about with very little effort. In contrast, the view maintained here is that all costs ("mental effort" included) should be kept out of the assessment of value.

3. See Rosenberg (1982), Chapter 3, for a well-formulated exposition of the "continuous view", and a critique of what he aptly calls the "heroic theory of invention."

4. Similarly, patents are often considered to signify distinct, clearly delimited segments of technical advance. Some do, particularly those associated with breakthroughs; but as will be argued extensively in Chapter 5, most patents do not and are instead slight variations around a few central themes.

is that once the magnitude of innovations has been equated with their value, it is very hard to disentangle the contribution of specific innovations to the observed flow of social gains, particularly since most technical advance comes about by way of many small, often unrecorded improvements. Moreover, the pervasiveness of externalities casts serious doubt on the feasibility of assigning benefits to specific, narrowly defined innovations, and hence on the very possibility of assessing their value separately (even the distinction between fields is often blurred by the presence of externalities). This is true of the cost side as well: the R&D expenditures (within, say, given firms and even fields) also constitute a flow that defies clear-cut segmentation. Thus any sort of analysis involving the costs and benefits of innovations should be conducted within a framework that stresses continuity as a crucial feature of the innovative process.

1.1.1   Product versus Process Innovations

So far the discussion has referred to innovation in general, but in fact the concern here is with the measurement of *product* rather than *process* innovations. Past research efforts have focused almost exclusively on the assessment of the latter, even though it is by now widely recognized that product innovations have become the dominant form of technical change (see for example Mansfield, 1968). This manifest bias seems to stem from the fact that process innovations are conceptually and empirically easier to deal with, because they can be represented as parametric changes in production functions and hence as cost reductions (or productivity increases) in the production of given products. By contrast, product innovations take place in dimensions other than prices and quantities and their empirical study often requires data that are alien to economists and hard to grasp.

Griliches's (1958) landmark work on the social returns from the introduction of hybrid corn firmly established the methodology for the assessment of process innovations at the microlevel, and numerous studies of productivity growth have done as much at the industry and macrolevels. The literature on product innovations is very scanty, however, with only a handful of studies attempting to tackle them empirically, most notably Mansfield et al. (1977) and Bresnahan (1986). The earlier work analyzes the welfare impact of 17 product innovations, but does so by treating them in fact as process innovations, that is, it computes the benefits from the implied price reductions in performing given services. Bresnahan's study, assessing the social gains from computerization in financial services, comes closer in aim and focus to the work here. Still, important differences in method should be noted: whereas Bresnahan bases the analysis on the observed changes in hedonic price indices (apparently a justified strategy in the case of mainframe computers), I attempt to assess the welfare impact of changes in the qualities of products directly, by making a full-fledged analysis of demand for those changing qualities.

It is important to note that despite its prevalence and intuitive appeal, the distinction between product and process innovations is by no means unambiguous: many advances primarily affecting production processes consist in fact of quality improvements in capital goods, whereas others are embedded in products that can serve both in production and in final consumption (such as personal computers, communication systems and devices, and so on). This suggests that a meaningful classification cannot be based just upon the intended use of innovations, and certainly not upon the physical form they take. As will be discussed at length in section 1.5 below, the issue is more complex, having to do primarily with the nature of technical advance (whether or nor it amounts to mere repackaging, for example), and the type of characteristics of products. The discussion in section 1.5 leads to a clear-cut distinction between the two types of innovations, and hence we are on firm ground in assuming hereforth that product innovations are indeed a well defined concept, and that they cannot be represented as process innovations for purposes of measurement.

Finally, it is important to note that economists are not the only ones who are interested in the basic question of quantifying innovations: others in academia, in the business world, and in government have an interest in it as well. A special issue of *Technological Forecasting and Social Change* that was devoted to the measurement of technical change provides a good idea of the range of disciplines with an interest in the topic, and a sense of the diversity of perspectives on it.[5] Virtually all of the papers in that issue base their proposed measures on the observed changes in the attributes of innovative products, some of them in the

5. The issue is based on a conference on the subject supported by the National Science Foundation that took place at the University of Dayton in the fall of 1983 (see *Technological Forecasting and Social Change*, 1985).

context of elementary hedonic-type equations. From the point of view of an economist, though, it is disturbing that most of the papers lack well-defined criteria (or, more formally, well-specified "objective functions") with which to evaluate the changes in attributes. Thus, for example, measures of displacements in "state of the art surfaces" (that is, the frontier in characteristics' space—see Dodson, 1985) are interesting and informative, but cannot provide an idea of the magnitude of innovation. Again, any such measure ought to be derived from a clear definition of innovations and a set of criteria (preferably explicit) congruent with such definition; unfortunately, those basic elements are lacking in most of these studies.

1.2   A Method for Measuring Innovations

The methodology to be used here in measuring product innovations draws from the characteristics approach to demand theory (Lancaster, 1971 and 1979), hedonic price functions (Griliches, 1971; Rosen, 1974), discrete choice models (McFadden, 1981), and the welfare analysis that goes with these models (Small and Rosen, 1981). The basic idea is fairly simple: consider a technologically dynamic product class as it evolves over time, and assume that the different brands in it can be described well in terms of a small number of attributes (quality dimensions) and price. Product innovation can then be thought of in terms of changes over time in the set of available products, both in the sense that new brands appear, and that there are improvements in the qualities of existing products.

Now, if the number of brands in the set is finite, and at least some of their attributes are "not combinable" (ruling out a continuous budget set in characteristics space), then the appropriate framework for modeling the demand side would be that of discrete choice. By applying such models to data on the distribution of sales per brand and on the brands' attributes and prices, one can estimate the parameters of the demand functions and, under some restrictions, of the underlying utility function. The magnitude of innovation occurring between two periods can then be calculated in terms of the benefits of having the latest choice set rather than the previous one, as measured by the corresponding increments in consumer surplus. Clearly, the procedure involves some sort of weighting of the changes in characteristics by their marginal utilities, that is, the magnitude of innovation thus measured is meant to capture both the relative valuations of attributes by consumers and the physical changes in the products themselves.

1.2.1 A Formal Definition of the Magnitude of Innovations

As mentioned above, one of the building blocks of the proposed methodology is the characteristics approach. The common feature of the various models associated with it is the view of products as bundles of attributes that enter explicitly in the utility function of consumers, rather than as abstract entities having only a quantity dimension. Such a conceptual framework is ideally suited for the analysis of product innovations: first, it vastly reduces the dimensionality of the optimization problem confronting agents in markets for differentiated and technologically progressive products, since a relatively small number of characteristics can span a much larger and ever growing number of products. Second, it allows one to analyze substitution effects explicitly, and hence to derive the demand for new—actual or potential—products. More generally, the representation of products as vectors in attributes' space rescues the notion of product quality from the sterile domain of exogenously given tastes, thus allowing the analytical separation of quality changes from changes in preferences.[6] Quite surprisingly, though, the characteristics' approach has rarely been applied to the study of product innovations: most existing applications have to do instead with static product differentiation.

In order to formalize these ideas, I define a product (or brand) within a given product class[7] as $s_i \equiv (z_i, p_i)$, p_i being its price and $z_i = (z_{i1}, z_{i2}, \ldots, z_{im})$ the vector of relevant characteristics.[8] Thus the choice set from which

---

6. In traditional demand analysis the qualities of products are embedded in the structure of preferences, and therefore quality changes manifest themselves as changes in taste and cannot be disentangled from them. An important implication of being able to separate the two is that the assumption of stable preferences (defined over attributes rather than over a given set of goods) is then much more plausible, even in the face of a changing universe of products.

7. By product class I mean a well-defined set of close substitutes located in a common space of attributes, and comprising a separable utility branch. The practical problems of drawing the boundaries of related product classes will be tacked below, when discussing the nested multinomial logit model.

8. They are labeled relevant in the sense that they appear as arguments in the utility function of consumers.

the consumer selects the preferred brand in period t is $S_t = (s_{1t}, s_{2t}, \ldots, s_{nt})$.

Here product innovation simply means that changes occur over time in the set S_t, in the form of improvements in existing products, and/or additions of new products to the set: let me denote those changes by ΔS.[9] Clearly, though, this is just a first step. Given the lack of commensurability among attributes, both within and across product classes, ΔS cannot by itself render meaningful economic measures of product innovations. Thus, for example, if the set S_t refers to computers, how should one relate an increase in, say, speed of computation to an expansion in storage capacity? Moreover, how should one go about comparing those advances with an improvement in the gas mileage of cars, or in the fidelity of a stereo set? It is plain that this problem resembles the one that arises in the construction of any aggregate measure of economic performance (such as GNP): without appropriate price indices, the rate of change of individual outputs are of little help. Furthermore, prices are supposed to reflect both marginal benefits and marginal costs, so that the resulting value measures have normative significance. Similarly, what one needs to know in the present context is, say, not just how much faster or smarter computers are today, but what is the worth of such improvements to consumers, and how much it costs to bring them about.

Thus what is needed is a "surplus" or net social benefit function $W(S_t)$, such that the extent of product innovation (which is, to insist, tantamount to the social gains accruing from it) would be measured by

$$(1.1) \qquad \Delta W_t = W(S_t) - W(S_{t-1}).$$

If, for example, $W(\cdot)$ were linear in the characteristics (certainly not the case in the analysis below), the problem would reside in finding a set of "marginal utility" coefficients β_j, such that the changes (innovations) occurring from one period to the next in the set of products offered to consumers would be evaluated by

$$\Delta W_t = \sum_i^n \sum_j^m \beta_j [(z_{ij})_t - (z_{ij})_{t-1}].$$

9. Actually, ΔS may involve at times "negative" product innovation, that is, the deterioration of existing products or the net contraction of the choice set. Likewise, and as explained below, ΔS is meant to include also changes in prices and not just in attributes. The above definition was intended to be general and encompass those possibilities as well.

Clearly, the main problem resides in obtaining estimates of something akin to the β_j coefficients. Since attributes are not traded independently, such estimation will have to rely on an indirect piece of evidence, namely, the relative frequencies of actual choices (that is, the market shares of the different products in S_t), which presumably reflect the structure and distribution of preferences in attributes space. Thus, for example, if consumers choose TV sets having sharp images more often than sets with large screens (controlling for all other attributes and price), then the β_j for "image quality" will be large relative to the one for "screen size." That, in turn, will be reflected in the amount of social benefits from innovation in TV technology, which are to be computed as some function of the observed improvements in image quality and screen size, weighted by their respective marginal values. The main task ahead is thus to model the demand for products in S_t, so as to be able to estimate the parameters of the corresponding $W(\cdot)$ function, and compute the ΔW_t of eq. 1.1.

1.2.2   *The Scope of* ΔW *and Its Limitations*

Two comments with respect to scope: first, in principle the function $W(\cdot)$ stands for what is usually called the "total surplus" function, that is, the sum of consumer and producer surplus. There is, however, a key difference between those two components in the present context: profit (producer surplus) is a well-defined magnitude whose measurement does not pose special difficulties, except for the practical problem of reconciling accounting with economic profits. If the appropriate data are available (certainly a big "if," but in principle there is no reason why they should not be), then there is nothing to estimate: the dollar figures for profits associated with the innovation can be incorporated as such to ΔW. The problem lies entirely in the specification and estimation of the changes in consumer surplus: those are certainly not observable to the naked eye but require instead an elaborate methodology. In laying out such methodology I will therefore ignore profits altogether, and associate ΔW with gains from innovation that are not appropriated by the innovating firms, but passed on to consumers.

Second, ΔS was meant to comprise not only changes in attributes but also changes in prices, and hence ΔW_t refers to the net social benefits from having set S_t rather than S_{t-1}, all things considered (one can think of price as another characteristic, and the corresponding coefficient as the marginal utility of income). It could be argued, though, that this is too broad a measure, and that one ought to separate the impact of changes in characteristics (that is, the pure product innovation component) from the welfare effect of price changes. After all—so the argument goes—price changes usually reflect phenomena that have little to do with innovation per se, such as demand shifts, the entry or exit of firms, changes in input prices, and so on.

Although such a view is not without merit, the broad definition of ΔW will be retained here, primarily for pragmatic reasons. To begin with, almost any plausible $W(\cdot)$ function will not be additive-linear in its arguments, and therefore it is not clear how the two effects could actually be sorted out without resorting to arbitrary procedures (local approximations would be helpful only for small changes, and not for discrete displacements of the choice set). Furthermore, much of ΔS consists of adding new products and discarding outmoded ones. Clearly, it is meaningless to talk of a separate price effect for those "births" and "deaths," since by definition there is no prior or posterior reference point to which the current price of the new good (or the last price of a displaced brand) could be compared.[10] In any case, the whole point of this methodology is to deal with technologically dynamic sectors, that is, with classes of products where innovation is the dominant force propelling most of the observed changes, be they in characteristics or in prices. Quite apart from the practical difficulties just discussed, it is apparent that for those sectors the broad definition is indeed the most appropriate.

Now to the limitations of the approach. First, the measure ΔW_t actually excludes the possibility of *directly* assessing the *initial* impact of radical innovations. That is, the measure cannot gauge the benefits associated with the first-time appearance of entirely new products that do not fit into existing product classes, but found instead new classes of their own. The reason is plain: in order to compute ΔW, an S_t and a $W(S_t)$ must exist to begin with; that is, something to compare the innovation to (the null set does not qualify for obvious reasons), and a yardstick to evaluate

---

10. This problem applies not only in the case of radically new products. In many instances it is very difficult to distinguish between a change in an existing product from, say, s to s' on the one hand, and the birth of s' and the simultaneous death of s on the other.

the difference between old and new. By definition, neither exists in the case of radical innovations.[11]

It could be argued that any new product, however revolutionary, could be seen as belonging in some way or another to existing product classes[12] and be therefore amenable to this kind of welfare analysis. That may well be the case at some ultimate level of abstraction, but the relevant issue is, once more, pragmatic rather than conceptual: is there enough in common between the breakthrough and existing product sets so that the innovation could be meaningfully evaluated in the context of preferences already defined over those sets? Or, alternatively, does the new product's appearance bring about a reformulation of preferences, very much the way quality changes do in the context of traditional demand theory? If the latter is true, then one cannot estimate directly the gains resulting from the introduction of the radical innovation, that is, from the discrete jump between not having anything of the kind, and having the first commercial units (of course, one can estimate the benefits stemming from improvements from then on, provided only that enough different brands of the new product appear in the market to make the parameters of the emerging preferences statistically identifiable). However, this limitation is not unsurmountable: in fact, it *is* possible to obtain indirect estimates of those initial gains by relying upon the interaction over time between innovation and diffusion (see Chapter 4).

The second limitation of the approach is that, by confining attention to the evaluation of changes within a given set S_l, one is implicitly leaving out spillover effects, that is, improvements in other product sets (or production processes) resulting from the original advances in S_l. In principle, nothing in the approach itself precludes the inclusion of such externalities: if there were information tracing those ripple effects from, say, ΔS_l to ΔS_k, then one could compute also ΔW_k, add it to ΔW_l, and assign the total to the innovations in the l sector. However, it is very unlikely

11. It is interesting to note that Kuznets had foreseen this limitation long ago: "If an invention involves a new product, a rough approximation to its economic magnitude seems to be possible only if the new product can be treated as a substitute for the old one so that it again becomes feasible to estimate the additional yield and seek for a defensible economic basis for evaluating it" (Kuznets, 1962, p. 28).

12. To put it differently, it can be argued that there is a limited number of higher-level, all-encompassing "wants" *à la* Karl Menger (1950), or utility branches *à la* Gorman (1959), so that any conceivable object, if desired and consumed at all, will fall by necessity into one of those categories.

that such information could be obtained, and moreover, it is extremely hard to determine how much of ΔS_k comes from ΔS_l, as opposed to independent innovations in the k sector itself. Likewise, in time the once specific and localized advances underlying ΔS_l become part of the general stock of knowledge, making the identification of a causal nexus between innovations in different sectors, and the proper assignment of down- (or up) the-line benefits a rather hopeless task. Thus, and at least in this respect, the measures derived only from ΔS_l should be regarded as lower bounds to the true social gains generated by innovations in any given product set.[13]

1.3   The Formal Derivation of the Surplus Function

The measure ΔW_l stands for the gains, in terms of consumer surplus, generated by changes over time in the set of available products. To gain a better understanding of it, consider first the simple case of set S_l consisting of a single product having just one quality dimension, q.[14] Denoting the demand function by $x(p,q)$, and disregarding income effects, the benefits to consumers of a small quality improvement are:

$$(1.2) \qquad \frac{\partial W}{\partial q} = \int_p^\infty \frac{\partial x(s,q)}{\partial q}\, ds,$$

or, for a sizable change from, say, q to q',

$$(1.2') \qquad \Delta W = \int_p^\infty [x(s,q') - x(s,q)]ds.$$

Note that (1.2) and (1.2') measure the additional area under the demand curve brought about by its upward shift in response to the change in quality. In other words, (1.2) stands for the consumer's *mar-*

---

[13]However, an innovation might also have what could be regarded as "negative externalities," in the sense that its appearance may render existing products obsolete before their time or, more generally, it may speed up the depreciation of the social stock of knowledge. It is not as yet clear whether and how these effects should be taken into account.

[14]For a detailed analysis of various versions of this case see Willig (1978); see also Spence (1965) for a particular application of the same construct.

ginal willingness to pay for quality improvements. This is precisely the conceptual tool needed to evaluate product innovations, and it is worth keeping it in mind, since the interpretation of ΔW will be basically the same in coming models.

It is interesting to note also that the problem of assessing the quality of products is very similar to the problem of valuing a fairly common type of public goods: those "attached" to private goods or services, so that their value depends upon the use of the related private goods. Classic examples are: size of telephone network (a public good), and telephone calls (a private good); air safety and air travel; local amenities and residence, and so on. In fact, one can think of those public goods as formally equivalent to the relevant quality dimensions of the related private goods, and vice versa. Thus an analysis analogous to the one applied to product innovations can be used to ascertain consumers' valuations of such public goods, that is, to elicit their "truthful revelation of preferences" (see Bradford and Hildebrandt, 1977).

1.3.1 Discrete versus Continuous Models

In general, the function $W(S_t)$ (and hence ΔW) results from integrating under an appropriately defined demand system, whose features depend in turn upon the nature of the choice set S_t. The main distinction to be made in this context is between continuous and discrete sets, each leading to a markedly different modeling strategy. The analysis here will be conducted on the assumption of discreteness, but first it is worth commenting briefly on the continuous case.

Strictly speaking, "continuous" refers to choice sets having infinitely many products that span a continuous spectrum in attributes space. More pragmatically, continuity can be taken to mean that there is a sufficiently large number of contiguous products (and corresponding markets) so that, for all practical purposes, consumers and producers can be thought of as engaging in marginal optimization. In his seminal paper of 1974, Rosen examined this case thoroughly, derived the "hedonic price function" as an equilibrium relationship, and put forward a research strategy for the identification and estimation of the underlying supply and demand functions for the attributes of products. If these demand functions could indeed be consistently estimated in such a way, one would obtain the $W(\cdot)$ function simply by integrating under them, and then use that function to evaluate product innovations. Of course, this method would be warranted only in those instances where at least the mild version of the continuity assumption is empirically justified.[15] It is important to emphasize that in the present context this assumption cannot be taken lightly, since Rosen's proposed econometric procedure involves the estimation of first-order conditions for utility maximization.

Even when the continuity assumption is justified, the implementation of Rosen's approach poses serious econometric difficulties, as first pointed out by Brown and Rosen (1982). Epple (1987) thoroughly examined these difficulties and established the conditions for consistent estimation, in the form of restrictions on the relationship between measured variables (for example, observed attributes of products) and the random components of the various equations. As Epple points out, though, the conditions are fairly stringent and it is not clear at this stage whether they leave much room for actual applications.

In the discrete case it is assumed that the choice set consists of a finite number of different brands, these being located far enough from each other in attributes space so as to preclude marginal adjustments.[16] There is good reason to believe that this is the case that corresponds more closely to technologically progressive products: product-specific R&D constitutes a fixed cost, and hence in any innovative sector a finite number of brands (thus also of firms) will be in equilibrium. (This is just a straightforward monopolistic-competition type of argument.) Moreover, the number of brands in equilibrium will be inversely related to the size of those fixed costs, so the more R&D-intensive a product class is, the smaller (*ceteris paribus*) will be the expected number of competing products. Since this is borne out by what we commonly observe in the real world, we are on safe grounds in characterizing innovative sectors as having discrete choice sets.

In addition to being a property of the choice set, discreteness is commonly used also to describe a certain behavioral pattern, that is, when consumers purchase a single unit of a single product out of the set, making the choice exclusively qualitative rather than quantitative (incidentally, note that neither aspect of discreteness entails the other). I will

---

[15]It seems that the housing market is one of the few cases that can be reasonably assumed to be continuous. And in fact, many of the applications of this approach have been on such markets (for example, Palmquist, 1984).

[16]As already mentioned, characteristics are assumed to be noncombinable (the related notion of nonconcatenability is discussed extensively in section 1.5), hence ruling out the possibility of spanning a piece-wise continuous choice set from a finite number of brands, as in Lancaster (1971).

assume throughout that discreteness holds also in this second sense, although the analysis can be easily extended to accommodate cases of continuous/discrete choice as well (see for example Hanemann, 1984).

Having set the problem this way, one can now draw from the extensive literature on discrete choice to specify the demand side and derive the surplus function. In order to set the stage for the subsequent analysis, the basics of those models are briefly reviewed below (I rely for that purpose primarily on McFadden, 1981).

1.3.2 The Multinomial Logit Model

The basic hypothesis underlying discrete choice models of demand for differentiated products is that consumers maximize a random utility function,

(1.3)
$$\max_{i,x} U_i = U(z_i, x; h) + \varepsilon_i$$

$$\text{s.t.} \quad p_i + x = y \quad \text{and} \quad s_i \varepsilon S,$$

where x stands for a composite "outside" good with unit price, h is a vector of observable attributes of the individual, y is income, and ε_i an independently and identically distributed (i.i.d.) random disturbance (for notational simplicity the subscripts for individuals and for time have been omitted everywhere). The error term ε_i encompasses unobserved (and presumably less important) attributes of the individual and the product, and perhaps also an idiosyncratic and irreducible element of randomness in tastes. Individual choices thus cannot be predicted with certainty, but depend upon the—unobserved—realizations of ε_i. From the researchers' point of view, this implies having to construct probabilistic rather than deterministic demand functions, conditional on S and h.

The problem stated in (1.3) is formally solved in two stages: first, the consumer chooses the optimal quantity of x given s_i; then she chooses the optimal brand $s_i \varepsilon S$. Since only one unit of the product is purchased (by assumption), the first stage is trivial, that is, the optimal quantity of the outside good (conditional on s_i) is just $x^* = y - p_i$. Substituting it for x in (1.3) renders the conditional indirect utility function,

(1.4) $\quad V_i^c = V(z_i, y - p_i; h) + \varepsilon_i \equiv V_i + \varepsilon_i = \max_x U_i,$

which the consumer maximizes in the second stage: $\max_i V_i^c$, s.t. $s_i \in S$. Given the discreteness of S, product s_i will be chosen iff $V_i^c \geq V_j^c$ for all $j \neq i$, that is, iff

$$V_{i-j} \equiv [V(z_i, y - p_i; h) - V(z_j, y - p_j; h)] \geq (\varepsilon_j - \varepsilon_i).$$

Denote the density function of the residuals $f(\varepsilon_i)$ and the corresponding cumulative distribution $F(\varepsilon_i)$. Recalling that the residuals are assumed to be i.i.d., the probability of choosing s_i can then be defined as

$$(1.5) \quad \pi_i \equiv Pr(s_i \mid S, h) = \int_{-\infty}^{\infty} \Pi_{j \neq i} F(\varepsilon_i + V_{i-j}) \cdot f(\varepsilon_i) d\varepsilon_i.$$

The exact form of π_i will depend, of course, upon the distribution of the error terms: if, for example, they are normally distributed, then (1.5) is just the cumulative normal, and the resulting model is the Probit. On the other hand, if the residuals conform to the type I extreme-value (or Weibull) distribution, then π_i will be logistic, that is,

$$(1.6) \quad \pi_i = \exp(V_i) \Big/ \sum_{j=1}^{n} \exp(V_j) \qquad i = 1, \ldots, n.$$

This is the well-known conditional multinomial logit model, hereafter referred to as MNL. The Probit and the logit—and some variants of them—have been and remain the most commonly used choice models, at least within the random utility framework. In the present case the Probit had to be discarded from the outset for pragmatic reasons: the models to be estimated involve choice sets of up to twenty alternatives, whereas with available software the Probit can successfully handle only up to four or five. Thus the MNL will be used throughout, taking account of its limitations, which stem primarily from the underlying assumption of "Independence of Irrelevant Alternatives" (this will eventually lead to the nested MNL).

The n equations in (1.6) constitute a system of probabilistic demand functions of the individual, that is, π_i stands for the probability that consumer h will choose product i, given the price and attributes of i relative to those of all other products. It is easy to prove that this is indeed a well-behaved demand system, exhibiting all the properties of conventional (that is, deterministic) demand functions; hence the notion of consumer surplus applies to it as well and can be computed by integration. The task is greatly simplified by disregarding income effects; thus the underlying utility function is specialized to be additive-separable in the group products (those in S) and in the outside good x, rendering a conditional indirect utility function of the form $V_i^c = \alpha(y - p_i) + \phi(z_i, h) + \varepsilon_i$, where α stands for the (constant) marginal utility of income. Substituting in (1.6),

$$(1.7) \quad \pi_i = \frac{e^{\alpha(y - p_i) + \phi(z_i;h)}}{\sum_{j=1}^{n} e^{\alpha(y - p_j) + \phi(z_j;h)}} = \frac{e^{-\alpha p_i + \phi(z_i;h)}}{\sum e^{-\alpha p_j + \phi(z_j;h)}}, \quad i = 1, \ldots, n.$$

Thus income drops out altogether from the choice probabilities, since it affects the utility level of all alternatives equally, but not their relative desirability (note, however, that y can still appear as a personal attribute in $\phi(\cdot)$). The identity of Hicksian and Marshallian demand functions in (1.7) allows one to obtain the surplus function $W(S,h)$ simply by computing the line integral,

$$W = -\int_{s=0}^{1} \sum_{i}^{n} \pi_i \left[\psi(s)\right] \psi_i' \, ds,$$

where ψ is any path of prices such that $\psi: [0,1]$, $\psi(0) = [0,0, \ldots, 0]$, and $\psi(1) = [p_1, p_2, \ldots, p_n]$ (for convenience the arguments z and h are deleted). In particular,

$$(1.8) \quad W = \int_{p_1}^{\infty} \pi_1(s, \infty, \infty, \ldots, \infty)ds + \ldots$$

$$+ \int_{p_i}^{\infty} \pi_i(p_1, p_2, \ldots, p_{i-1}, s, \infty, \ldots, \infty)ds$$

$$+ \ldots + \int_{p_n}^{\infty} \pi_n(p_1, p_2, \ldots, p_{n-1}, s)ds.$$

Applying it to (1.7), we arrive at

$$(1.9) \quad W(S, h) = \ln\left[\sum_{i=1}^{n} \exp(-\alpha p_i + \phi(z_i, h))\right]/\alpha + y,$$

where y obtains as the constant of integration. It is easy to verify that $\partial W/\partial p_i = \pi_i$, and hence that (1.9) is indeed the correct surplus function (by virtue of Roy's identity).[17] The gains from innovations occurring from period $t-1$ to t can then be computed as follows:

$$(1.10) \quad \Delta W_t = \ell n \left[\sum_i^{n_t} \exp(-\alpha p_{it} + \phi(z_{it},h)) \right]/\alpha$$

$$- \ell n \left[\sum_i^{n_{t-1}} \exp(-\alpha p_{it-1}\phi(z_{it-1},h)) \right]/\alpha.$$

Equations (1.7) and (1.9) refer to the demand and surplus functions of the individual consumer. Given a distribution of personal attributes $g(h)$, the corresponding market-wide functions can be easily obtained by integration. Thus the market demand function for product i will be

$$(1.11) \quad X_i^d = N \int_{-\infty}^{\infty} \pi_i(h)g(h)dh,$$

where N is the size of the population of consumers (as shown in chapter 4, N could be made endogenous). The aggregate surplus function can be computed either by applying the line integral (1.8) directly to (1.11)—recall that income effects are ignored—or by integrating (1.9) over $g(h)$, that is,

$$W^T = \int_{-\infty}^{\infty} W(S;h)g(h)dh.$$

1.3.3 Properties of the MNL Surplus Function

Since the surplus function (1.9) is the key to the computation of welfare gains from innovation, its main properties are worth examining in detail. First, note that even though the consumer ends up buying one unit of one specific product, the surplus function refers to the whole set S, that is, it is calculated as if the consumer were to buy fractions π_i of each and

---

17. The function $W(\cdot)$ in (1.9) is usually referred to in the discrete choice literature as the inclusive value of the choice set.

every product in the set. This seemingly puzzling feature stems directly from the randomness of the utility function: note that the unconditional indirect utility function V^u is also a random variable, since $V^u = \underset{i}{\text{Max }} V_i^c = \alpha(y - p_i) + \phi(z_i;h) + \varepsilon_i$, and that is true not only ex-ante but also ex-post. In other words, even if one knows which brand the consumer chooses, the exact magnitude of V^u will still be unknown to the researcher, simply because the realizations of ε_i's are not observable. Thus the only meaningful welfare measure is the expected value of V^u, that is,

$$E(V^u) = \alpha y + E\{\underset{i}{\max}[-\alpha p_i + \phi(z_i;h) + \varepsilon_i]\},$$

which is equal by construction to the consumer surplus, as shown in (1.9) for the case of the MNL. The function $W(S,h)$ should therefore be interpreted as a money measure of the *expected maximum utility*, accruing to consumer h when choosing a product from set S. This feature and consequent interpretation of the surplus function are very convenient in the present context, for they allow one to trace the welfare effects of innovations in the entire set of products, regardless of what product each consumer actually purchases.

The second set of properties of the surplus function specified in (1.9) come to light in the following, previously unnoticed decomposition of it:[18]

$$(1.12) \quad W(S, h) = \sum_i^n \pi_i V_i + \left[-\sum_i^n \pi_i \ell n \; \pi_i\right] = E(V_i) + \psi,$$

where $E(V_i)$ stands for the expected value of the deterministic component of the conditional indirect utility function (that is, $V_i = -\alpha p_i + \phi(z_i,h)$) and ψ for the well-known entropy measure. Note, first, that this formulation resembles a "mean-variance" utility indicator (recall that ψ is in fact a measure of dispersion): $W(\cdot)$ increases with the mean utility of the choice set, and decreases with its spread. Second and more impor-

---

18. This is done as follows: starting from $\pi_i = \exp(V_i)/\Sigma\exp(V_j)$ and taking logs, one gets $\ell n \; \pi_i = V_i - \ell n[\Sigma\exp(V_j)]$; multiplying both sides by π_i, summing over i, and rearranging terms renders eq. (1.11). For expositional convenience, α is omitted from $W(\cdot)$ throughout the discussion.

tant, (1.12) brings to light the existence of a taste for "horizontal variety" embedded in the entropy measure. In other words, the preferences underlying (1.9) are such that the welfare of the consumer is enhanced by the proliferation of seemingly identical brands, which may differ only in their unobserved (and thus presumably less important) attributes. To see this, assume that set S consists of product 1 and m variants of product 2; then from (1.9),

$$W = \ell n \, [\exp(V_i) + m \exp(V_2)], \qquad \partial W / \partial m = \pi_2 > 0,$$

which means that utility increases by replicating "irrelevant alternatives." As an example, consider the case where S refers to personal computers, comprising at first just an IBM PC and a clone. A taste for horizontal variety means that consumers would be better off if one were to add to the set other clones having identical z's and prices as the one already there, but carrying different labels (and perhaps also different *unobserved* characteristics). The extent to which this is an appropriate characterization of the preferences of consumers in specific choice situations is of course an open empirical question.

To demonstrate that such taste for variety is in fact associated with the term ψ, I differentiate (1.12) with respect to m for the same hypothetical case as before (the final result has to be of course the same), that is, $\partial W / \partial m = \partial E(V_i) / \partial m + \partial \psi / \partial m$; now, as shown in appendix 1.1

$$\frac{\partial E(V_i)}{\partial m} = \pi_1 \pi_2 (V_2 - V_1) \gtreqless 0 \qquad \text{as } V_2 \gtreqless V_1, \qquad \text{and}$$

$$\frac{\partial \psi}{\partial m} = \pi_2 [1 - \pi_1 (V_2 - V_1)] > 0,$$

that is, $E(V_i)$ increases with m if the nonrandom component of the utility of the good being replicated, V_2, is greater than that of the other good. Clearly, the reason is that when $V_2 > V_1$, additions of irrelevant alternatives (that is, of V_2) augment the probability of ending up with the product that yields the highest expected utility. This is the conventional effect that obtains just as if the probabilities π_i were exogenous, and consumers behaved according to expected utility. On the other hand, $\partial \psi / \partial m$ is always positive, capturing the pure taste-for-variety effect. This is more evident in the extreme case where there is only horizontal variety, that is, where $V_i = \bar{V}$ for all i, and then

$$W = \bar{V} + \ell n\ m, \qquad \frac{\partial W}{\partial m} = \frac{\partial \psi}{\partial m} = 1/m > 0.$$

Thus it may be of interest, for example, to decompose the gains ΔW into the two components $\Delta E(V_i)$ and $\Delta \psi$ and, since the latter stands for the benefits resulting only from increased variety, one may want, for some purposes, to net them out and use the partial measure $(\Delta W - \Delta \psi)$.

1.4 The Construction of Quality-Adjusted Price Indices on the Basis of ΔW

One of the potentially important applications of the measures ΔW_t is to use them as the basis for the construction of "real" price indices for technologically dynamic sectors. The procedure suggested here for that purpose involves relying on the expenditure function dual to (1.9), and using it to compute the hypothetical price change that would have resulted in the same welfare effect (measured by ΔW) as the innovations that actually took place. In that sense the proposed index belongs to the class of "cost-of-living"—or Konüs—indices (see Diewert, 1987). Consider the function

$$V = \frac{y}{P} + W(S) = \frac{y}{P} + \ell n \left[\sum_{i=1}^{n} \exp(-\alpha p_i + \phi(z_1)) \right]/\alpha,$$

where $\bar{P}$ is the price of all goods other than those in S (that is, the price of the numeraire, implicitly assumed before to be unity), and the prices p_i appearing in $W(S)$ are now "real," that is, $p_i = \tilde{p}_i/\bar{P}$, where $\tilde{p}_i$ are nominal. Note that V is homogenous of degree zero in prices and income, and convex in prices. Thus, and as shown in McFadden (1981), V is in fact an indirect utility function, and is therefore invertible to a (concave) expenditure function, $e(S, V^0) = \bar{P} \cdot [V^0 - W(S)]$. Given that $\bar{P}$ will not play a role in the forthcoming analysis, we can ignore it and write

$$(1.13) \quad e(V^0, p, Z) = V^0 - \ell n \left[\sum_{i=1}^{n} \exp(V_i) \right]/\alpha,$$

where p stands for the vector of prices of all brands in S, and Z for the matrix of their attributes. Assume now that innovations occur from period $t-1$ to t, taking the form of improvements in the attributes of some of the products in the choice set (their prices may change as well). Using (1.10) and (1.13), the welfare gains from those innovations would be measured by

$$\Delta W_t = \ell n \left[\sum_{i=1}^{n} \exp(V_{it}) \right] / \alpha - \ell n \left[\sum_{i=1}^{n} \exp(V_{it-1}) \right] / \alpha \Rightarrow$$

(1.14) $$\Delta W_t = e(V^0, p_{t-1}, Z_{t-1}) - e(V^0, p_t, Z_t).$$

Thus ΔW as expressed in (1.14) measures the analog in the present context of a *compensating variation*, that is, it answers the question "how much income could be taken away from the consumer so as to leave him indifferent between facing the old choice set, and the new (improved) one but with the lesser income?" However, since $e(\cdot)$ is linear-additive in V (recall that income effects were assumed away), then the reference utility level (or the income level in the dual) does not matter, and hence the compensating and equivalent variations are one and the same. Thus we can omit V^0 from (1.14) and write:

(1.14)' $$\Delta W_t = e(p_{t-1}, Z_{t-1}) - e(p_t, Z_t).$$

We can now define two different price indices that would reflect the quality changes embedded in S_t vis-à-vis S_{t-1}. The first requires that we solve for δ_t out of

(1.15) $$\Delta W_t = e[p_{t-1}, Z_{t-1}] - e[(1 - \delta_t) \cdot p_{t-1}, Z_{t-1}],$$

keeping in mind that ΔW_t in equation 1.15 is a known magnitude, and so are the parameters of the expenditure function. That is, δ_t is the hypothetical average price reduction that would have had the same welfare consequences as the innovations that actually took place. In other words, consumers would have been equally well off if they had been offered the *old* set of products at prices lower by a factor of δ_t, as they actually are by virtue of having the *new* set that incorporates the better qualities (they would be indifferent between $[(1-\delta_t) \cdot p_{t-1}, Z_{t-1}]$ and

$[p_t, Z_t]$). From a computational viewpoint, the values of δ_t can be obtained from (1.15) with methods of iterative search.[19] However, if one is willing to use a somewhat more restrictive notion of average price change, then δ_t can be computed in a much simpler way. The price of each brand at time t can always be written as $p_{it} = \bar{p}_t + \Delta p_{it}$, where $\bar{p}_t$ is the average across brands. Now, suppose that the changes in prices from period $t-1$ to t take the form $p_{it} = (1 - \delta_t)\bar{p}_{t-1} + \Delta p_{it-1}$, that is, the distribution of prices moves leftward by a factor of $(1 - \delta_t)$ but the variance remains the same. It is easy to show that in such a case (1.15) simplifies to[20]

$$(1.16) \quad \Delta W_t = \delta_t\, \bar{p}_{t-1},$$

and hence δ_t obtains immediately as the ratio $\Delta W_t / \bar{p}_{t-1}$. To reiterate its meaning, this ratio stands for the average price reduction that would be equivalent, from a welfare viewpoint, to the innovations valued ΔW_t. This is a very convenient result for computational purposes, and it may help clarify the meaning of the measure ΔW_t itself (in particular, it may be easier to visualize ΔW_t as a displacement along the price dimension). Once the series $\{\delta_t\}$ has been obtained, a quality adjusted price index can be computed simply as $I_t^1/I_{t-1}^1 = (1 - \delta_t)$, with $I_0^1 = 100$ (the superscript is meant to distinguish between the two alternative indices).

The second price index obtains by solving for φ_t from

$$(1.17) \quad \Delta W_t = e[(1 + \varphi_t) \cdot p_t, Z_t] - e[p_t, Z_t].$$

That is, if prices of the improved products had been $(1 + \varphi_t)$ times higher than actual prices, then the implied price reduction of $\delta_t' = \varphi_t/(1 + \varphi_t)$ would be equivalent, from the point of view of its welfare effects, to the quality improvements that took place. Thus $(1 + \varphi_t)\cdot\bar{p}_t$ can be interpreted as the reservation price for the innovations embedded in S_t: if the products in that set were offered at an average price of $(1 + \varphi_t)\cdot\bar{p}_t + \varepsilon$ (for any small $\varepsilon > 0$), the consumer would prefer to have the older set instead.

19. Note from (1.14)′ and (1.15) that this is the same as solving for δ_t out of $e[(1 - \delta_t)\cdot p_{t-1}, Z_{t-1}] = e[p_t, Z_t]$.

20. Recall that $W = \ell n[\Sigma_i \exp(\phi_{it} - \alpha p_{it})]/\alpha$, where $\phi_{it} = \phi(z_{it})$. Given $p_{it} = \bar{p}_t + \Delta p_{it}$, $W = \ell n[\Sigma_i \exp(\phi_{it} - \alpha\bar{p}_t - \alpha\Delta p_{it})]/\alpha = \ell n\{[\Sigma_i \exp(\phi_{it} - \alpha\Delta p_{it})] \exp(-\alpha\bar{p}_t)\}/\alpha = -\bar{p}_t + \ell n[\Sigma_i \exp(\phi_{it} - \alpha\Delta p_{it})]/\alpha$. Therefore, given $\bar{p}_t = (1 - \delta_t)\bar{p}_{t-1}$, (1.15) reduces to $\Delta W_t = \bar{p}_{t-1} - (1 - \delta_t)\bar{p}_{t-1} = \delta_t\bar{p}_{t-1}$.

Again, on the assumption that the price change is just a displacement in the mean price, φ_t would obtain simply from

(1.18) $(1 + \varphi_t) = (\Delta W_t + \bar{p}_t)/\bar{p}_t \rightarrow \varphi_t = \Delta W_t / \bar{p}_t,$

implying a percentage price reduction of

(1.19) $\delta'_t \equiv \varphi_t/(1 + \varphi_t) = \Delta W_t/(\Delta W_t + \bar{p}_t).$

The associated price index would be $I_t^2/I_{t-1}^2 = 1/(1+\varphi_t) = (1 - \delta'_t)$. Comparing the two indices, it can be shown that $\delta'_t \leq \delta_t$, that is, the first index, will always show a larger "quality-ajusted" price reduction. This is easily seen in the case where $\bar{p}_t = \bar{p}_{t-1} = \bar{p}$:

$$\delta_t = \frac{\Delta W_t}{\bar{p}} > \frac{\Delta W_t}{\Delta W_t + \bar{p}} = \delta'_t,$$

That is, ΔW_t (to be interpreted here as a notional average price discount equivalent to the quality improvements) would certainly represent a higher percentage of the base price $\bar{p}$ than of the necessarily higher "reservation price" $(\Delta W_t + \bar{p})$.[21] In general, though, $\bar{p}_t \neq \bar{p}_{t-1}$, but the above inequality will still hold. When $\bar{p}_t = (1+\lambda_t)\cdot\bar{p}_{t-1}$, it is easy to show that $\delta' = \delta_t/(1 + \lambda_t + \delta_t)$, and hence that $\delta'_t < \delta_t$;[22] notice also that the difference between the two indices grows with λ_t.

Clearly, the two indices are equally legitimate and have equally well defined welfare interpretations. A technical difference, however, makes the second index the only feasible one when innovations are "drastic," that is, when the ΔW's are very large (relative to prices). Note that there is no reason whatsoever for ΔW_t to be smaller than $\bar{p}_{t-1}$ (in other words, there is no reason for the *value* of innovations to be bounded by the average price of the products embodying those innovations), and hence it may happen that $\Delta W_t > \bar{p}_{t-1}$ (that is, that $\delta_t > 1$). What that would

---

21. This is the same sort of discrepancy as the one that may arise when computing the elasticity of, say, a demand function along a segment (for a discrete price change), rather than at a point.

22. This is so provided that, if $\lambda_t < 0$ (that is, if there is an average price reduction), then $|\lambda_t| \leq \delta_t$. But that is always the case (unless there is a quality deterioration): if the qualities of products don't change from $t-1$ to t but $\bar{p}_t = (1-\lambda)\bar{p}_{t-1}$, then $\Delta W_t = \lambda\bar{p}_{t-1}$, and hence $\delta_t = \lambda_t$. If at the same time qualities improve, then $\delta_t > \lambda_t$.

mean is simply that even if the products that existed in period $t-1$ were to be given away for free, consumers would still prefer to have the more advanced products and pay their full price. In other words, in order for consumers to be indifferent between facing the period t choice set and that of period $t-1$, they would have to be offered the $t-1$ products for free, plus a "bribe" (or "negative price") of $(\Delta W_t - \bar{p}_{t-1})$ dollars. Negative prices are not allowed, however, so one could not use in such a case I_t^1, since $\delta_t > 1$ would imply a negative value for the index. On the other hand, if ΔW_t is larger than $\bar{p}_t$ and hence $\varphi_t > 1$, the second index is still well defined: the hypothetical reservation prices that would make the consumer indifferent to the choice between the improved (but more expensive) products and the older set can be as high as necessary.

Consequently, if innovations in a given field are at times very substantial, there is no choice but to use the second index only. Conversely, if a field consistently displays just incremental innovations, it may be worth considering some sort of average between the two indices, and/or using the average of the mean price in the two periods to compute either index. Finally, it is worth noting that those indices can accommodate well cases of "negative" innovations, resulting in negative values of ΔW_t. That would be the case, for example, if there were no change in the qualities of products, but prices *rose* by λ percent: it is easy to see that in such a case $\delta'_t = \delta_t = -\lambda$; in other words, both indices would faithfully and equally reflect the price hike.

1.5 ΔW-based Indices versus Hedonic Prices

Having constructed price indices based on the measures ΔW, one should step back and ask whether one really needs the rather complicated method outlined above to obtain reasonably good deflators for rapidly changing goods: would not indices based on hedonic price regressions do the job just as well?[23] It is important to note that this question is in fact equivalent to asking whether or not there is a meaningful distinction between

---

23. The hedonic method is certainly much simpler, its data requirements are more modest, and it has the extra advantage of having already gained some official acceptance (for example, the U.S. Bureau of Economic Analysis, in collaboration with IBM, uses the hedonic method to compute a price index for computers). Thus, if both methods were roughly equivalent, surely one would not hesitate in taking the hedonic approach.

process and product innovations: as I shall argue below, the use of hedonic price indices (instead of ΔW-based indices) is justified only when "quality" is merely a redefinition of quantity, and hence "product innovation" is just process innovation in disguise.

1.5.1   Quality-Adjusted Price Indices in the "Repackaging" Case

The answer to the question just posed can essentially be found in the classic work by Fisher and Shell (1972) on the theory of price indices (even though the question was not quite put in those terms there): hedonic-based price indices (or a price/performance ratio if "quality" is unidimensional) would suffice to account for quality change only in the repackaging case. If the choice set consists of one good only (say, good 1), and quality can be fully accounted for with one parameter θ, repackaging implies that the corresponding argument in the utility function is just θx_1. That is, θ stands for the amount of services provided by the good, and hence "quality change" (meaning $\theta_t > \theta_{t-1}$) amounts essentially to a redefinition of units. In such a case one can define a price-performance ratio p_1/θ such that, for any θ,

$$(1.20) \quad e(V^0, p_1, p_2, \ldots, p_n; \theta) = e(V^0, p_1/\theta, p_2, \ldots, p_n),$$

and the implied quality-adjusted price index would simply be $(p_{1t}/\theta_t)/(p_{1t-1}/\theta_{t-1})$. Thus, if θ were easily observable (as when it is indeed just a matter of redefining units), accounting for quality change would be a very simple matter. It is important to notice that in such a case the distinction between process and product innovations all but vanishes (as does the quality-quantity dichotomy): by defining the relevant price as p_1/θ rather than just p_1, it is clear that technical change that brings about a reduction in costs, leading in turn to a decrease in the unadjusted price p_1 (that is, a *process* innovation), is exactly equivalent to a product innovation that results in the enhancement of θ.

When the choice set consists of $n > 1$ brands, repackaging implies that the corresponding branch of the utility function takes the form $U(\sum_{i=1}^{n} \theta_i x_i)$. Clearly, if $U(\cdot)$ is common to all consumers, then in order for more than one brand to be purchased in a cross-section it has to be the case that $p_i/p_j = \theta_i/\theta_j$. Denoting by $\tilde{p}_0$ the quality-adjusted price of the reference variety, one can always write $p_i = \tilde{p}_0 \, \theta_i$. Furthermore, if θ_i is not one-dimensional but depends upon a vector of attributes $\bar{z}_i$ (see for example Deaton and Muellbauer, 1980), then

$$(1.21) \quad \log p_i = \log \tilde{p}_0 + \log \theta(\bar{z}_i),$$

which is one of the forms that estimated hedonic price functions commonly take. In a two-year panel, for example, the term $\log \tilde{p}_0$ would obtain as the coefficient of a time dummy variable and can be taken as a sufficient price index in the sense of (1.20) above (that is, $\tilde{p}_t$ would be the equivalent in this context of the price-performance ratio p_t/θ_t).[24] To insist, the point is that the hedonic price function by itself merely allows us to account for more than one attribute in computing price indices, but such indices can serve as sufficient indicators of quality change only in the highly restrictive context of the repackaging case.

1.5.2 Product Innovations, Repackaging, and the Nature of Characteristics

To gain a better understanding of what lies behind the repackaging case (and hence be able perhaps to assess its empirical relevance), it is worth examining carefully the notion of quality implied by it, and the sort of attributes of products that would support such notion. I resort for that purpose to the distinction between concatenable and nonconcatenable characteristics (see Trajtenberg, 1979)[25], the former being formally defined as

$$z_{ij} = f^j(x_i), \qquad \frac{\partial z_{ij}}{\partial x_i} \neq 0 \qquad \text{for } x_i \geq 0,$$

24. Even this simple case is subject to several qualifications. In particular, if the budget constraint in attributes space is nonlinear (as it is most likely to be), then the estimation of (1.21) involves what can be construed as errors of aggregation.

25. This terminology, borrowed from the theory of measurement (see Krantz et al., 1971), was meant to focus attention on the physical properties that underlie the different kinds of measurement, and their implications for economic behavior. Concatenation is an operation by which objects are connected with respect to some common attribute, allowing for extensive measurement (for example, placing rods edge to edge for the measurement of length).

and the latter as

$$z_{ij} = g^j(\omega_i), \qquad \frac{\partial z_{ij}}{\partial x_i} = 0 \qquad \text{for all } x_i \geq \omega_i,$$

where ω_i denotes the "natural unit" of product i and x_i its quantity. Typical examples of concatenable characteristics are proteins in food products or the carrying capacity of vehicles; in other words, the quantity of the characteristics available to the consumer is a monotonic function, usually linear, of the quantity of the product(s) consumed. Nonconcatenable characteristics, on the other hand, are much closer to the intuitive notion of quality, that is, they are properties inherent in the product itself and do not vary with its quantity (for example, speed of vehicles, aperture of photographic cameras, and so on). Therefore, different amounts of characteristics can be obtained only by switching products, not by adjusting the quantities consumed.

Similar distinctions have been made in the literature,[26] and the various "characteristics models" available can thus be categorized, at least retroactively. Thus, for example, the original model of demand for characteristics developed by Lancaster (1971) clearly corresponds to products that have only concatenable attributes. On the other hand, Rosen (1974) and Lancaster's second model (1979), among others, have addressed the nonconcatenability case. However, the relevance of this sort of distinction for the conceptualization of innovations has not been well established.

It is easy to see that when the product in question has just one relevant attribute, then concatenability entails the simple repackaging case, that is, the utility branch is just $U(z)$, $= b\, x_1$, where b is the per-unit amount of the characteristic, obviously identical to θ in (1.20) above. Since concatenability implies that the amount of the characteristic available to the consumer can be added up both over units of one product and over units of different products, the case of product variety obtains in a straightforward manner ($z = \Sigma\, b_i\, x_i \equiv \Sigma\, \theta_i\, x_i$). When the θ_i's (and hence utility) depend upon more than one characteristic, concatenability and repack-

26. These distinctions, however, are made in an informal, implicit manner (when explicit, the distinction has been referred to in a variety of ways, such as combinable versus noncombinable, additive versus nonadditive, and so on). Moreover, the different types of attributes are simply assumed, not explained in terms of more primitive elements.

aging are equivalent only under more restrictive assumptions regarding the form of the utility function (see Muellbauer, 1974). However, concatenability of the composite quality indicator $\theta(\bar{z}_i)$ is still a sufficient condition for repackaging.

Thus in order to have a distinct and meaningful notion of product innovation, some of the product characteristics (at least one) have to be nonconcatenable. Otherwise the choice set would be homogeneous of degree zero in prices and characteristics, which in turn would imply that consumers are necessarily indifferent to the choice between price reductions and proportional increases in the per-unit quantity of all characteristics (regardless of their preferences). When that is so the distinction between process innovations (associated with costs and hence price reductions) and product innovations (linked to changes in attributes) all but vanishes, at least from the viewpoint of their effects.

To illustrate the argument, consider the case where there is a change in product $s_i = (z_i, p_i)$ such that $s'_i = (\lambda z_i, \lambda p_i)$, $\lambda > 1$. If all characteristics were concatenable, then the transition from s_i to s'_i would not be regarded as an innovation at all because it is inconsequential for behavior, and what is more important here, for welfare (it is clear that $V(s_i, y) = V(s'_i, y)$, where V is the indirect utility function and y is money income). However, if some of the z's were nonconcatenable, then the same change will certainly qualify as an innovation and probably have a sizable welfare impact. To sum up, product innovation is inextricably related to, and presupposes the existence of, a distinct quality dimension (that is, distinct from a mere redefinition of units). Since nonconcatenability is essential for the notion of quality, it is by extension a *sine qua non* for the notion of product innovation.

The obvious question is, what do we gain by stating the problem in terms of concatenability rather than repackaging? The intention is to make the distinction empirically applicable, by focusing on observable properties of attributes. Thus, when weighing whether technical advances in a specific field should be assessed as if they were merely cost reductions, or whether they ought to be treated as product innovations instead (hence necessitating the methodology put forward here), one should first establish what the relevant attributes of the goods in question are. Second, one should examine whether those attributes exhibit the concatenability property, that is, see if it is possible to "join" (if not physically then at least conceptually) two or more units of the good with respect to each of the attributes, so that the summing operation $z_i = \Sigma$

$b_{ij}x_j$ is well-defined and meaningful in terms of utility. If the answer is positive, then one is on firm ground estimating quality-adjusted price indices on the basis of hedonic price functions and using them to assess the magnitude of innovations. Otherwise, product innovation is the name of the game, and the approach outlined in previous sections is called for. In contrast, note that the notion of repackaging in itself does not lead to a well-defined test having empirical relevance (at least it is not obvious how one would go about testing for it).

Put this way, it is quite clear that few cases would pass the strict concatenability test. It would thus be more realistic to devise rules such that the choice of method for the assessment of innovations would depend upon the type most of the attributes correspond to. Still, it seems likely that a large number of products would fail even a more lenient test of this sort, and hence that we may be missing a great deal because of the prevailing practice of forcing product innovations into the narrow mold of price-performance ratios (or simply by ignoring them). Thus the claim that conventional price indices may actually be accounting quite well for innovation (see for example Triplett, 1975) needs to be given a good hard look once again.

1.5.3   Assessing the Performance of Hedonic-Based Price Indices

One of the intended uses of the price index based on the measures $\Delta W_i'$s is for it to serve as a test criterion for other indices and, in particular, for hedonic-based indices. That is taken up empirically in Chapter 4, where both indices are computed and compared for the case of CT scanners. However, to gain a better sense of what those comparisons may entail, it is worth examining in a heuristic manner how hedonic price indices are likely to perform in various stylized situations.

Quite clearly, a price index that purports to account faithfully for product innovations should measure the change ("distance," in money metric) in the attainable utility level before and after the innovation. Consider now the case where there is a downward shift in the hedonic function, as shown in figure 1.1a, and assume that the shift is entirely supply-determined. In the simplest possible situation (abstracting from discreteness, aggregation problems, and income effects), the distance between the indifference curves labeled W_t and W_{t+1} would be a good approximation to the monetized welfare gains associated with the inno-

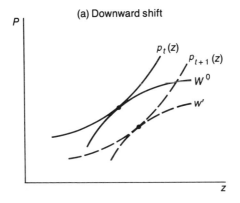

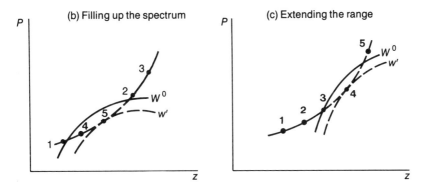

Figure 1.1 Alternative Effects of Innovation on Hedonic Price Functions

vations that induced the displacement in the hedonic function. The coefficient of a time dummy in a hedonic regression pooling adjacent years will thus accurately measure those gains, and the resulting quality-adjusted price index can then be taken as a faithful indicator of the changes occurred.

To illustrate this equivalence, assume that there is only one attribute, z, and that innovation consists of augmenting the quantity of that attribute in all brands by the same absolute magnitude, Δz; if prices remain unchanged, that will result in a parallel displacement of $p(z)$ as in figure

1.1a. Evaluating this change with the measure ΔW of equation (1.10), and further assuming that $V(\cdot)$ is linear in z,

$$\Delta W = \ell n \left\{ \sum \exp[-\alpha p_i + \beta(z_i + \Delta z)] \right\} / \alpha$$

$$- \ell n \left[\sum \exp(-\alpha p_i + \beta z_i) \right] / \alpha = \beta \Delta z / \alpha.$$

Now if the hedonic function is also linear, that is, $p_i = \bar{p} + \gamma z_i$, it follows that the implied price index will change by $\Delta \bar{p} = \gamma \Delta z.$[27] Thus $\Delta \bar{p}$ and ΔW are proportional to each other and, under a suitable normalization, they will be identical. This is of course a highly simplified case, but the gist of the argument applies in more complex situations as well.

By way of contrast, consider figure 1.1b. Innovation in this case consists of the filling-up of the spectrum of products: in the base period only brands 1, 2, and 3 exist, but in the second period products 4 and 5 are added to the choice set. As the figure suggests, there will be no change whatsoever in the hedonic price function, so a price index based on it will altogether fail to register the innovations. A measure such as ΔW will certainly be positive, however, and could in fact be quite large. Figure 1.1c illustrates a similar situation, except that innovation takes the form of extending the range of available products by introducing higher quality brands, priced (approximately) in accordance to the base hedonic function. Again, this type of innovations will leave no trace in a hedonic index, whereas the actual gains may be substantial. Moreover, in the last two cases ΔW may be positive, and at the same time the hedonic-adjusted price index might actually *increase* (for an empirical finding of that nature, see Alexander and Mitchell, 1985).

It should be clear that the three stylized types of changes described are equally legitimate as instances of product innovations, and a priori it would appear that they are equally likely. However, there is some evidence to the effect that the last two are more prevalent during the initial

---

27. Similarly, if z enters both in the utility function and in the hedonic equation as $\log z$, then a proportional change in the z of all brands ($z_{i+1} = \lambda z_i, \lambda > 1$, for all i) will render the same result.

stages of the product cycle, whereas the first tends to occur later on, in the wake of widespread imitation and price competition. If this is so, adjusting for quality changes with the aid of hedonic price functions may be a reasonable first approximation for well-established sectors, but not for tracing the emergence of new ones. Indeed, one of the main findings from the empirical study here is that the bulk of the gains from innovation in CT occurred very early on in the development of the field. If this result is typical (and there is room to believe so), then the picture painted by price indices may systematically misrepresent a great deal of what goes on in the technologically progressive sectors of the economy.

The potential for discrepancies is aggravated by two practical problems: first, the collection of data on new products by official agencies usually starts well after their initial stages, and second, the norm is to chain-link them at the point of their inclusion in the index. In light of the previous discussion it is clear that both practices, dictated to a large extent by pragmatic considerations, are very likely to further diminish the reliability of hedonic-based price indices as indicators of innovation.

Of course the quality of the answer depends first of all upon the type of question asked: if one is interested in the average price change over time of a constant bundle of attributes within a given product class, the hedonic technique will render a fairly good answer. Is that also a good measure of the value of innovations in the field? Except for some special cases, the answer is, most likely not, not even as an approximation. This answer has a bearing upon a much wider issue, namely, that the main economic statistics explicitly or implicitly used as indicators of our well-being seem to be increasingly removed from such welfare parallels. As Griliches (1979) and others point out, conventional measures such as real income (adjusted, say, for total factor productivity growth) can hardly capture changes such as the increasing weight in GNP of services having ill-defined prices (health care, education, and so forth), the growing dependence of our well-being upon environmental factors (good and bad), and yes, the constant appearance of new and improved goods. The measures of innovation and the associated price indices developed in this chapter could thus help expose the limitations of conventional measures, while contributing to the design of economic indicators more closely and more directly linked to our welfare.

Appendix 1.1   The Decomposition of $W(\cdot)$ and the "Taste for Horizontal Variety"

As shown in section 1.3.3, the surplus function can be decomposed as follows:

$$(1.22) \quad W(S,h) = \sum_{i}^{n} \pi_i V_i + \left(-\sum_{i}^{n} \pi_i \ell n \pi_i \right) \equiv E(V_i) + \psi.$$

Now, suppose set S consists of product 1 and m variants of product 2. Then $\pi_i = \exp(V_i)/[\exp(V_1) + m \exp(V_2)]$, $i = 1, 2$. Differentiating the first term of (1.22),

$$\frac{\partial E(V_i)}{\partial m} = -\pi_1 \pi_2 V_1 + \pi_2 V_2 (1 - m\pi_2),$$

but $(1 - m \pi_2) = \pi_1$, hence

$$(1.23) \quad \frac{\partial E(V_i)}{\partial m} = \pi_1 \pi_2 (V_2 - V_1) \gtrless 0 \qquad \text{as } V_2 \gtrless V_1$$

Now to the second term,

$$\frac{\partial \psi}{\partial m} = -[-\pi_1 \pi_2 \ell n \pi_1 - \pi_1 \pi_2 + \pi_2 \ell n \pi_2 - m\pi_2^2 \ell n \pi_2 - m\pi_2^2]$$

$$= \pi_1 \pi_2 (1 + \ell n \pi_1 - \ell n \pi_2) + m\pi_2^2.$$

But $(\ell n \,\pi_1 - \ell n \,\pi_2) = V_1 - V_2$, hence

$$(1.24) \quad \frac{\partial \psi}{\partial m} = \pi_2 [1 - \pi_1 (V_2 - V_1)] > 0.$$

Clearly, if $V_1 > V_2$ then (1.24) is positive. Conversely, if $V_1 < V_2$, then for $\partial \psi/\partial m$ to be positive it is necessary that $\pi_1 (V_2 - V_1) < 1$, that is, that $(V_2 - V_1) < 1/\pi_1 = 1 + m \, exp \, (V_2 - V_1)$. But that is always true, since for any x, $x < exp(x)$.

2

The Case of CT Scanners

The empirical work is approached here through the case-study method, that is, the in-depth and thorough analysis of a particular innovation as it evolves over time. I have chosen for that purpose the case of Computed Tomography (CT) scanners, one of the most remarkable innovations in medical technology of recent times. This chapter raises the curtain on the empirical study with a mostly descriptive overview of this technology: its origins and evolution, the market for CT scanners, the diffusion process, and a detailed account of the quality dimensions of CT and of the data gathered for this study.

One of the leading premises here is that the study of technological change, particularly at the microlevel, requires a good grasp of the facts of technology, not just of the purely economic dimensions of innovations. Indeed, and as will become clear in the coming sections, the process of acquiring ample knowledge of the technology itself proved to be crucial in gathering the data, in selecting and measuring the relevant characteristics of CT scanners, in understanding the evolution of the innovation and the market, and so forth. More generally, as the pace of technical advance accelerates and technologies become more sophisticated, the need to invest heavily in getting a grasp of them grows ever more pressing, for those who wish to study their economic impact.

2.1 The Ongoing Revolution in Diagnostic Technologies

Just as the post-World War II years witnessed the proliferation of the "wonder drugs" (the new biochemical compounds that proved extremely effective in fighting an array of much dreaded illnesses), the last couple

of decades have seen the unfolding of unprecedental advances in diagnostic imaging technologies.

Roentgen's discovery of x rays in 1895 and the subsequent development of radiography opened a new era in the history of medicine: for
the first time the trained eye could peer into the human body, without
having to cut it open, in search for the signs of disease. However, and a
long series of gradual improvements notwithstanding, conventional
radiography remained severely limited in its ability to provide useful
diagnostic information. Meanwhile, as cancer and cardiovascular ail-
ments became the major health threats, displacing traditional infectious
diseases, the ever-present need for more powerful and accurate imaging
devices grew in urgency, fostered also by the rising emphasis on preven-
tive medicine and the exacting requirements of biomedical research.

Some of the basic ideas for new diagnostic modalities were formulated
already in the early fifties (the concept of ultrasonography goes back in
fact to the forties, following the development of the radar and the so-
nar), and a few of those were actually implemented in the sixties, such
as ultrasound, rectilinear scanners, and Gamma cameras. However, it
was not until the advent of microelectronics and powerful minicompu-
ters in the early seventies, coupled with significant advances in electro-
optics and nuclear physics, that the revolution in imaging technologies
started in earnest. Computed Tomography scanners came to epitomize
this revolution[1] and set the stage for subsequent innovations, such as
Positron Emission Tomography (PET), Digital Subtraction Angiography
and Digital Fluoroscopy (two members of the newly evolving family of
Digital Radiography), major advances in Nuclear Medicine and Ultrasound, and the wonder of the eighties, Magnetic Resonance Imaging
(previously known as Nuclear Magnetic Resonance).

This formidable array of rapidly advancing technologies allows physicians to scrutinize the human body to an extent never before thought
possible: they can render exceedingly clear pictures of most structures
in the body (including soft tissues), pinpoint elements as small as half a
millimeter, perform dynamic studies of various organs (including the
heart), map the metabolism of the brain, analyze the chemical composition of living tissues, and so on. All that has been accomplished while

1. This is the official denomination of the technology, as adopted by the Radiological
Society of North America in late 1975. Previously it was called Computerized Axial
Tomography, Computer Assisted Tomography, EMI Scanner, and other designations.
The abbreviation C.A.T. (rather than CT) is still used occasionally.

significantly reducing the risks and discomfort to patients and the need for invasive procedures. However, the wider impact of those innovations on the practice of medicine and their long-term effect on health outcomes remain to be assessed.

The following comparisons will give us some idea of the remarkable pace at which diagnostic imaging technologies have grown over the past two decades, and of the place of CT within that context (see table 2.1 and figure 2.1). In 1987 the U.S. market for those technologies stood at about 2.3 billion dollars, whereas it amounted to just 280 millions in 1972, at the start of their "take-off" (the world market is about twice the size of the U.S. market). In real terms, using the capital equipment price

Table 2.1   The U.S. Market for Diagnostic Imaging Technologies (current $ millions)

Year	X ray	CT	Ultrasound	Nuclear medicine	MRI	Total
1972	245	—	3	32	—	280
1973	276	5	8	42	—	331
1974	311	27	20	56	—	414
1975	350	82	50	75	—	557
1976	393	170	75	85	—	723
1977	440	208	82	100	—	830
1978	492	122	90	117	—	821
1979	550	141	99	137	—	927
1980	625	190	113	157	—	1,085
1981	725	328	171	134	—	1,358
1982	949	404	229	164	9	1,755
1983	934	543	237	152	50	1,916
1984	1,050	350	280	145	120	1,945
1985	1,025	304	313	149	337	2,128
1986	1,000	300	340	152	458	2,250
1987[a]	1,000	280	375	155	510	2,320

[a]Estimates.

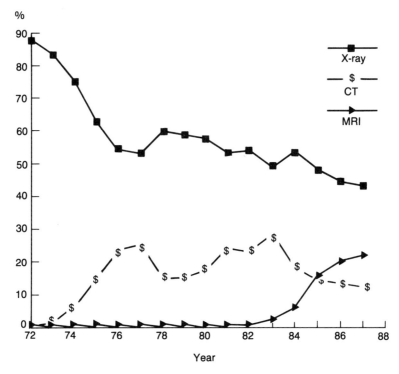

Figure 2.1   Distribution of Shares in the U.S. Market for Imaging
            Technologies

index as a deflator, that means an average rate of growth of over 8 percent per year over a period of fifteen years, making it one of the fastest
growing subsectors in the economy.[2] At the same time, the composition
of the market has changed dramatically, reflecting the successive waves
of innovations in the area: whereas in 1972 x-ray equipment was by far
the dominant imaging modality, accounting for almost 90 percent of the

2. For the sake of comparison, the electronic computing equipment industry (SIC
3573), one of the fastest growing sectors in manufacturing, grew in real terms at an
annual rate of 9 percent over the period 1973–1982, whereas the imaging market grew
over the same period at a rate of 10 percent per year. The comparison is not exact in
that the later refers to the US market, whereas the former refers to the value of ship-
ments of the US industry (the difference being in the value of exports and imports),
but the figures are in the right ballpark whatever the definition used.

market, by 1987 it amounted to less than 50 percent.[3] By contrast, CT managed to capture 25 percent of the market in the first five years following its introduction, fell briefly in the late seventies but recovered quite fast, peaking again in 1983 with over 28 percent of the market. Since then, though, it has been declining steadily (both in absolute and in relative terms), as it cedes pride of place to Magnetic Resonance Imaging (MRI), the current technological wonder.

2.2   The Story of CT Scanners

Computed Tomography is a highly sophisticated imaging modality that produces cross-sectional pictures of internal organs of the body, using a special configuration of x rays, detectors, and computers. It has been hailed, in and outside medicine, as one of the most remarkable innovations of recent times, comparable to the invention of radiography. Public recognition of the significance of the innovation climaxed in 1979, when the Nobel Prize in Medicine was awarded to the two scientists who pioneered the system: Godfrey N. Hounsfield of EMI Ltd. in the United Kingdom, and Allan M. Cormack of Tufts University in the United States.[4]

2.2.1   *The Development of Computed Tomography*

The invention of CT scanners is in many ways a typical case of serendipity; it was not the result of a conscious search for a better diagnostic technology, but rather the accidental outcome of research in a much more basic and broader area. Hounsfield, an engineer, began his work

3. In fact, the share of conventional x ray is declining much faster, since about half the market for x-ray systems consists now of various digital radiography systems.

4. Cormack, a physicist, was interested primarily in the mathematical problem of reconstructing an image from data on line integrals, although he was aware of its potential for medical diagnosis. From 1955 to 1963 he worked out a mathematical solution, constructed a very rudimentary scanner that used gamma rays, and performed scans of a phantom built of aluminium and lucite. He published the results in the *Journal of Applied Physics* in 1963 and 1964, but these went largely unnoticed (incidentally, the mathematical problem had been solved back in 1917 by Radon, the famous Austrian mathematician). Hounsfield, who actually designed and built the first operational CT scanner, apparently was not aware of Cormack's work.

at the Central Research Laboratories of EMI Ltd. in 1967.[5] At the time he was not involved with anything having to do with medicine or diagnostics; rather, he was doing research in the area of pattern identification and computer storage techniques and, in particular, on the problem of loss of efficiency in the transmission of large amounts of information from one medium to another. One typical instance of the problem was the loss of valuable information in radiology because of the relative insensitivity of film to x rays. This led Hounsfield to the idea of detecting the information carried by x rays with the aid of crystals rather than film, and to the realization that it would thus be possible to obtain images with far greater contrast than conventional x-ray pictures. At this point CT was born.

After devising some models for the computerized reconstruction of images, Hounsfield sought the support of the head of EMI's Central Research Laboratories for the project. Although EMI was known primarily for its records division, its laboratories had a long tradition of excellence in applied as well as basic research, which had led in the past to important innovations in communications, electronics, radar systems, and so on. Thus despite EMI's having nothing to do at that point with medical technologies, Hounsfield received full backing for the continuation of the project. Later on, a committee of prominent British radiologists and representatives of the British Department of Health and Social Security was formed to assess the project. Their enthusiastic endorsement brought in early 1970 the official support of the department. From then on events ran quickly: a first prototype was built and installed at the Atkinson Morley's Hospital in London, in September 1971. A year later, the EMI Head Scanner and the first series of brain scans done at the Atkinson Hospital were shown at the Radiological Society of North America meetings in Chicago, generating enormous interest. Commercial production followed soon after, and in June 1973 the first system in the United States was installed at the Mayo Clinic in Rochester, Minn. Meanwhile, Robert Ledley of Georgetown University Medical Center in Washington, D.C., developed a whole-body scanner (called ACTA scanner), and installed the first unit at the Georgetown Center in February 1974 (the system was later acquired and marketed by Pfizer).

5. See Berggren (1985) for a detailed account of Hounsfield's initial work on Computed Tomography at EMI.

2.2.2   Competition, Market Structure, and Technical Progress in CT

Aware of the revolutionary nature of the innovation and anticipating a vast market, a number of U.S., European, and Japanese companies rushed to enter the new field (see tables 2.2 and 2.3). In the period 1973–1978, 15 firms stepped in, ranging from the giants in electronics (General Electric, Siemens, Philips), to pharmaceutical companies (Pfizer, Searle, Syntex), to small, specialized firms (AS&E, Elscint). The process of rapid entry culminated in 1977, with the number of competitors at a peak of 13 firms, and the Herfindahl index dropping to an all-time low of 0.22. As table 2.3 reveals, this initial burst of action in the market manifested itself also in the number of new scanner models introduced, which peaked in 1977 as well. Since then, however, the number of players has gradually contracted, stabilizing at a total of 8 firms by 1981, with just one exit and one entry taking place from 1982 to 1988.

As is commonly the case in new markets, the relative position of firms changed dramatically over time. The most notable changes were, first, the exit of EMI in 1980, after having dominated the market for about five years; second, the gradual fall of Technicare from a position of close second to its exit in 1986; and third, the rise of General Electric from 1976 onwards to a position of undisputable dominance after the early eighties.

As the dust settled, it became clear that the firms that prevailed in this very competitive market were, almost exclusively, those that had from the start a deep involvement in the market for conventional x rays. The main reason seems to reside in marketing complementarities rather than in any sort of strict technological advantage: firms with a significant share of the x-ray market had access to a large customer base (CT scanners and conventional x rays are both aimed at the same users, namely radiologists), and could therefore take advantage of scale economies in marketing, servicing, and customer support, rely on long-term ties with users, and exploit their already established reputation. Once the pace of technical advance in CT started to abate in the late seventies, and as the market suffered its first serious downturn, the factors just mentioned became dominant, displacing technological excellency and innovativeness in determining the long-term performance of firms.

Clearly, competition in the CT market took primarily the form of fierce product rivalry, each firm trying to capture a share of the growing market by offering ever-improving performance. The result was a stag-

Table 2.2   Firms in Computed Tomography

Firm[a]	Entry[b]	Exit	Total units sold[c]	Max. market share (year)	Patents[d] in CT
EMI	1973	1980	596	100.0 (73)	123
Artronix	1975	1979	34	3.7 (76)	4
G.E.	1975	—	466	40.6 (81)	52
Pfizer	1975	1981	118	11.3 (75)	5
Technicare	1975	1986	534	39.0 (78)	16
AS&E	1976	1978	13	2.9 (77)	5
Picker	1976	—	82	10.7 (80)	11
Syntex	1976	1978	31	5.9 (76)	5
Varian	1976	1978	15	2.1 (76)	7
Elscint	1977	—	56	8.5 (80)	3
Philips	1977	—	n.a.	n.a.	50
Searle	1977	1978	6	1.3 (77)	1
Siemens	1977	—	54	14.6 (81)	51
CGR	1978	1979	1	0.3 (78)	6
Omnimedical	1978	—	45	7.1 (80)	0
Toshiba	1979	—	7	3.3 (81)	18
Interad	1982	—	—	—	0
Imatron	1984	—	—	—	4

[a]In addition to Toshiba, at least two other Japanese companies manufacture CT scanners, but they are virtually absent from the U.S. market.

[b]The year of entry corresponds in most cases to the date of announcement of the first CT scanner or the date of the first order received by the firm. However, in a few cases the effective entry of the firm in the market occurred later (for example, Siemens announced its first scanner in November 1974, but the system failed and the firm actually entered the U.S. market only in 1977; Pfizer acquired the Acta scanner only in 1975, and so on).

[c]Up to June 1981.

[d]Total number of patents granted up to December 1986.

Table 2.3 Selected Indicators of the Market for CT Scanners

Year	# of firms	Net entry[a]	Herfindahl index	# of models[b]	# of new models[b]	Herfindahl for patents[c]
1973	1	1	1.00	1	1	1.00
1974	1	0	1.00	1	1	0.77
1975	5	4	0.42	5	4	0.21
1976	9	4	0.36	14	11	0.32
1977	13	4	0.22	23	14	0.22
1978	11	−2	0.27	23	6	0.15
1979	10	−1	0.22	22	5	0.15
1980	9	−1	0.26	17	2	0.29
1981	8	−1	0.25	14	3	0.27
1982	9	1	n.a.	16	8	0.37

[a]Number of entries minus number of exits.
[b]Philips's scanners are not included.
[c]Index of concentration of patents by year of application.

gering pace of technological advance (see table 2.4). By 1980 the main performance dimensions of CT had improved by factors of 5 to 50; for example, scan time dropped from five *minutes* to a couple of *seconds* (opening the possibility of scanning not just the brain but almost any organ in the body), spatial resolution improved dramatically to less than one millimeter, and so on. At the same time the basic design of CT systems underwent four "generational" changes, going from a single detector, single pencil-beam that could take 28,000 readings per scan, to a full ring of several hundred stationary detectors (2,400 in the most ambitious model) that could perform close to one million readings and process the information in a few seconds. Mirroring those advances and the underlying nature of competition in the field, the price of body scanners went up from less than $400,000 in 1975 to about one million dollars by 1981; on the other hand, the price of head scanners dropped from the same initial amount to $100,000–150,000 by 1979.

Not surprisingly, about 80 percent of the innovative activity in CT was carried out by firms that were active in the market for CT scanners (at

Table 2.4   Average Prices and Characteristics of CT Scanners, 1973–1982

Year	Price[a] ($ thousand) Head	Body	Speed[b] (seconds) Head	Body	Resolution[c] (millimeters) Head	Body
1973	310	—	300	—	3.1	—
1974	370	—	300	—	1.7	—
1975	379	365	285	195.0	1.8	1.6
1976	374	471	105	63.0	1.7	1.5
1977	354	573	95	19.0	1.7	1.3
1978	167	620	96	7.1	1.6	1.2
1979	154	667	150	6.6	1.5	1.1
1980	154	739	115	5.5	1.5	1.0
1981	150	827	115	4.9	1.5	0.8
1982	150	850	115	2.6	1.5	0.7

[a]Weighted average of all scanners in the market (annual sales as weights).
[b]Minimum scan time, simple average.
[c]Spatial resolution, simple average.

least for a while). Moreover, they were responsible for an even larger fraction of the important innovations in the field (see table 2.5).[6] Research on CT done at universities, government agencies, and by private individuals was sparse and had little impact. Over 50 percent of all patents in CT were awarded to residents of the United States, followed by Germany (19 percent), the U.K. (13 percent), and Japan (7.5 percent). Although Computed Tomography originated in England, the United States became almost immediately the prime locus of innovative activity in this area, reflecting primarily the fact that it accounts for a full half of the world market for imaging technologies.

2.2.3   Why CT Scanners as Case Study?

Although the choice of a specific innovation for a case study hardly needs formal justification, it is worth spelling out the reasons that make

6. These statements are based on patent counts and counts weighted by citations: see Chapter 5 for a thorough discussion of the merits of those measures as indicators of innovative activity and of important innovations.

Table 2.5 Distribution of CT Patents by Type of Assignee and Country of Inventor

Type of assignee	Type of assignee			
	No. of patents	% of patents	% of patents weighted by citations	Average citations per patent
Firms in CT	364	79.8	88.9	2.2
Other firms	44	9.6	5.4	· 1.1
Universities	21	4.6	3.3	1.4
Private inventors	20	4.4	1.9	0.8
Government agencies	7	1.5	0.4	0.6

Country	Country of inventor	
	% of patents	% of patents weighted by citations
United States	52.4	60.6
Germany	19.1	13.3
United Kingdom	13.2	14.8
Japan	7.5	5.9
The Netherlands	3.3	2.1
France	2.6	2.1
Other (6 countries)	1.9	1.2
Total	100.0	100.0

CT scanners a case particularly well suited to the goals of this project because this can tell us something about the requirements, potential significance, and limitations of this line of research.

1. Computed Tomography is, to repeat, a major innovation that had a profound and lasting impact on its field; to be sure, this is by no means a prerequisite, but it certainly makes the case study more appealing. Moreover, the technology improved dramatically over time, suggesting that the welfare gains stemming from those advances had been substantial. As that proved indeed to be the case, a more compelling argument

can be made regarding the need for such welfare measures (and their underlying methodology) for assessing the dynamic performance of technologically progressive sectors.

2. CT scanners are undoubtedly a product rather than a process innovation, according to the criteria set in Chapter 1. That is, the performance characteristics of CT (speed, resolution, reconstruction time, and so on) are clearly nonconcatenable, in that a larger number of scanners cannot deliver more of these attributes.

3. The technology is recent enough so that, aside from the methodological and empirical insights that may be generated, the study could be of relevance for outstanding policy issues as well (for example, the ongoing debate on the handling of new medical technologies, particularly of their diffusion).

4. CT scanners constitute a distinct, well-defined product (or product class), a fact that greatly facilitates the empirical analysis. By contrast, many other products take the form of modular systems or have a wide range of different configurations, making it very difficult to determine the standard unit of the product, and consequently, to assess price and quality dimensions uniformly across the different models or brands. Likewise, in those cases it becomes exceedingly hard to establish the boundaries of the product class, both in a cross-section and over time, and hence to delimit the scope of the empirical inquiry.

5. Because CT scanners commanded so much public attention, large amounts of data were gathered by various government and public institutions. Thus it seemed a priori that the heavy data requirements of this type of research could be met with relative ease. Likewise, since the users of CT are hospitals and clinics, it was reasonable to assume that data on "who bought what and when," and on the attributes of users would in principle be available in some form.

6. The number of competing CT models was particularly well suited to the estimation of the Multinomial Logit Model. A larger number would have made the computations quite cumbersome, whereas fewer models would have prevented the inclusion of variables of interest.

So much for the merits of the case. As to the drawbacks, at least two deserve to be mentioned at the outset: first, the expectations regarding the availability of data turned out to be overly optimistic. Second, as will be discussed in detail in Chapter 4, the various imperfections afflicting the market for health care make the interpretation of the welfare measures more elusive and problematic.

2.3 Diffusion and Regulation

In contrast to the traditionally cautious and often reluctant attitude of the medical profession to the adoption of innovations (see Russell, 1979), the diffusion of CT scanners in the United States proceeded at a very rapid pace (see tables 2.6 and 2.7). In fact, compared to a set of 20 innovations in various fields for which diffusion studies have been performed, CT ranks fifth in terms of diffusion speed, and it is by far the fastest of the medical innovations in the set.[7] As is usually the case, larger hospitals adopted the new technology much faster than smaller ones (see figure 2.2): by 1984, barely over a decade after the appearance of CT, virtually all large hospitals (more than 400 beds) had CT scanners, but only about 3 percent of hospitals with fewer than 100 beds.

Undoubtedly, the immediately apparent diagnostic merits of CT scanners, particularly in brain studies, provided the main stimulus for their rapid proliferation.[8] Yet it is equally clear that the system of third-party reimbursement on a fee-for-service basis (which prevailed up to 1983) greatly facilitated the process and may have provided hospitals and clinics with financial incentives to acquire the technology. Other extraneous motives having to do with the nature of rivalry among health-care providers (such as professional status, recruitment of highly qualified medical personnel, and so on) may have fostered its adoption as well.

The rapid diffusion of CT happened at a time of mounting concerns regarding the fast-rising costs of health care in the United States, and hence it brought to the forefront the intricate issue of how to allocate resources for the acquisition and use of this kind of new, very sophisticated, but very expensive medical technologies. Clearly, this is but one aspect of the general problem of allocating resources to health care, in view of the various types of market failures that characterize this sector,

7. The comparison was carried out in Trajtenberg and Yitzhaki (1989), using the Gini's mean difference as the measure of diffusion speed. The main advantage of the Gini is that its estimation does not require one to assume a particular functional form for the distribution of adoption times, thus avoiding potential misspecification biases. In fact, we show that in the case of CT scanners the use of the logistic distribution (the one most commonly used in diffusion studies) would have resulted in an upward bias of about 50 percent in the estimate of speed. Moreover, the Gini allows for consistent comparisons across different diffusion studies.

8. The rapid spread of the technology was greatly helped by the fact that CT procedures are not invasive (except for the use of contrast materials in some procedures), and hence present relatively low risks, other than the known dangers of exposure to x rays.

Table 2.6   Sales of CT Scanners by Type and Year

Year	Unit sales	Body scanners (%)	Private clinics (%)	New adopters (%)	Hospitals[a] with scanners (%)
1973	16	0.0	6.2	100.0	0.5
1974	74	0.0	17.3	98.4	2.4
1975	221	44.8	18.1	97.2	8.1
1976	374	76.2	21.4	81.7	15.8
1977	389	85.1	19.0	82.5	24.2
1978	251	72.3	24.3	82.1	29.1
1979	278	70.0	23.0	75.6	34.3
1980	306	81.7	28.8	57.0	38.1
1981	426	88.7	22.3	45.5	42.7
1982	503	94.9	19.7	45.1	48.2
1983	639	96.0	21.3	42.3	54.5
1984[b]	390	91.5	33.1	38.8	57.3

[a]Community hospitals with more than 100 beds.
[b]The data for the last quarter of 1984 are incomplete.

Table 2.7   Diffusion of CT Scanners by Hospital Size in Selected Years

Hospital size (number of beds)	Number of hospitals	% of hospitals with CT			
		1975	1978	1981	1984
100–199	1,417	0.4	7.3	15.2	29.2
200–299	719	5.6	27.1	44.1	64.0
300–399	384	13.3	49.7	71.1	84.6
400–499	244	23.0	70.1	88.9	97.1
500 +	329	39.2	81.2	93.0	100.0
All	3,093	9.1	30.0	42.9	57.0

Note: the purchases of CT scanners are dated by the orders, not the installations.

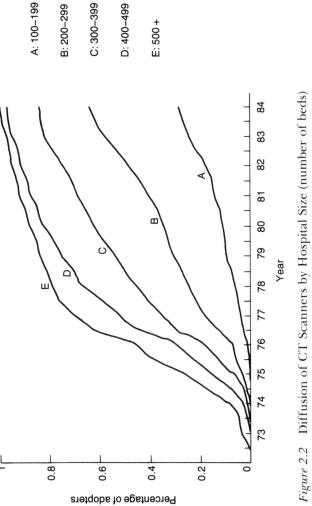

A: 100–199

B: 200–299

C: 300–399

D: 400–499

E: 500 +

Figure 2.2 Diffusion of CT Scanners by Hospital Size (number of beds)

and society's implicit commitment to provide a minimal level of health care to all. The issue is even more complex in the case of diagnostic technologies, essentially because of the difficulties in evaluating the impact of diagnostic procedures on health care outcomes.

Just because the diffusion of a particular innovation is very fast, it does not necessarily follow that it is overly fast from the viewpoint of social welfare. It is actually very difficult to determine the optimal adoption path of any innovation, primarily because of the various externalities that are usually at work along the diffusion process, having to do with the spread of information, cost reductions due to learning-by-doing, and so on. These difficulties are aggravated when the technology improves rapidly over time, as was the case with CT, since faster adoption could then result in the premature obsolescence of most of the installed base (clearly, the more expensive the innovation, the more acute this problem will be). Therefore, normative statements to the effect that the diffusion of an innovation was "too fast" (or "too slow") should be taken with a great deal of caution.

Be it as it may, the prevailing perception in the mid-seventies was that CT scanners were indeed spreading too fast. That provoked an intense public debate, which in turn motivated a series of studies on the cost-effectiveness of new medical technologies in general, and of CT in particular.[9] More important, it prompted the government to take a series of regulatory measures, primarily through the implementation of Certificate of Need (CON) requirements and Section 1122 of the Social Security Act. Essentially, those measures were meant to restrain the spread of CT scanners, by having special agencies at the state level review applications for new scanners and set approval criteria according to "need" (given the number of scanners already in the area and their utilization), costs, and so on. As shown in detail in appendix 2.1, regulation did have a noticeable impact on the extent of diffusion: states with stricter regulatory controls had indeed a lower percentage of adopters, at least until mid-1981. Conversely, relatively more scanners were installed privately in states where the regulations were enacted early and had a wide scope.

9. In fact, during the Carter administration Congress established a new agency for that purpose, the National Center for Health Care Technologies (NCHCT). Major studies were undertaken also by the Office of Technology Assessment (OTA) of the U.S. Congress (OTA, 1976, 1978, 1981), the National Academy of Sciences (1977), and the American Hospital Association (1976).

Thus an unintended by-product of regulation seems to have been the proliferation of private providers of CT services relative to hospitals.

Partly as a consequence of the actual implementation of the regulatory measures, and partly because of the previous rush to buy CT scanners in anticipation of those measures, the overall diffusion of CT slowed down significantly in 1977–1979.[10] This hiatus did not last long, however. The regulatory controls were eased substantially in the early eighties, primarily because of sustained pressure from the medical profession, difficulties in implementing the regulatory measures, rapidly mounting evidence regarding the benefits of CT for an ever expanding range of uses (thanks to the accumulation of experience and to advances in the technology), and the antiregulatory political climate associated with the Reagan administration. Following this crumbling of regulation and a major reshuffling of the industry, the market rebounded and embarked on a second growth and diffusion wave that peaked in late 1982. Since then it has declined steadily, though, for various reasons: first, the introduction in October 1983 of the new prospective reimbursement system based on diagnosis-related groups forced hospitals to weigh carefully the acquisition of expensive diagnostic technologies, and effectively removed any purely financial incentive to do so. Second, the diffusion process is rapidly approaching an asymptotic stage: as said above, most large hospitals have already adopted CT and, barring unforeseen technological developments, it is very unlikely that large numbers of small hospitals will do so. Third, Magnetic Resonance Imaging is rapidly emerging as the imaging modality of the future, and there is no doubt that to some extent it is displacing or at least outcompeting CT in terms of budgets and priority in acquisition.

Diffusion processes are commonly described in the aggregate by the time path of the cumulative percentage of adopters, $F(t)$. Moreover, those processes are often parametrized by assuming that $F(t)$ corresponds to some specific distribution, such as the logistic. As its history indicates, though, the diffusion process of CT scanners has been subjected to severe shocks that made its path anything but smooth. In these circumstances the course followed by $F(t)$ is not very revealing and, more important, it would be highly misleading to try to characterize the pro-

10. Actually, not only first-time purchases dwindled, but the CT market as a whole experienced a sharp downturn in 1978–79 (recall tables 2.1 and 2.2.).

cess over the entire period by imposing on it any given functional form. As argued in Trajtenberg and Yitzhaki (1989), the hazard rate is a more sensitive tool and hence its time path may offer a better summary description of the diffusion process (in this context the hazard rate, $h(t)$, stands for the conditional probability of adopting at time t, having held out until then). As can be seen in figure 2.3, the hazard rate captures very well indeed the main features of the process as outlined above: the acceleration of the first few years peaking in late 1976, the sharp drop afterwards, and the second wave in the early eighties. The variability of the process as manifested in the plot of $h(t)$ is in fact quite striking and rather atypical. If nothing else, it should sound a note of warning as to the marked impact that government intervention might have on diffu-

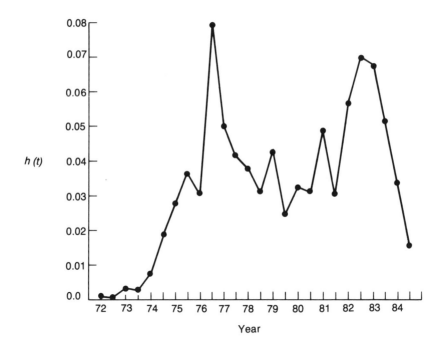

The hazard rate is defined as $h(t) = \dfrac{f(t)}{1 - F(t)}$, where $F(t)$ is the cumulative distribution of adopters, and $f(t)$ the corresponding density (that is, $f(t) = \partial F(t)/\partial t$).

Figure 2.3   The Conditional Probability of Adoption of CT Scanners (Hazard rate)

sion, considering how elusive optimal diffusion paths are, and how little is usually known about them when those decisions are made.

So far I have referred to the diffusion of CT in the United States nationwide; however, the distribution of scanners across states has been quite uneven, as is the case also with installations in hospitals versus private clinics (see table 2.8). Thus, for example, the average percentage of hospitals with scanners by the end of 1984 was 59.1 percent (with a standard deviation of 18.6 percent), with some small states such as Alaska and Nevada having reached 100 percent adoption, whereas others had less than one third (Minnesota, Vermont, and Wyoming). The average percentage of scanners installed in private clinics was 20.4 percent, with a range of 0 to 50 percent, and a standard deviation of 11.2 percent. On a national basis there was one CT scanner per 61,200 inhabitants (private scanners included), but again, there were marked disparities across states in that respect.

Finally, to gauge the determinants of the timing of adoption for individual hospitals, I run a simple regression of adoption time on various attributes of hospitals for all community hospitals that had adopted scanners by the end of 1984. As shown in appendix 2.2, the size of the hospital (by number of beds) and its degree of sophistication (as captured by the percentage of advanced facilities it offered) had the largest impact on the timing of adoption: hospitals located one standard deviation above the mean in terms of size were likely to adopt some 10 months earlier than the average, and those with 20 percent (one standard deviation) more advanced facilities than the mean almost 14 months earlier. Government control of hospitals seems to retard adoption, but its influence is not statistically significant; on the other hand, the profit motive does have a significant impact, that is, for-profit providers were likely to adopt almost one year earlier than not-for-profit hospitals.

2.4 Technical Aspects

2.4.1 Principles of Operation

The imaging process of conventional x rays builds on the differences in density of structures—organs, tissues—in the body: the denser a structure, the more energy it absorbs as the x rays pass through it, and hence the more attenuated the beam will be when it hits the radiographic film. Thus very dense material such as bone will show in white, areas contain-

Table 2.8 Distribution of CT Scanners in the U.S. by State and Ownership

State	Number of hospitals[a]	Hospitals with CT	Private clinics with CT	Total number of CTs[b]	% of hospitals with CT	% of private clinic CTs	Population per scanner (thousands)
Alabama	63	33	5	55	52.4	9.1	72.5
Alaska	4	4	1	7	100.0	14.3	72.1
Arizona	27	18	15	46	66.7	34.8	66.8
Arkansas	35	17	4	33	48.6	15.2	71.1
California	287	213	104	554	74.2	28.9	46.6
Colorado	31	26	6	53	83.9	15.1	60.2
Connecticut	29	20	8	38	69.0	23.7	83.0
Delaware	6	4	2	9	66.7	33.3	68.2
D.C.	13	11	2	27	84.6	7.4	23.1
Florida	148	94	47	232	63.5	28.0	47.6
Georgia	67	39	26	101	58.2	27.7	57.8
Hawaii	12	9	0	12	75.0	0.0	86.4
Idaho	12	8	2	15	66.7	13.3	66.6
Illinois	172	106	24	205	61.6	19.5	56.2
Indiana	73	38	9	70	52.1	14.3	78.5
Iowa	45	20	6	37	44.4	18.9	78.5

Kansas	36	16	3	32	44.4	9.4	76.3
Kentucky	47	33	12	66	70.2	22.7	56.4
Louisiana	57	33	12	73	57.9	20.5	61.1
Maine	15	8	1	12	53.3	8.3	96.3
Maryland	41	32	10	69	78.0	23.2	63.0
Massachusetts	90	45	7	82	50.0	9.8	70.7
Michigan	125	51	10	84	40.8	11.9	107.8
Minnesota	65	22	13	72	33.8	37.5	57.8
Mississippi	39	23	3	34	59.0	8.8	76.4
Missouri	78	50	7	105	64.1	6.7	47.6
Montana	15	9	1	15	60.0	6.7	54.9
Nebraska	22	15	2	27	68.2	11.1	59.4
Nevada	7	7	3	19	100.0	21.1	48.3
New Hampshire	13	7	2	10	53.8	20.0	97.8
New Jersey	95	57	17	114	60.0	34.2	65.9
New Mexico	12	12	7	29	100.0	27.6	49.2
New York	237	101	67	238	42.6	33.2	74.6
North Carolina	73	31	14	79	42.5	25.3	78.1
North Dakota	15	8	3	17	53.3	17.6	40.4
Ohio	147	89	26	169	60.5	18.3	63.6

Table 2.8 (continued)

State	Number of hospitals[a]	Hospitals with CT	Private clinics with CT	Total number of CTs[b]	% of hospitals with CT	% of private clinic CTs	Population per scanner (thousands)
Oklahoma	36	21	9	49	58.3	22.4	67.6
Oregon	27	23	7	49	85.2	16.3	54.6
Pennsylvania	195	116	25	212	59.5	14.6	56.1
Puerto Rico	33	3	6	13	9.1	61.5	n.a.
Rhode Island	12	7	3	11	58.3	27.3	87.5
South Carolina	38	17	2	29	44.7	6.9	113.9
South Dakota	12	6	2	9	50.0	22.2	78.3
Tennessee	68	42	13	98	61.8	14.3	48.2
Texas	168	95	72	284	56.5	30.6	56.6
Utah	11	9	4	23	81.8	21.7	70.6

Vermont	7	1	2	4	14.3	50.0	132.5
Virginia	70	38	7	72	54.3	12.5	78.3
Washington	46	31	22	72	67.4	31.9	60.4
West Virginia	31	11	5	30	35.5	20.0	65.0
Wisconsin	83	34	8	65	41.0	15.4	73.3
Wyoming	3	1	1	6	33.3	16.7	85.5
All states	3093	1764	669	3866	57.0	22.7	61.2
Average	59	34	13	74	59.1	20.4	67.5
Standard deviation	62	39	20	94	18.6	11.2	22.9

[a]Taken from the 1980 survey of the American Hospital Association.

[b]This figure refers to the total number of scanners *sold* and hence may be biased upward, since some of those scanners may have already been scrapped. Recall also that some users have several scanners.

Note: All figures refer to community hospitals with more than 100 beds, and to CT scanners installed through the end of 1984.

ing air or gas will appear in black, and tissues of intermediate density in various shades of gray. Such a procedure has two main shortcomings: first, it collapses a three-dimensional body into a two-dimensional plane, superimposing all structures in the third dimension (depth). The visual information reflects therefore the average absorption along the path of the x-ray beam, rather than that of each structure of interest. Second, the x ray is not sensitive to small differences in density and cannot deliver images of soft tissue such as the liver or pancreas, not to speak of the brain.

CT scanning, while based on the same physical principle, namely, the differential energy absorption of body structures, overcomes those limitations by using a radically different approach. The target area is not a plane but a series of contiguous, very thin slices or cross-sections of the body; accordingly, the x rays are radiated not as a cone but as a very narrow, collimated beam. After passing through the body, the x-ray beam hits an array of detectors—rather than a radiographic film—that read and quantify the outcoming energy, and pass this digitized information to a computer. Instead of taking a single snapshot, the procedure is repeated many times by rotating the x-ray source and the detectors around the body, and taking readings at each step (angle) in the rotation. The data thus gathered are processed by a computer, and the reconstructed picture is displayed on a cathode-ray tube (see figures 2.4 and 2.5).

Figure 2.6 shows schematically the basic scanning configurations (or geometries) of the different generations of CT scanners: first-generation systems consist of a single detector[11] and an x-ray source generating a pencil-like beam, both mounted at opposite ends of a frame called gantry. The scan is performed in a series of consecutive, dual-movement steps: first, the beam "translates" across—or traverses—the body in a rectilinear fashion, then the gantry shifts (rotates) 1° of arc and traverses again, and so forth until completing a 180° rotation. Second-generation scanners are based on the same translate/rotate principle, but have a multiple-pencil beam and multiple detectors (up to 50). They gather more information in each traverse, and the rotational increments between traverses can be much larger (up to 10°), reducing substantially the time it takes to complete a scan. Third- and fourth-generation scan-

---

11. Some systems scanned two contiguous slices simultaneously and hence had two detectors.

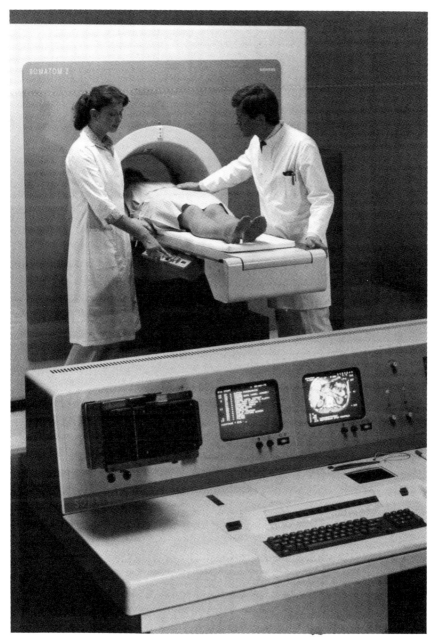

Figure 2.4   A Typical CT Body Scanner

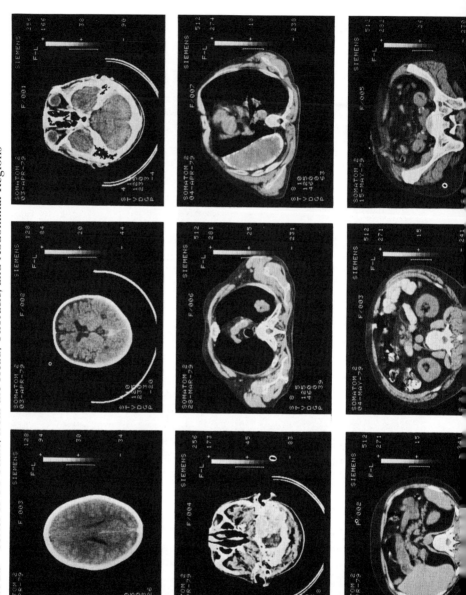

Figure 2.5   Series of CT Scans, from the Head, Thoracic, and Abdominal Regions

ners do away with the dual motion (and its inherent mechanical slowness) and perform instead a 360° rotational sweep. That requires a much larger number of detectors (several hundreds), and a fan-shaped beam opening in a wide angle so as to encompass the whole diameter of the body. The difference between third- and fourth-generation systems is that the latter have a full ring of stationary detectors and only the x-ray source rotates, whereas in the former the ring of detectors rotates as well.

There are two types of CT systems, as we recall: head and whole-body scanners.[12] One can perform scans of the brain only, the other can be used to image any section of the body. From a technological viewpoint they are identical, except that head scanners are slower and less sophisticated than body scanners, and their scan geometry is of the translate/rotate type (first or second generation), rather than of the more advanced third and fourth generations.[13] Although the majority of CT procedures actually performed are brain scans,[14] body scanners have dominated the scene from 1976 on, both in sales and in terms of technological advance (recall tables 2.4 and 2.6).

2.4.2   Selection of Characteristics

A major problem in empirical research dealing with products' characteristics is the selection of the minimal set of relevant attributes, that is, of characteristics that have a direct and significant impact on actual choices, and hence qualify as arguments in the utility function of consumers (the vector z in the notation of chapter 1). The selection is difficult because characteristics are usually traded in the form of indivisible bundles (that is, products) rather than separately, and are therefore not

12. General Electric attempted to develop a breast scanner in 1975, but clinical studies done on the first prototypes were not successful, and the project was abandoned.

13. Except for one model, the Artronix Neuro Scanner, which used a third-generation configuration (Artronix exited the market in 1979). An additional difference between the two types of scanners is that the aperture of the gantry in head scanners is much smaller than in whole-body scanners, for obvious reasons.

14. Brain scans were the more frequent procedure, at least until the early eighties: according to a study conducted in 1978 by the *Radiology/Nuclear Medicine Magazine* and the Technology Marketing Group, Inc., the ratio of brain to body procedures was 4 to 1 (79 percent and 21 percent respectively). A survey by the Massachusetts Department of Public Health found the distribution to be 74 percent and 26 percent for the fiscal year 1980.

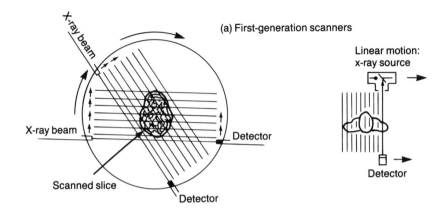

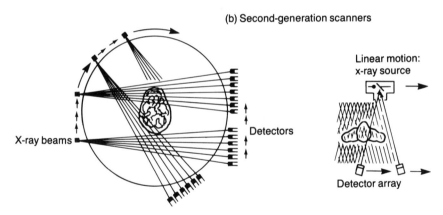

Figure 2.6   Four Generations of CT Scanners

directly observable as individual entities in the market. Instead, the researcher has to learn of them from a variety of direct and indirect sources, such as descriptive brochures, consumer surveys, advertising messages, and the examination of the product itself. These sources typically contain technical descriptions of a large number of quality dimen-

(c) Third-generation scanners

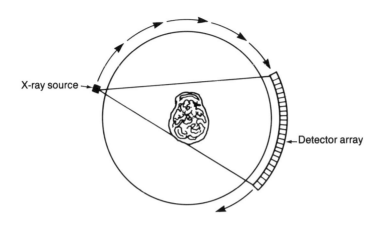

(d) Fourth-generation scanners

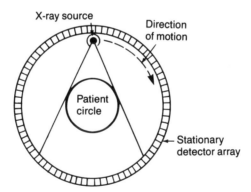

Figure 2.6 (continued)

sions, but seldom offer decisive evidence regarding their relative importance for consumer choice. Statistical arbitration may, of course, help in
the selection process, but it will rarely be conclusive, and an element of
arbitrariness is likely to remain.

As a start, a distinction is often made between "technical" (x) and "performance" (z) characteristics, the two being connected via some "transformation function" $z = f(x)$; see for example Otha and Griliches, 1976.
This is analogous to the input-output distinction, the presumption being
that consumers are interested only in z, not in the underlying technical
aspects associated with the x vector. In practice, though, it is fairly difficult to differentiate between them conclusively, since some of the x's
may serve both as inputs and as performance characteristics in their own
right, or may be classified either way depending on the level of aggregation, or on the type of consumers buying the product.[15] Nevertheless,
and with those caveats in mind, the distinction is useful and may serve
as a preliminary criterion for the selection of the characteristics to be
included in the analysis.

A related problem is that characteristics are often highly correlated,
reflecting the fact that products are not uniformly distributed in attributes space, but tend instead to be bunched in a few, closely knitted
groups, or stratified on quality levels. However, this may actually help
reduce the many dimensions of performance to a manageable number,
either by resorting to statistical constructs such as principal components
(see Dhrymes, 1971), or simply by discarding attributes deemed to be of
minor importance that are highly correlated with the main ones.

At first sight it would seem that the identification and selection problems had to be particularly severe in the case at hand: in other studies
of this kind the researcher, being also a consumer, usually has first-hand
knowledge of the products examined (for example, consumer durables,
transportation modes, and so on), and hence can resort to personal
experience or introspection for guidance. That is certainly not the case
with CT scanners: the area of use (diagnostic medicine) and the technological sophistication of the systems are both far removed from common experience and competence. To be sure, I invested heavily in learning about medical technologies in general and CT in particular, and that
proved indeed to be critical for grasping the innovation and its perfor-

---

15. For example, it is often the case that the more educated consumers are, the more
they will tend to consider technical attributes in making their choices.

mance dimensions. However, once I had achieved a basic understanding of the technology, the identification and preliminary selection of relevant attributes of CT scanners proved, quite surprisingly, not to be a major stumbling block.

2.4.3 Quality Dimensions of CT Scanners

By all accounts, the most important performance characteristics of CT scanners are image quality and scan time. Among the host of other potentially relevant attributes, only reconstruction time and gantry tilt have been considered here (the latter proved to be of no statistical significance and was eventually discarded). Three major difficulties prevented the inclusion of additional attributes. First, data were not available for some of those attributes covering a sufficiently large number of scanners. Second, the variance in cross-sections was too small; that is, some of the features of interest were incorporated in most CT scanners at roughly the same time so their effect within a given period could not have been successfully estimated. Third, some of the attributes were of a qualitative nature: their inclusion would have required the use of many dummy variables, with the consequent loss of precious degrees of freedom. In any case, a preliminary statistical examination showed that many of the excluded attributes are indeed highly correlated with the included ones, and therefore not much is lost by leaving them out. Following is a description of the attributes included in the analysis.

(i) Scan Time. The length of time it takes a CT scanner to complete a scan is the crucial factor determining the clarity of the images obtained (that is, the presence and extent of blurring and of motion "artifacts") and hence the range of organs that can be scanned successfully. To obtain clear images, the organ scanned has to be as still as possible for the length of the scanning procedure. However, patients have little control over internal body movements: they can hold their breath for no more than 20 seconds on average, and of course many organs are subject to involuntary motions. Thus the shorter the scan time, the less will be the extent of distortions caused by those unavoidable motions (this is equivalent to the importance of speed in photography).

Clearly, the importance of scan time increases with the extent of motion in the organs of interest, the two extremes being the brain and the heart. Because the head can be effectively immobilized for a substantial length of time and has virtually no internal motion, the brain can be successfully scanned even with scan times of several minutes. On the other hand, the scanning of the heart requires speeds of the order of one-hundredth of a second (this has already been achieved with Cine CT systems), or alternatively, the synchronization of the emission of x rays with the heart beat (this is called gated CT).

The advantages of faster scan times have to be weighed against the reduction in the number of ray measurements made, with the consequent detrimental effect on resolution (this is again analogous to the tradeoffs encountered in photography). Scan time will be referred to as speed, and defined as the minimum scan time possible in a scanner (most scanners can be operated at several speeds), measured in seconds.

(ii) Image Quality. The output of a CT procedure consists of a series of computer-generated pictures displayed on a TV-like screen. Thus the acid test for the performance of a CT scanner is the quality of the received images, that is, the accuracy and richness in detail of the pictures, and hence the extent to which they visually convey useful diagnostic information. Clearly, such a notion of image quality is not well defined and does not lend itself easily to objective assessment. In fact, there is a voluminous literature in radiology and medical physics on this issue, and the evaluation of the image quality of most imaging modalities, including CT scanners, is still an open, controversial question.

Bringing in econometric tools to bear on the issue, I designed a procedure to estimate indices of image quality (very much like total factor productivity indices) and applied it successfully to experimental data on 6 scanners (the procedure and results are discussed in appendix 2.3; the complete version is in Trajtenberg, 1984). Unfortunately, and despite intense efforts, it was not possible to gather the extensive data needed to estimate indices of image quality of all CT scanners marketed up to 1982 (about 50 different models). Short of a comprehensive indicator, measures of spatial resolution were used instead as proxies for image quality.

Spatial resolution refers to the ability of an imaging system to record detail and distinguish small objects. More precisely, it is defined as the size of the smallest object that can be just visualized in high-contrast regions, where there are pronounced differences in density between the object and its surroundings. This, I repeat, is just one dimension of the imaging performance of a system (although it is usually correlated with the other dimensions) and can be taken only as a partial indicator of image quality. Still, it is the best proxy for which fairly good data were available for most scanners. Spatial resolution will be denoted RESOL and measured in millimeters; smaller values indicate better resolution.

(iii) Reconstruction Time. This refers to the interval between the end of the scan and the display of the image: it is the amount of time it takes the computer to process the massive amount of information generated during the scan, and reconstruct mathematically the final picture. Faster reconstruction times obviously increase the efficiency of CT scanners on two counts: reducing the overall time of a CT examination and thereby increasing the number of patients that can be scanned per working day (the so-called "patient throughput"), and enhancing the operator's ability to monitor and adjust the system in the course of a given examination. Reconstruction time is denoted RTIME and, as with scan time, it is defined as the minimum of the available range, measured in seconds.

(iv) Gantry Tilt. As we saw in figure 2.4, during a scanning procedure the patient lies horizontally on a table that moves into the gantry's aperture. The orientation of the slice scanned thus depends upon the position of the gantry relative to the table. Normally, it stands at a 90° angle so the slices are perpendicular to the body; in some scanners, though, the gantry can be tilted backward or forward, so as to scan oblique sections. The relevant measure is thus the tilting range, that is, the sum of the maximum forward and backward tilt, in degrees.

Aside from these performance characteristics, detailed data were gathered also on technical attributes, such as number and type of detectors, matrix size, object diameter, slice thickness, and so on. But beyond its descriptive uses, it is yet unclear whether and how this information could contribute to the analysis, since pervasive collinearity precludes their inclusion in the econometric models along with performance characteristics. Beyond the attributes of the scanners themselves, it is quite likely that the behavior of buyers is influenced by firm-related variables, such as servicing, customer support, reputation, advertising, range of products offered, and so on. Data on most of those variables were also gathered, but they have been used only to a very limited extent—much remains to be done to exploit this important information fully.

2.5 Data and Sources

A distinctive feature of this project is that it required the gathering of very large amounts of data (most of them unfamiliar to economists), from a wide variety of disparate sources. The aim was to gather all relevant data, rather than be satisfied with sampling, primarily because, in the absence of reliable information on the population as a whole (such as total sales of scanners by year, total number of brands per period, and so on), it was virtually impossible to determine what a representative sample should consist of.

This section describes in some detail the various data sets and their sources. Since much of the underlying material is quite technical, tedious details are omitted whenever possible, to focus instead on aspects of the data that are of direct relevance to the empirical analysis conducted in the coming chapters.

2.5.1   An Overview of the Data

The main data sets consist of:

(i) The characteristics and prices of all CT scanners marketed in the United States since the introduction of Computed Tomography in 1973.

(ii) Installation data, that is, the identity of all hospitals and clinics in the United States that acquired CT scanners, the dates when the scanners were ordered and installed, and the precise scanner models bought.

(iii) Attributes of hospitals, such as size, affiliation, services offered, budget, and so on.

(iv) Information about the manufacturers of CT scanners, including patents and R&D expenditures.

Much quantitative and qualitative information on other aspects of CT was collected as well: the CT technology itself, its scientific basis and medical impact, and its history; regulatory policies and their effects; institutional and economic factors affecting the provision of diagnostic services; issues surrounding the development and use of medical technologies in general and imaging modalities in particular; worldwide market trends, and so on. This body of information provided the essential background needed to understand the industry, greatly facilitated the collection of the principal data sets,[16] and will, I hope, serve for further research in this area.

---

16. It was crucial to demonstrate close familiarity with the field when requesting information from manufacturers, hospitals, government agencies and the like, in order to gain credibility and ensure their cooperation.

The main data sources were:

a. A highly detailed questionnaire sent to all CT manufacturers, and follow-up contacts with officers from those companies.

b. Articles in the scientific literature (in radiology and medical physics); journals related to the medical sector, such as *Modern HealthCare* and *Diagnostic Imaging;* reports by consulting companies (Arthur D. Little, Eberstadt, and others), and a variety of other publications.

c. Material collected by various government agencies, primarily by the Bureau of Radiological Health (BRH) at the Food and Drug Administration (FDA), the Office of Technology Assessment of the U.S. Congress (OTA), and the U.S. Patent Office.

d. The annual surveys of hospitals by the American Hospital Association.

e. Personal contacts with hospitals, researchers, and faculty in various medical schools.

A comment on the questionnaire to the firms producing CT scanners is pertinent. As is usually the case, it was quite difficult to secure their cooperation, particularly since most of the information requested was very specific, and the firms regarded it as confidential (of course, assurances of nondisclosure were given). Nevertheless, all but two of the firms that were still active in the CT market at the time of this project eventually answered the questionnaire, at least partially. Some were in fact extremely helpful (particularly Technicare), devoting significant amounts of time and resources to the gathering of the information requested and to further clarifications. Unfortunately, almost half the companies had already exited the market by then (1981–82), and hence could not—or would not—respond (with the exception of Varian). Some firms had sold their CT operation and no longer had the pertinent records (EMI, Pfizer); in others the personnel that had been involved with CT had left and could not be located (Syntex, Searle). Those that responded to the questionnaire were Elscint, General Electric, Omnimedical, Picker, Siemens, Technicare (formerly Ohio Nuclear), Toshiba, and Varian; those that did not were Artronix, AS&E, CGR, EMI, Pfizer, Philips, Searle, and Syntex.

Of the nonresponders only CGR and Philips are still in the market; the former is active primarily in Europe and up to 1982 had apparently sold just one system in the United States. Philips posed the most serious problem, and in the end had to be excluded from the analysis: the infor-

mation was too scanty and unreliable and the company refused to coop-
erate. As for EMI, a substantial part of their installation data was eventually supplied to us by Omnimedical, the firm that purchased part of
EMI assets in the United States in late 1980.

All of the data sets cover the time span from the beginning of Computed Tomography in 1973 to mid-1981; those are the nine years
included in the econometric analysis of discrete choice, and hence in the
computations of welfare gains from innovation. In addition, some of the
sets have been updated, primarily the installation data, which includes
now all scanners installed up to the end of 1984 (but without the precise
scanner model), and the patents data, updated up to the end of 1986.
However, these additional data have been used mostly for descriptive
purposes, as in this chapter, and still remain to be integrated fully in the
analysis.

A comment about dating the information: by far the most important
annual event in the market for imaging equipment is the annual meeting
of the Radiological Society of North America (RSNA), which takes place
in November (in the past few years the meetings have been held in Chicago). Not only is this a massive scientific conference (the meetings are
attended by some 20,000 people), but a very large-scale commercial
exhibit is held at the same time. Firms announce and display their latest
systems and invest heavily in promoting their equipment; by all accounts
those exhibits define what the market will be like in the following
months, until the next meeting.[17] Thus a year is herein defined as the
period between November 1 (of the previous year) and October 31.

2.5.2 Characteristics and Prices of CT Scanners

From 1973 to 1982, 70 different models of CT scanners were developed
and announced in the United States, but only about 50 of them had any
sales. The data on the characteristics and prices of those 50 models come
from a variety of sources (see table 2.10 in appendix 2.4). The multi-
plicity of sources underlies the difficulties encountered; for example, in
many cases the information was partial, incomplete, and even contradic-
tory, the definitions were not uniform, and so on. It was particularly
hard to obtain reliable data on prices, primarily because of discrepancies

---

17. I attended the 1980 meetings held in Dallas, Texas, and that proved to be an
important step in understanding the market and the technology.

between list and sale prices, and changes in the latter over time. Of course, the aim was to obtain, whenever possible, actual sale prices; and indeed, most figures in the data refer to transaction rather than list prices, but some inconsistencies may have remained.

The other major difficulty was to get consistent measures of spatial resolution, to be used here as proxy for image quality. As a first step, I composed a table with the best available estimates of the spatial resolution of each scanner, based on the sources mentioned above, and on a special survey conducted by the Bureau of Radiological Health of the Food and Drug Administration (furnished to me in May 1981 by Lee Goldman of the Radiological Systems Section at the bureau). Later, Philip Judy of the Harvard Medical School, who helped me at various stages of this project, examined the figures in detail and made some adjustments on the basis of his research in the area. The few scanners for which information was too scanty and unreliable were excluded from the econometric analysis altogether; still, it is possible that some inaccuracies might have remained for those included. Appendix 2.4, table 2.10, lists the set of CT scanners included in the analysis, their attributes, prices, and unit sales (by year); table 2.11 in the same appendix lists those excluded, specifying the reasons (the only omissions of any significance are Philips and the later Elscint models).

Although the data cover scanners marketed up to 1982, a check of the 1982–1987 issues of *Diagnostic Imaging* revealed that, except for the systems introduced by Imatron in 1984, there have not been major changes in the set of CT models offered in the market.

2.5.3   Installation Data

The most arduous and time-consuming task was the assembly of data on who bought what and when. The starting point was a fairly comprehensive list of installations gathered by the Office of Technology Assessment (OTA) of the U.S. Congress, and furnished to me by D. Banta (then its director), and an updated listing from the FDA covering all installations up to 1981.[18] However, the OTA listing did not specify the precise scanner model (it only identified the manufacturer) and, worse still, the FDA

18. OTA gathered the data to prepare its reports on CT scanners in 1978 and 1981. The Food and Drug Administration requires all users to report on installations of CT scanners, including installation date and type of system.

list consisted only of the names and addresses of users and the installation dates, with no references to the scanners themselves (except for the
distinction between stationary and mobile systems). The companies'
answers to the questionnaire furnished much additional information,
particularly in terms of specific CT models and in distinguishing
between new installations and upgrades. The combined data sets were
carefully examined (each of the more than 2,000 observations was cross-
checked) and in order to close the gaps, several hundred hospitals and
clinics across the United States were contacted by telephone. I am confident that the data set thus assembled covers virtually all CT installations up to mid-1981 (including upgrades), and that it is highly accurate.
The main items included are: name and address of the hospital or clinic,
and type of ownership (some scanners are located in a hospital but
owned by a private group); manufacturer and precise scanner model;
whether stationary or mobile;[19] and date scanner was ordered and date
when installed.

Because for most scanners only the installation date was available, the
order date was inferred from the average delivery lag reported by the
companies (only one major manufacturer, Technicare, supplied precise
order dates for each installation). When no other information was available, the lag was assumed to be of six months. The reason for insisting
on obtaining this piece of information is that the order date is in fact the
relevant one for analyzing choices: it is when the purchasing decision
was made. This is also the relevant date for the firms, so sales are dated
throughout according to order date.

The installation data set was updated with a listing provided by
the FDA in July 1985, covering all installations from 1981 to the last
quarter of 1984. This listing, however, does not provide information on
the scanner model installed, only on whether it was a head or whole-
body system. The tables showing figures on sales, diffusion, and so
forth up to 1985 are based on these data. The complete set includes
4,260 entries, of which 3,868 are installations proper, and the
remaining 392 are upgrades (that is, refurbished scanners); those
included in the econometric study (to mid-1981) total 2,050 installations.

---

19. Most scanners are installed in fixed locations, but a few (5.6 percent of all scanners in the United States) are installed in special vans, serving a number of hospitals in
a given area.

2.5.4 Attributes of Hospitals

The American Hospital Association (AHA) conducts a yearly survey of all hospitals in the United States—more than 7,000—covering a wide range of issues (the 1980 survey contains more than 400 data items). The surveys for 1973, 1977, and 1980 were obtained for the present study, thus covering the period of interest, and merged with the installation data, so that the entry for each hospital that acquired a CT scanner was augmented with detailed information on its attributes.

Given the large number of variables included in the AHA surveys, it was necessary to select a small set of characteristics that could be regarded a priori as being relevant for the choice of CT scanners. After a rather tedious sorting process, approximately 20 variables were selected, covering size, classification, type of facilities available, utilization, and finances. In particular, two summary variables were created: ADV (for advanced), and RAD (for radiation therapy). The first was meant to capture the degree of sophistication of the hospital, and consists of the first principal component of the following attributes: (a) the percentage of advanced facilities offered by the hospital, out of a list of 17 such facilities included in the AHA surveys, such as open-heart surgery, intensive care unit, and so forth; (b) medical school affiliation; (c) residency program; and (d) cancer program. Clearly, the underlying hypothesis was that hospitals with a higher value of ADV would choose more sophisticated scanners. The second variable, RAD, is simply $(R1 + R2 + R3)/3$, where the R's are dummy variables for x-ray, cobalt, and radium therapy. The presumption was that hospitals with a wider range of radiation therapy services will tend to put a higher value on the resolution of CT scanners, since they are used in radiation therapy treatment to increase the locational precision of the treatment.

Appendix 2.1   The Impact of Regulation on the Diffusion of CT Scanners

In the mid-seventies, the U.S. government enacted a series of regulatory measures aimed at slowing down the spread of new medical technologies so as to hold down costs. The rationale and adequacy of those policies have been widely debated, but the debate has suffered from the lack of good evidence regarding the effects of the regulatory measures. However, a large-scale study of Certificate of Need (CON) programs under-taken by the U.S. Department of Health and Human Services in 1981 made a serious effort to construct quantitative indicators of various aspects of those programs that were deemed of relevance for the assess-ment of their effects. These indicators, coupled with the detailed data on CT scanners gathered for this study, offered an excellent opportunity to examine anew the extent of the impact of the regulations on the dif-fusion of CT. A related issue to be examined here is the indirect effect of regulation on the spread of private installations of CT scanners.

Because the regulatory programs varied considerably across states (the indicators from the DHHS study are computed state by state), the sim-plest way to approach those issues is to estimate various diffusion param-eters for each state and regress them on the available measures of reg-ulation. The diffusion parameters used below were computed for the period 1972-1981 and refer to the diffusion of CT scanners in commu-nity hospitals with more than 100 beds.

Diffusion Parameters

Three parameters of diffusion will be used here in an effort to capture various aspects of the diffusion process that may have been affected dif-ferently by regulation: first, the extent of diffusion, to be denoted P, for the proportion of hospitals that had adopted CT scanners by 1981. The ceilings used are those reached in each state by Diagnostic Radioiso-topes, a previous innovation in diagnostic technology (see Trajtenberg and Yitzhaki, 1989). The second parameter is the mean adoption time (denoted MEANT), computed as the simple average of the number of months elapsed from November 1972 (the beginning of the process) to the time of adoption. The third is the speed of diffusion (SPEED), com-puted as the Gini's expected mean difference of the distribution of adop-tion times, normalized to take into account the differences in P across states. Finally, in order to assess the impact of regulation on the spread of private installations, I will make use of the percentage of private clin-ics out of the total population of adopters (PRIV).

Regulation Variables

The following four measures will be used:
    (i) AGE: Year in which CON legislation became effective. Presumably,

the earlier the program was enacted, the stronger its impact on diffusion, since there was more time to develop review criteria and the tools to implement them.

(ii) PLAN: Existence and extent of specific CT planning criteria, as of August 1976. It takes the following values: 0 is nonexistent; 1 is regional only; 2 is statewide.

(iii) ACTIV: Index of the extent of "activism" of CON programs. A high score indicates that the program was relatively rigorous, that it was centralized, made an explicit attempt to constraint hospitals, and had well defined standards. Conversely, low scores indicate a less active approach, including programs with ill-defined objectives, lacking firm operating standards, and so on.

(iv) LIMIT: Index of the extent of CON limitations: higher scores were assigned to programs having liberal exemptive provisions, or having been slowly implemented. Low scores indicate a larger scope and effectiveness.

ACTIV and LIMIT were computed in the DHHS study mentioned above as factor scores, applying discriminant analysis to a data set gathered specifically for that purpose. Data on AGE and PLAN were obtained from the DHHS study, from OTA (1978), and from specific material provided to me by the Bureau of Health Planning of the DHHS (for more details, see Trajtenberg, 1983, chap. 9). Notice that the first two variables have to do primarily with the enactment of regulatory measures, whereas the last two are indicative of their actual (or ex-post) strength and effectiveness.

Regression Results

The diffusion parameters are regressed separately on each pair of regulatory measures: ACTIV and LIMIT, and AGE and PLAN. Severe multicollinearity did not allow the inclusion of the four variables in one equation (AGE is highly correlated with ACTIV, and PLAN with LIMIT). The sample includes only the 28 states that enacted CON programs before 1977, since the DHHS study computed the measures ACTIV and LIMIT just for those states. Quite clearly, the estimated equations are misspecified, in that explanatory variables other than those related to regulation are omitted. However, and given that regulatory policies were largely independent of other factors affecting diffusion, it is hoped that the potential biases resulting from this misspecification error are not substantial.

The results are presented in table 2.9: both ACTIV and LIMIT had a significant impact on the extent of diffusion, but their effect on the other diffusion parameters is barely noticeable. On the other hand, AGE and PLAN had no effect on diffusion, but had a very strong impact on the percentage of CT scanners installed in private clinics. Thus, regulation did curtail the diffusion of CT scanners, in the sense that it limited the percentage of hospitals with CT within states, at least up to 1981. However, it was not the mere enactment of the measures that did that (AGE and PLAN), but rather the effectiveness with which they were implemented, as reflected in the measures ACTIV and LIMIT. On the other hand, the parameters of the distribution of adoption times within the period (that is, the mean adoption time and the Gini, given P_i) were influenced only slightly by the presence and extent of regulation. The

Table 2.9 Regressions of Diffusion Parameters on Regulation Variables

| Dependent variable | On ACTIV and LIMIT | | | | |
	Intercept	ACTIV	LIMIT	R^2	d.f.
P	0.47 (17.2)[a]	−0.07 (−2.4)	0.05 (1.9)	.27	25
MEANT	64.63 (51.1)	0.006 (0.0)	−2.11 (−1.6)	.10	23
SPEED	26.27 (19.6)	2.21 (1.5)	0.15 (0.1)	.09	23
PRIV	0.21 (10.3)	0.02 (0.8)	0.05 (2.3)	.19	25
	On PLAN and AGE				
	Intercept	AGE	PLAN	R^2	d.f.
P	−0.41 (−0.4)	0.01 (1.0)	−0.01 (−0.3)	.04	25
MEANT	69.15 (1.7)	−0.07 (−0.1)	0.51 (0.3)	.005	23
SPEED	61.36 (1.5)	−0.51 (−0.9)	0.94 (0.6)	.05	23
PRIV	1.18 (2.3)	−0.02 (−2.1)	0.08 (3.8)	.46	25

[a] *t*-ratios are in parentheses.

finding regarding the impact of AGE and PLAN on PRIV suggests that the earlier and wider adoption of regulatory measures were seen by the private sector as signals of a tougher future regulatory environment: they anticipated as a consequence fewer CT scanner installations in hospitals, and hence a larger market for themselves. The proliferation of private installations of CT scanners can thus be seen, at least to some extent, as an unanticipated by-product of the regulatory measures themselves, that reversed in part the intended effect of those measures.

Appendix 2.2 Determinants of the Adoption Time of CT for Individual Hospitals

The variables used are as follows:

TMOR: number of months elapsed from November 1972 to the time when the first CT scanner was ordered.

BEDS: Number of beds in the hospital.

GOV: Dummy variable; 1 means controlled by the government; 0 means nongovernment.

FP: Dummy variable; 1 means for profit; 0 means not for profit.

PAF: Percentage of advanced facilities (such as for organ transplant, neurosurgery, and so on), out of 29 such facilities listed by the American Hospital Association in 1980.

Sample Statistics of the Variables:

Variable	Mean	Standard Deviation	Range
TMOR	76	36	0–142
BEDS	333	204	31–1900
GOV	0.16	0.37	0–1.00
FP	0.10	0.30	0–1.00
PAF	0.54	0.20	0.03–1.00

Regressing the time of adoption on the attributes of hospitals, for all community hospitals that had adopted CT by the end of 1984 ($n = 1757$, t-values in parentheses),

$$TMOR = 131.9 - 0.05 \text{ BEDS} + 2.5 \text{ GOV} - 11.8 \text{ FP} - 68.5 \text{ PAF},$$
$$(62.5) \ (-12.5) \qquad (1.3) \qquad (-4.9) \quad (-15.0)$$

$$R^2 = 0.37$$

Appendix 2.3   The Assessment of Image Quality

The discussion here centers on resolution, which is the most important dimension of image quality (save for the blurring of the image already discussed in the context of scan time); other dimensions, including uniformity, linearity, and artifactual behavior, are ignored. In broad terms, resolution refers to the ability of a system to record detail, that is, to distinguish (or resolve) objects having different densities. In general, the size of the smallest object that can still be visualized is a function of the contrast between the object and the background: the sharper the contrast is, the finer the details that can be recorded. In CT scanners, as in conventional radiography, contrast refers to differences in densities (or linear attenuation) and is commonly measured in percentage terms. This relationship is depicted in figure 2.7(a): the curve R-R represents the imaging "frontier" of a system, that is, it indicates the maximum resolution possible (the smallest lesion detectable) at every contrast level or, conversely, the minimum perceivable difference in densities given the size of the object. The asymptote $\bar{r}$, denoting high-contrast or spatial resolution, represents the absolute maximum of attainable resolution, and thus reflects the limiting geometrical capabilities of the system (ultimately, $\bar{r}$ is constrained by the size of the pixels—picture elements—in the reconstruction matrix). The other asymptote, $\bar{c}$, called density, low-contrast (or just contrast) resolution or detectability, is a function of the photon "noise" in the scan, that is, of the statistical fluctuation in the number of emergent photons, which results both from the randomness inherent in the behavior of x rays, and the physical limitations (or imperfections) of the system itself.

The curve R-R, however, is not a unique characterization of a system, for its location depends upon radiation dose (that is, upon the intensity of the x-ray beam): larger doses will shift the curve inward, thus improving detectability within the limits imposed by $\bar{r}$ and $\bar{c}$ (see figure 2.7).[20] The imaging capabilities of a CT scanner can therefore be summarized by a function $\phi(C, R, D; F_i) = 0$, where C stands for contrast, R for resolution, D for dose, and F_i for a scanner specific constant. In fact, a

---

20. Theoretically, $\bar{r}$ and $\bar{c}$ are invariant with respect to dose, but it seems that in practice the measured values may well depend on it.

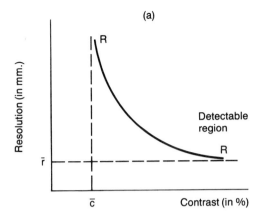

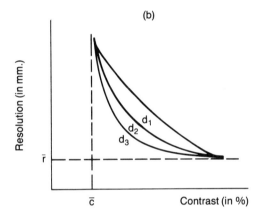

Figure 2.7 The Trade-off between Resolution and Contrast in CT

precise expression for such function can be derived from the physical principles of CT, as follows:

$$(2.1) \quad RC^{1/2}D^{1/3} = F_i.$$

A real scanner may, however, deviate in various ways from the idealized (or frictionless) behavior implied in eq. (2.1), so this equation should be regarded only as a guide, or starting hypothesis, for empirical research. In other words, the assessment of the imaging performance of scanners calls for the gathering of data on R, C, and D, so as to estimate an equation of the form:[21]

$$(2.2) \quad r = f_i - \beta_1 c - \beta_2 d + \varepsilon$$

where the variables are now in logs, and ε is an error term, assumed to be i.i.d.[22] An economist would immediately associate eq. (2.2) with a production function, and therefore think of f_i as analogous to measures of total factor productivity (provided of course that the technology embedded in the coefficients β_1 and β_2 is the same for all scanners). And indeed, the estimates of the f_i's (or some transformation of them) constitute well-defined indices of image quality, which can be used to characterize the relative performance of different scanners.

Having thus put forward a consistent methodology, I sought to obtain the data needed for implementing it. That required sampling the behavior of all 50 different models of CT scanners, using elaborate laboratory procedures for the generation of the raw data and for their interpretation (for example, the scanning of specially designed "phantoms" under a variety of operational modes). Two leading figures in the field, Gerald Cohen of the University of Texas Medical School and Philip Judy of the Harvard Medical School, were very receptive to the criticisms leveled against the prevailing line of research, and to the proposed alternative. Cohen provided me with data on seven scanners that he had gathered and analyzed in a previous study, so I could test the feasibility and presumed merits of the approach. The results were highly encouraging, and were eventually published in *Medical Physics* (see Trajtenberg, 1984). In light of them, Cohen agreed to participate in the project, provided only that adequate funding could be obtained. But the magnitude of the study called for a large budget, and the efforts to secure sufficient support were not successful. The data requirements thus had to be downgraded, settling eventually for a measure of spatial resolution.

---

21. Actually, this is not the correct functional form, for it ignores the extra curvature due to the asymptotes $\bar{r}$ and $\bar{c}$. This problem was addressed in Trajtenberg (1984) by adding a quadratic term to eq. 2.2 and, alternatively, by estimating a piece-wise linear regression.

22. Resolution (r) was chosen as the dependent variable precisely because the error associated with it is indeed purely a measurement error, uncorrelated with the other variables. This elementary point has been overlooked in previous studies conducted on this subject.

It is worth commenting briefly on the impressions left by this incursion into a far-removed discipline (for an economist) such as medical physics. First, it is quite clear that economists are very well equipped in terms of statistical models and tools, and therefore may have something to contribute when crossing interdisciplinary boundaries. By contrast, researchers in radiology and medical physics have a rather poor background in statistical methods, a fact that shows clearly in the abundance of rather basic statistical flaws in published scientific articles.[23]

Second, economists seem to have a much broader and open-minded conception of what empirical research is all about, that is, an iterative (and often inconclusive) process by which tentative hypothesis are formulated on the basis of theoretical considerations, tested against data subject to errors, revised accordingly, and so forth. The approach prevailing in medical physics is, by contrast, much narrower and dogmatic, in the sense that theoretical models are for the most part taken literally, with only shy attempts to truly test them (or question their validity) in the context of empirical research. Quite clearly, this affected the quality of previous studies of imaging performance, not only of CT scanners, but of ultrasound and digital radiography as well. It is comforting to realize that the inherent weaknesses of economics as a scientific discipline, namely the scarcity of immutable theoretical principles and the qualitative nature of the few available laws, may have well been a source of strength, for they compel economists to develop a cunning empirical approach and sophisticated statistical methods.

Appendix 2.4   Data on CT Scanners

Table 2.10 lists all CT scanners included in the econometric analysis, their characteristics, prices, and yearly sales; it concludes with a schematic list of the sources used in collecting the data on characteristics and prices. Table 2.11 presents the few scanners excluded, and the reasons for their exclusion.

---

23. For example, some studies take eq. 2.1 as a given, and compute the values of F simply by plugging in a set of values for C, R, and D, instead of estimating the equation with F as one of the parameters. Others estimate the coefficients β_1 and β_2 one at a time using bivariate regressions (hence obtaining biased estimates because of underlying correlations between the variables), and go on to compute the F's in the same fashion.

Table 2.10 Characteristics and Prices of CT Scanners

Firm	Scanner	Date of introduction[a]	Speed[b]	Resolution[c]	Rtime[d]	Price	Residual price[e]	Sales[f]
		Year-73		Scanner type: head				
EMI	Mark I	11/72	300	3.13	300	310	—	16
		Year-74		Scanner type: head				
EMI	Mark I	11/72	300	3.13	300	360	—	62
EMI	CT 1000	7/74	300	1.67	30	380	—	12
		Year-75		Scanner type: body				
Pfizer	ACTA 0100	7/74	270	1.79	1	350	—	25
Technicare	Delta 50	9/74	120	1.43	15	370	—	74
		Year-75		Scanner type: head				
EMI	CT 1000	7/74	300	1.67	30	380	—	120
G.E.	CT/N 1st Gen.	1/75	270	2.00	10	320	—	1
		Year-76		Scanner type: body				
AS&E	AS&E CT scanner	1/76	5	0.91	60	625	14.66	1
EMI	CT 5000	11/75	20	1.43	100	495	2.10	149

G.E.	CT/T	11/75	5	2.00	200	595	9.10	10
Pfizer	Acta 0150/0200	11/75	270	1.79	1	375	13.37	17
Syntex	System 60-Body	11/75	60	1.67	150	400	−2.38	16
Technicare	Delta 50	9/74	120	1.43	15	380	−5.86	50
Technicare	Delta 50FS	6/76	15	1.35	15	515	−28.01	34
Varian	VSS	6/76	6	1.79	120	575	−2.98	8
		Year-76	Scanner type: head					
Artronix	Neuro-CAT 1110	11/74	9	1.67	120	270	—	14
EMI	CT 1000	7/74	300	1.67	30	380	—	17
EMI	CT 1010	11/75	60	1.52	10	410	—	31
G.E.	CT/N 2nd Gen.	11/75	120	2.00	30	360	—	4
Syntex	System 60-Head	11/75	60	1.67	150	345	—	6
Technicare	Delta 25	6/76	80	1.52	15	400	—	17
		Year-77	Scanner type: body					
AS&E	AS&E CT Scanner	1/76	5.0	0.91	60	688	46.05	11
Elscint	700/705 (Scan-Ex)	11/76	10.0	1.25	10	600	16.82	1
EMI	CT 5005	11/76	20.0	1.43	20	550	45.50	87

Table 2.10 (continued)

Firm	Scanner	Date of introduction[a]	Speed[b]	Resolution[c]	Rtime[d]	Price	Residual price[e]	Sales[f]
		Year-77	Scanner type: body					
G.E.	CT/T 7800	11/76	4.8	1.35	90	582	9.41	74
G.E.	CT/T 8800	8/77	4.8	0.77	35	695	12.75	17
Pfizer	Acta 0200FS	11/76	18.0	1.25	30	500	−24.73	31
Picker	Synerview 120	4/77	12.0	1.25	30	525	−24.95	2
Searle	Pho-Trax 4000	11/76	5.0	1.00	40	556	−78.77	5
Siemens	Somatom	11/76	5.0	1.67	1	645	19.69	1
Syntex	System 60-Body	11/75	60.0	1.67	150	400	29.08	4
Technicare	Delta 50	9/74	120.0	1.43	15	380	−18.79	7
Technicare	Delta 50FS	6/76	15.0	1.35	15	520	−17.43	37
Technicare	Delta 2005	5/77	5.0	1.35	25	566	−29.58	2
Technicare	Delta 2010	5/77	2.0	1.35	25	625	−27.57	29
Technicare	Delta 2020	5/77	2.0	1.00	30	740	42.51	16
		Year-77	Scanner type: head					
Artronix	Neuro-CAT 1110	11/74	9	1.67	120	270	—	13
EMI	CT 1010	11/75	60	1.52	10	425	—	20

			Year-78					
EMI	CTR 100	4/77	300	1.67	30	225	—	5
Siemens	Siretom 2000	11/76	60	2.00	1	420	—	1
Syntex	System 60-Head	11/75	60	1.67	150	345	—	5
Technicare	Delta 25	6/76	80	1.52	15	400	—	12
		Scanner type: body						
AS&E	AS&E CT Scanner	1/76	5	0.91	60	688	63.41	1
Elscint	700/705 (Scan-Ex)	11/76	10	1.25	10	615	19.65	4
EMI	CT 5005	11/76	20	1.43	20	550	36.59	19
EMI	EMI 7070	11/77	3	0.77	15	655	−68.39	4
G.E.	CT/T 7800	11/76	5	1.35	90	604	49.34	12
G.E.	CT/T 8800	8/77	5	0.77	35	722	52.65	63
Pfizer	Acta 0200FS	11/76	18	1.25	30	525	−1.51	10
Picker	Synerview 120	4/77	12	1.25	30	525	−24.55	5
Picker	Synerview 300	11/77	1	1.11	30	650	−58.62	0
Picker	Synerview 600	2/78	1	1.00	30	715	−9.28	4
Searle	Pho-Trax 4000	11/76	5	1.00	40	556	−67.52	1
Siemens	Somatom	11/76	5	1.32	1	750	49.17	2
Technicare	Delta 50FS	6/76	15	1.35	15	450	−97.68	11

Table 2.10 (continued)

Firm	Scanner	Date of introduction[a]	Speed[b]	Resolution[c]	Rtime[d]	Price	Residual price[e]	Sales[f]
		Year-78		Scanner type: body				
Technicare	Delta 2005	5/77	5	1.35	25	570	−23.65	1
Technicare	Delta 2010	5/77	2	1.35	25	660	14.26	9
Technicare	Delta 2020	5/77	2	1.00	30	751	66.12	18
		Year-78		Scanner type: head				
Artronix	Neuro-CAT 1110	11/74	9	1.67	120	270	—	4
CGR	ND 8000	6/77	20	1.25	20	500	—	1
EMI	CT 1010	11/75	60	1.52	10	400	—	3
EMI	CTR 100	4/77	300	1.67	30	180	—	8
Omnimedical	Omni-4001	11/77	120	1.52	5	150	—	5
Siemens	Siretom 2000	11/76	60	2.00	1	420	—	0
Technicare	Delta 25	6/76	80	1.52	15	400	—	2
Technicare	Delta 100	11/77	120	1.39	30	132	—	46
		Year-79		Scanner type: body				
EMI	CT 5005	11/76	20.0	1.43	20	480	11.89	8

		Year-79		Scanner type: head				
EMI	EMI 7070	11/77	3.0	0.77	15	757	−2.30	9
EMI	EMI 6000	11/78	5.0	1.00	40	580	−43.20	10
G.E.	CT/T 7800	11/76	4.8	1.35	90	629	96.96	12
G.E.	CT/T 8800	8/77	4.8	0.60	35	751	17.22	73
Pfizer	Acta 0200FS	11/76	18.0	1.25	30	470	−16.04	13
Pfizer	Pfizer/AS&E 0450	11/78	5.0	0.91	30	685	30.68	11
Picker	Synerview 120	4/77	12.0	1.25	30	475	−44.34	1
Picker	Synerview 300	11/77	1.0	1.11	30	650	−97.06	1
Picker	Synerview 600	2/78	1.0	1.00	30	770	2.21	16
Siemens	Somatom	11/76	5.0	1.32	1	800	73.18	3
Siemens	Somatom 2	11/78	3.0	0.75	1	850	−31.08	4
Technicare	Delta 50FS	6/76	15.0	1.35	15	450	−65.56	4
Technicare	Delta 2010	5/77	2.0	1.35	25	648	−11.08	4
Technicare	Delta 2020	5/77	2.0	1.00	30	775	64.15	8
Toshiba	TCT-60A	11/78	4.5	0.71	35	720	14.36	0
EMI	CT 1010	11/75	60	1.52	10	350	—	5
EMI	CTR 100	4/77	300	1.67	30	140	—	2

Table 2.10 (continued)

Firm	Scanner	Date of introduction[a]	Speed[b]	Resolution[c]	Rtime[d]	Price	Residual price[e]	Sales[f]
		Year-79	Scanner type: head					
Omnimedical	Omni-4001	11/77	120	1.52	5	150	—	12
Technicare	Delta 100	11/77	120	1.39	30	137	—	61
		Year-80	Scanner type: body					
EMI	EMI 7070	11/77	3.0	0.77	15	860	68.58	8
EMI	EMI 6000	11/78	5.0	1.00	40	600	-13.07	0
G.E.	CT/T 7800	11/76	4.8	1.35	90	653	168.58	7
G.E.	CT/T 8800	8/77	4.8	0.60	35	780	-35.88	107
Pfizer	Acta 0200FS	11/76	18.0	1.25	30	350	-43.47	1
Pfizer	Pfizer/AS&E 0450	11/78	5.0	0.91	30	685	29.34	7
Picker	Synerview 120	4/77	12.0	1.25	30	475	36.95	4
Picker	Synerview 300	11/77	1.0	1.11	30	650	-106.65	1
Picker	Synerview 600	2/78	1.0	1.00	30	870	73.46	28
Siemens	Somatom 2	11/78	3.0	0.75	1	930	67.04	12
Technicare	Delta 50FS	6/76	15.0	1.35	15	300	-99.83	6
Technicare	Delta 2010	5/77	2.0	1.35	25	465	-144.75	1

Technicare	Delta 2020	5/77	2.0	1.00	30	789	68.66	4
Technicare	Delta 2020HR	4/80	2.0	0.50	30	890	−95.33	7
Toshiba	TCT-60A	11/78	4.5	0.71	35	785	26.38	0
		Year-80		Scanner type: head				
Omnimedical	Omni-4001	11/77	120	1.52	5	150	—	13
Technicare	Delta 100	11/77	120	1.39	30	154	—	39
Toshiba	TCT-30	3/80	105	1.67	45	155	—	0
		Year-81		Scanner type: body				
EMI	EMI 7070	11/77	3.0	0.77	15	910	29.34	1
G.E.	CT/T 7800	11/76	4.8	1.35	90	703	147.28	1
G.E.	CT/T 8800	8/77	4.8	0.60	35	840	−13.66	85
Omnimedical	Omni-6000	11/80	5.0	1.00	45	645	−21.93	8
Pfizer	Acta 0200FS	11/76	18.0	1.25	30	300	−57.38	1
Pfizer	Pfizer/AS&E 0450	11/78	5.0	0.91	30	600	−109.10	1
Pfizer	PF-2400	11/80	2.5	0.50	15	1300	238.70	0
Picker	Synerview 600	2/78	1.0	1.00	30	935	−49.44	20
Siemens	Somatom 2	11/78	3.0	0.75	1	950	−8.43	31
Technicare	Delta 2020HR	4/80	2.0	0.50	30	890	−196.26	4
Toshiba	TCT-60A	11/78	4.5	0.71	35	850	40.88	1

Table 2.10 (continued)

Firm	Scanner	Date of introduction[a]	Speed[b]	Resolution[c]	Rtime[d]	Price	Residual price[e]	Sales[f]
		Year-81	Scanner type: head					
Omnimedical	Omni-4001	11/77	120	1.52	5	150	—	7
Technicare	Delta 100	11/77	120	1.39	30	145	—	14
Toshiba	TCT-30	3/80	105	1.67	45	155	—	6
		Year-82	Scanner type: body					
G.E.	CT/T 8800	8/77	4.8	0.60	35	840	−29.08	—
G.E.	CT 9800	11/81	1.3	0.50	20	1150	73.43	—
Interad	Interad	11/81	3.0	1.00	60	475	−99.52	—
Omnimedical	Omni-6000	11/80	5.0	1.00	45	695	133.41	—
Omnimedical	Quad 1	11/81	1.5	0.79	20	795	−12.51	—
Philips	Tomoscan 310	11/81	3.0	0.50	10	975	−92.49	—
Picker	Synerview 600S	9/81	1.0	0.71	12	950	31.13	—
Picker	Synerview 1200SX	9/81	1.0	0.42	20	1200	9.25	—
Siemens	Somatom DR	11/81	1.4	0.71	1	1025	−10.10	—
Technicare	Delta 2060	11/81	2.0	0.50	10	1100	9.84	—
Toshiba	TCT-60A	11/78	4.5	0.71	35	850	73.39	—
Toshiba	TCT-80A	11/81	2.7	0.83	60	600	−86.75	—

			Year-82	Scanner type: head					
Omnimedical	Omni-4001	11/77	120	1.52	5	162	—	—	—
Technicare	Delta 100	11/77	120	1.39	30	145	—	—	—
Toshiba	TCT-30	3/80	105	1.67	45	170	—	—	—

[a] Date of announcement of the scanner model in the market.
[b] Minimum scan time, in seconds.
[c] Spatial resolution, in millimeters.
[d] Reconstruction time, in seconds.
[e] Residual price, from hedonic price regressions (price and residual price are in $ thousands).
[f] Unit sales, according to date of order.

Sources:

(i) From CT manufacturers:

Answers to the questionnaire, and personal communications with their CT personnel.

Brochures and advertising in scientific journals.

Tables detailing competing CT scanners prepared as internal documents by Elscint, EMI (February 1977), and Syntex (March 1976).

(ii) Published material:

American Hospital Association, CT Scanners: A Technical Report, Chicago, Illinois, 1977.

A Health Planning Document: CT Scanning Systems (prepared for the Health Resources Administration by Arthur D. Little), Cambridge, Mass., November 1975.

R. A. Brooks and G. DiChiro, "Principles of Computer-Assisted Tomography (CAT) in Radiographic and Radioisotopic Imaging," Physics in Medical Biology, April 1976 (comparative table, p. 728).

Articles and reports in the American Journal of Roentgenology, Diagnostic Imaging, the Journal of C.A.T., Medical Physics, Modern HealthCare, and Radiology.

(iii) Unpublished material:

Donald Frey, Joseph Wise, and Paul Ross, "Evaluation of CT Units," Medical University of South Carolina, Charleston, South Carolina.

William R. Hendee and Robert K. Corak, "Specifications for CT Units," University of Colorado Health Sciences Center, February 1980.

Harvard Business School, Case study on CT scanners, 1978.

Office of Technology Assessment of the US Congress (OTA), background material for report on CT scanners, 1976.

Massachusetts Department of Public Health, C.O.N. division, Resource Inventory for CT Scanners, 1981 (includes estimated costs of purchased equipment).

Table comparing recent CT scanners, prepared as part of application for C.O.N. by unidentified hospital in Massachusetts.

Table 2.11   CT Scanners Not Included in the Empirical Analysis

Firm	Scanner	Reasons for exclusion
Artronix	Torso-CAT 1120	Resolution n.a.; only one unit sold
Artronix	"New Geometry"	Not marketed
CGR	CE10000	Resolution n.a.; not certain if actively marketed in the U.S. (no sales reported)
Elscint	XL 905, 1002	Unreliable data on resolution
Pfizer	0400	Not marketed
Philips	All scanners	No reliable data
Picker	First Synerview model (1976)	No reliable data; apparently no sales
Technicare	Delta 50 from 1978 to 1981	Outdated model by 1978; price not clear; few units sold to "fringe" users
Varian	V-360-3	Resolution n.a.

3

The Choice of CT Scanners and the Dynamics of Preferences

This chapter is devoted mainly to the detailed analysis of choice of CT scanners, laying the basis for the computation of social gains from innovation in CT. To be able to gauge the value of innovations in a particular field an analyst needs, first and foremost, to estimate the preferences of consumers for the attributes of the product (since innovation is taken to mean changes in attributes space). The way to obtain these preferences, in turn, is by analyzing actual choices. Thus a strong demand for systems that emphasize particular attributes would suggest that such attributes are highly valued by consumers. The analysis will be conducted with the aid of the multinomial logit model (MNL), which is particularly well suited for the purpose at hand. (Even so, much of this chapter deals with problems associated with the specification and actual implementation of the model.)

The first problem encountered when formulating the choice model is that one usually finds a close association between price and characteristics (as captured by the hedonic price function), and hence the inclusion of both as explanatory variables might seriously undermine the quality of the estimates. The solution put forward here involves estimating the hedonic functions first, and using the residuals from those regressions—rather than price—as independent variables in the choice model. The second issue is how to specify the decision tree in view of the existence of two different types of scanners: head and body. Having rejected the hypothesis that the two can be treated symmetrically, I specify a *nested* model, with separate branches for each scanner type. The estimation of such a model indicates that head and body CT scanners constitute in fact unrelated markets from the point of view of the choice behavior of users. This is an interesting finding in itself, and one that has important implications for the computation of gains from innovation.

The last section looks closely at the third issue: the finding that preferences for attributes of CT scanners appear not to be stable, but to change from year to year. Searching for clues, I examine the yearly changes of relative preferences (something akin to the ratio of the marginal utilities from any two attributes) in conjunction with the actual changes over time in the attributes of scanners, and find a close association between the two series, with a lag. This can be interpreted in terms of a dual inducement mechanism in the characteristics space: on the one hand, strong preferences for a particular attribute in one period seem to induce firms to enhance that attribute relatively more than others in the scanners offered in the following period; on the other hand, the relative intensity of preferences appear to respond to the changing mix of attributes available in the marketplace. Once again, those findings will have a bearing on the computation of social gains.

3.1   Specification Issues

3.1.1   Hedonic Price Functions, Multicollinearity, and the MNL Model

Recall that the typical MNL equation is of the form

$$(3.1) \quad \pi_i = \exp V_i / \sum_{j=1}^{n} \exp V_j.$$

If we disregard income effects and ignore the vector of personal attributes h, the indirect utility function in (3.1) takes the form $V_i = -\alpha p_i + \phi(z_i)$.[1] However, this specification overlooks an important feature of markets for differentiated products, namely, that prices and attributes usually exhibit a systematic relationship, embedded in the hedonic price function:

$$(3.2) \quad p_i = p(z_i) + \tilde{p}_i,$$

---

1. Recall that income y drops out of V_i, since it appears exponentiated both in the nominator and in the denominator of eq. (3.1).

where $p(z_i)$ is the systematic component and $\tilde{p}_i$ an independently and identically distributed error term, to be called residual price. The existence of such a relationship poses a serious multicollinearity problem in the estimation of the choice probabilities in (3.1); since both price and the vector z_i appear there as explanatory variables, their individual coefficients cannot be estimated with any precision. Of course, multicollinearity is a problem associated with the data entering the model, rather than with the model itself, and hence cannot be easily circumvented. The solution suggested in this case involves providing the functions V_i with more structure, which builds upon the role that the hedonic price function plays in the agents' optimization problem.

As formally shown by Rosen (1974), hedonic price functions are not a mere statistical regularity, but the result of simultaneous equilibria occurring in a string of contiguous markets for differentiated products. From the point of view of the individual consumer, the hedonic function is to be thought of as an exogenously given budget constraint (usually nonlinear), that is, it is the locus of feasible "consumption bundles" in price-attributes space, and should be incorporated as such in the analysis of consumer behavior. In the continuous case this is done in a straightforward manner (see Rosen, 1974): assuming a continuous and nonstochastic hedonic price function $p = p(z)$, and the same indirect utility function as above, one can simply substitute $p(z)$ for price in V_i, leading to the garden-variety maximization problem,

$$(3.3) \qquad \max_z V = \alpha[y - p(z)] + \phi(z),$$

which renders the first order condition $p'(z) = \phi'(z)/\alpha$ (notice that the index i is absent here because $p(z)$ is assumed to be continuous). The rather obvious point made explicit by (3.3) is that the consumer cannot independently choose both a vector z and a price p, but instead the choice of the former uniquely determines the latter. Incidentally, in the regression analysis proposed by Rosen and based upon the first order condition just stated (for the demand equations), only the characteristics z appear as explanatory variables, and therefore the collinearity problem does not arise.

In the discrete case the hedonic price function is, of course, neither continuous nor fully deterministic, but it still plays the role of a (stochastic) budget constraint, and should be brought into the analysis as such. Substituting the hedonic price function in (3.2) for p_i in V_i, and ignoring y,

$$V_i = -\alpha[p(z_i) + \tilde{p}_i] + \phi(z_i) = \phi(z_i) - \alpha p(z_i) - \alpha\tilde{p}_i,$$

or, defining $V^n(z_i) \equiv \phi(z_i) - \alpha p(z_i)$,

(3.4) $V_i = V^n(z_i) - \alpha\tilde{p}_i,$

where the term $V^n(z_i)$ can be interpreted as the net utility conferred by product i (that is, net of the expected cost of the product), and $\tilde{p}_i$ as an extra charge/discount resulting from random deviations of actual prices from predicted market equilibria. Once the problem is stated this way, the behavior of consumers is now seen to depend upon z_i and $\tilde{p}_i$, rather than upon z_i and p_i. In other words, given the existence of a hedonic function, the price variable largely replicates the information conveyed by z_i; therefore, only the component of p_i that is orthogonal to z_i (that is, $\tilde{p}_i$) can affect the choice behavior, thus qualifying as a legitimate explanatory variable in the choice model.

For equation (3.4) to offer an actual solution to the multicollinearity problem, a suitable specification for $V^n(z)$ needs to be found. The following straightforward proposition furnishes the required structure: $V^n(z)$ can be closely approximated by the sum of a linear and a quadratic form, provided only that it has an interior maximum. More formally, $V^n(z) \cong z'\beta + z'Gz$ where G is a symmetric matrix, if there is a $z^* > 0$ such that: $z^* = \arg\max V^n(z)$ (that is, if G is negative definite). If the proposition holds, the approximation $(z'\beta + z'Gz)$ obtains readily from a second-order Taylor expansion about z^*. Normally we would expect $\phi(z)$ to be concave (or quasi-concave), and the hedonic function to be convex (as has been found to be the case in many empirical studies), in which case $V^n(z)$ would necessarily meet the required conditions.[2] Figure 3.1 illustrates such a case for a one-dimensional z. Notice that, since the analysis refers to the discrete choice case, tangency between $\phi(z)$ and $p(z)$ is not required, and z^* does not necessarily stand for the actual choice. Rather, products in the vicinity of z^* have, *ceteris paribus*, a higher probability of

---

2. The function $p(z)$ may be concave and the stated conditions could still hold: all that is required, loosely speaking, is that $p(z)$ be more convex than $\phi(z)$. If that is not the case then the expected optimum z^* will be in a corner, and the suggested approximation will probably be less precise; likewise, in that case the estimated coefficients may turn out to have the wrong signs.

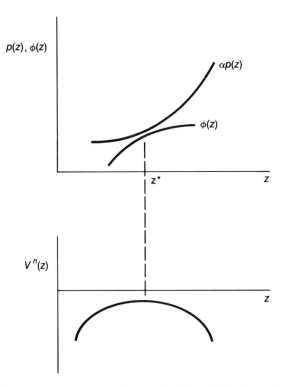

Figure 3.1   Quadratic Approximation to the Net Utility Function V''

being selected than those further apart (thus, the Taylor expansion is done about the expected, not the actual, optimum).

If, in addition, one assumes that the utility branch for characteristics takes the form $\phi(z_i) = \Sigma_j f^j(z_{ij})$, where $f^j(\cdot)$ is a quasi-concave function of the jth attribute (this is the working assumption in virtually all applications of the MNL), and furthermore, if the hedonic price function is of the class $p_i = \Sigma_j g^j(z_{ij}) + \bar{p}_i$, where $g^j(\cdot)$ is quasi-convex, then the approximation to the net utility function reduces to the simple quadratic form,

$$(3.5) \quad V''(z_i) = \sum_{j=1}^{m} \left[f^j(z_{ij}) - g^j(z_{ij}) \right] \cong \sum_{j=1}^{m} (a_j z_{ij} - b_j z_{ij}^2).$$

Simply put, if both the utility and the hedonic price functions are additive—separable in some transformations of the z_{ij}'s, then the interaction terms drop out of the quadratic form, leaving only the linear and squared terms. Given that the best fit achieved in this study for the hedonic function was with a linear-log form (see section 3.2 below), and since eq. (3.5) saves $m(m-1)/2$ degrees of freedom vis-à-vis the generalized quadratic form, the net utility will indeed be specified as in (3.5) in the estimation of the MNL model.

3.1.2 A Two-Stage Estimation Procedure

When equations (3.1) to (3.5) are combined, the following model emerges,

$$(3.6) \begin{cases} \pi_i = \exp V_i / \sum \exp V_j, \\[2mm] V_i = \sum_{j=1}^{m} (a_j z_{ij} - b_j z_{ij}^2) - \alpha \hat{p}_i, \\[2mm] \hat{p}_i = p_i - p(z_i), \end{cases}$$

implying a two-stage procedure. First, estimate the hedonic price function and compute the residuals $\hat{p}_i$; second, enter $\hat{p}_i$ as an independent variable in π_i and estimate the MNL model.[3] Quite clearly, this is not the most general formulation possible: a simultaneous-equation framework could be more appropriate, depending upon the presumed behavior of the supply side (such as the pricing and product design behavior of firms), and related issues such as whether list or transaction prices are used, the length of the periods analyzed (and hence the likelihood of within-period adjustments), and others. Such a framework may comprise a system of demand and supply equations, replicating in the context of discrete choice what Rosen (1974) suggested for the continuous case. Alternatively, it may include just the demand system as in (3.6), but estimated simultaneously with the hedonic price equation, rather than in two stages. In view of the specific features of the case at hand, and in order to avoid excessive complications, I abstract here from simultaneity issues. Formally, the working assumption that allows me to do that is that each choice set S_t, and hence each hedonic price function, are deter-

---

3. Cowling and Rayner (1970) also made use of residuals from hedonic regressions as explanatory variables in a demand equation, albeit in the context of a much simpler model.

mined at the beginning of each period and do not change throughout the course of the period. As described in Chapter 2, this corresponds quite closely to the case of CT scanners.

A related problem could present itself, however, when implementing (3.6): the residual price $\bar{p}_i$ is likely to be correlated with left-out attributes that affect the choice behavior—that is, that belong in $\phi(z)$—and hence its coefficient might overestimate the marginal utility of income, α. This issue will be dealt with in detail in Chapter 4, in the discussion of the results of the case study.

In concluding this section, it is interesting to note that the rather striking omission of hedonic price functions in the literature on discrete choice seems to have been quite fortuitous: the case originally and most often analyzed in that literature is the choice of transportation modes. In that context, however, the hedonic price function is virtually non-existent, for there is almost no relationship between fares and the attributes usually considered therein (driving time, route access, and so on). Thus the practical problem of multicollinearity that motivated the foregoing analysis simply did not arise. Quite clearly, though, the transportation case is, in that sense, the exception rather than the rule.

3.2 Estimating the Hedonic Price Functions

This section deals with the implementation of the first stage of the procedure suggested in (3.6) above: the estimation of the hedonic price functions and the subsequent computation of residual prices. As is commonly the case in hedonic price studies, there were no strong priors at hand regarding the functional form of the hedonic equation and, except for plausible arguments favoring convexity, there are virtually no theoretical guidelines to follow (see Griliches, 1971). The matter is thus to be decided by comparing the fit of alternative specifications (being mindful of the severe limitations of such criterion), and subsidiary considerations of a pragmatic nature. Three alternative specifications were considered:

(i) Double-log: $\ell n \; p_i = \beta_0 + \sum_j \beta_j \; \ell n \; z_{ij} + \varepsilon_i;$

(ii) Semi-log: $\ell n \; p_i = \beta_0 + \sum_j \beta_j z_{ij} + \varepsilon_i;$

(iii) Linear-log: $p_i = \beta_0 + \sum_j \beta_j \; \ell n \; z_{ij} + \varepsilon_i.$

The double-log and the semi-log are the two forms most commonly used in the literature, and are therefore natural candidates. To the best of my knowledge the third form has not been used before in hedonic studies, simply because characteristics are usually defined so that "more is better" (that is, so that $\partial U/\partial z > 0$, and hence $\partial p/\partial z > 0$), in which case the linear-log turns out to be concave and, as already said, that is rather implausible. On the other hand, if $\partial U/\partial z < 0$, then (iii) is necessarily convex, as are the other two forms.[4] As we recall from Chapter 2, the three main attributes of CT scanners, namely scan time, reconstruction time, and resolution, are defined so that "less is better" (that is, smaller values indicate a better scanner), and therefore in this case the linear-log form is indeed convex.

The three equations were estimated both for the joint set of head and body scanners (including a dummy variable for head scanners), and for body scanners only, for every year in the period 1976–1982 (1975 will receive separate treatment.)[5] Using the Box-Cox transformation to compare the alternative specifications, the linear-log emerged as the clear winner (see table 3.1): it ranked first—it had the smallest corrected mean squared error—in half the cases, second in 4 out of the 14 cases considered, and last in just 3 cases. The next best was the double-log, whereas the semi-log was far behind the other two. For most applications it probably would not make much of a difference whether the linear-log or the double-log were used, and the criterion of minimum squared error does not allow for fine distinctions. However, the linear-log also happens to be a convenient specification for the purposes here: first, its residuals are defined in the same units as price (since the dependent variable is in fact price, rather than log price as in the other two forms), and can therefore be incorporated directly in the MNL as an independent variable. Second, the linear-log is additive-separable in the z's (that is, in their logs), and thus eq. (3.5) holds indeed as an approximation to net utility. Therefore, all hedonic price equations will be specified hereafter as linear-log.

---

4. To be more precise, the semi-log is always convex, whereas the double-log depends upon the values of β_j; if $\beta_j < 0$ (that is, if $\partial U/\partial z_j < 0$) or if $\beta_j > 1$, then it is convex, whereas if $0 < \beta_j < 1$, it is concave.

5. Although 1982 was not included in the MNL analysis (for lack of data on choices), the hedonic regression was estimated for that year as well, since the residual prices from it will be needed to compute the welfare gains from innovation for 1981–82 (see Chapter 4).

Table 3.1   Hedonic Price Regressions: Box-Cox Comparisons

Year	Mean-squared error(MSE)		Price: geometric mean	Corrected MSE[a]		MSE Linear-log
	Double-log	Semi-log		Double-log	Semi-log	
			Head and body scanners			
1976	0.0338	0.0398	426.0	6,115	7,223	5,589
1977	0.0168	0.0176	486.4	3,985	4,176	2,584
1978	0.0734	0.0745	471.5	16,311	16,569	6,104
1979	0.0346	0.0532	497.1	8,552	13,136	4,054
1980	0.0288	0.0221	503.6	7,295	5,594	8,343
1981	0.0298	0.0390	541.0	8,729	11,401	15,603
1982	0.0177	0.0100	612.9	6,638	3,772	7,157
			Body scanners only			
1976	0.0008	0.0283	485.9	189	6,679	328
1977	0.0044	0.0098	562.6	1,402	3,098	1,591
1978	0.0097	0.0113	617.9	3,692	4,329	3,451
1979	0.0091	0.0107	642.5	3,764	4,413	3,280
1980	0.0333	0.0177	639.0	13,619	7,217	9,580
1981	0.0375	0.0229	767.6	22,090	13,522	19,728
1982	0.0152	0.0101	859.3	11,257	7,441	7,102

[a]Corrected MSE = MSE × (geometric mean of dependent variable)^2

Table 3.2 shows the two sets of estimated hedonic price functions (recall that SPEED stands for scan time, RESOL for spatial resolution, and RTIME for reconstruction time). Because these equations are only used here to generate the residual prices that go into the MNL model, the regression results are not analyzed here in any detail. Note only that the R^2's hover at about 0.85, and that the estimated coefficients are, with few exceptions, statistically significant. Thus the characteristics included are indeed of relevance in the market for CT scanners, accounting for most of the observed price variability. The relative good fits obtained indicate that the inclusion of both price and attributes in the MNL would

Table 3.2 Hedonic Price Regressions, Linear-Log Form, by Year

	1976	1977	1978	1979	1980	1981	1982
			Head and body scanners				
Intercept	657.2	831.5	880.1	905.0	861.3	1,062.7	840.3
	(5.3)[a]	(20)	(13.8)	(18.9)	(9.6)	(7.2)	(9.1)
Head dummy	−87.8	−75.2	−121.2	−123.8	31.5	209.7	24.7
	(−1.9)	(−2.3)	(−2.1)	(−1.8)	(0.3)	(1.0)	(0.1)
ℓn Speed	−37.3	−46.8	−66.9	−82.8	−110.9	−193.7	−73.6
	(−1.7)	(−4.2)	(−3.7)	(−4.6)	(−3.8)	(−3.2)	(−1.5)
ℓn Resol	−67.7	−226.5	−147.2	−189.2	−380.1	−335.0	−558.0
	(−0.6)	(−3.3)	(−1.5)	(−3.0)	(−4.6)	(−2.5)	(−5.7)
ℓn Rtime	−4.6	−33.3	−42.0	−39.7	−18.3	−21.4	−41.6
	(−0.2)	(−3.7)	(−2.7)	(−3.0)	(−0.8)	(−0.7)	(−1.8)
R^2	.65	.90	.86	.94	.91	.92	.96
df	9	16	19	15	13	9	10
			Body scanners only				
Intercept	790.1	808.4	834.0	914.2	873.8	1,071	858.4
	(20.7)	(20.6)	(13.8)	(20)	(8.5)	(6.2)	(8.9)
ℓn Speed	−75.2	−62.2	−56.8	−82.1	−109.9	−190.9	−55.9
	(−11)	(−5.7)	(−3.2)	(−4.8)	(−3.5)	(−2.8)	(−1.1)
ℓn Resol	−12.6	−161.8	−150.0	−198.6	−382.3	−333.8	−570.7
	(−0.4)	(−2.7)	(−1.8)	(−3.4)	(−4.2)	(−2.2)	(−5.7)
ℓn Rtime	−14.6	−19.9	−32.2	−43.0	−22.7	−25.4	−54.3
	(−2.5)	(−1.9)	(−2.0)	(−3.6)	(−0.8)	(−0.6)	(−2.1)
R^2	.98	.88	.66	.85	.81	.78	.90
df	4	11	12	12	11	7	8

[a]*t*-values in parentheses.

have resulted, as suspected, in a serious multicollinearity problem, and hence that the specification in (3.6) is amply justified.

3.3 The Estimation of the MNL

The second stage of the procedure suggested in (3.6) consists of the estimation of the MNL model, incorporating in it the residual prices obtained in the previous section as one of the independent variables. The MNL will be estimated separately for every year in the period 1975–1981; the model could not be estimated for 1973 and 1974, because during those two years there was in fact just one scanner in the market. To keep computational complexities at a manageable level, the estimated models do not include the vector h of individual attributes (except in the estimation of the MNL for 1975). In other words, the choice probabilities are estimated as functions of the attributes and prices of scanners only (those being common to all buyers), omitting the interaction between those variables and the individual h's. Otherwise the gains from innovation (ΔW_t) would have to be computed for *each buyer* in *each period*, and then integrated over h (recall eq. 1.10). Given that there are about 300 observations on average per annum, such procedure would increase the computational burden by an order of magnitude. Thus the results from the estimation of the MNL model refer to the representative user of CT scanners, which includes hospitals and private clinics. Likewise, the estimated equations do not include firm-related variables that may have a bearing on choices, but do not have a clear interpretation in terms of welfare, such as reputation (measured, for example, by cumulative sales), or advertising outlays.

3.3.1   Changes in the Choice Sets Within Periods

Most new models of CT scanners are introduced at the annual meetings, in November, of the Radiological Society of North America (RSNA), setting the stage for what the market for imaging equipment is going to be in the course of the year. Yet the choice sets do not remain constant within the "radiological year" from November 1 to October 31: some entries do occur after November, and the timing of exits is of course unrelated to the RSNA meetings.[6] Thus users purchasing scanners in the course of a given year do not necessarily face the same choice set, and just to assume that this is so may severely impair the accuracy of the results. In principle, the MNL does allow the choice set to vary across individuals; since the data gathered include the precise date (month/year) at which each buyer l ordered a scanner (denote it by t_l), one could define choice sets specific to each individual (that is, the set of scanners offered in the market at time t_l, net of entries and exits) and estimate the MNL accordingly. However, the software used here to estimate the MNL, the MLOGIT,[7] has an option that allows it to incorporate quite easily expansions in the choice set, but not contractions.[8] Moreover, in many cases the precise date of withdrawal of scanners from the market was not known with certainty, whereas announcement dates are for the most part well known. Thus within-period changes in the choice sets caused by new entries have been duly taken into account, but that is not so for exits: if a scanner was offered at the beginning of the year, it was assumed that it remained in the market throughout that year, even if it had been withdrawn earlier. It is conceivable that this asymmetry may have had some detrimental impact on the results, but it is virtually impossible to assess that with the tools used here.

3.3.2   Measures of Goodness of Fit for the MNL

In contrast to the widespread reliance on the R^2 in regression analysis, there is no universally accepted scalar criterion of fit for discrete choice

6. "Entries" and "exits" refer here to the introduction of new CT scanners to the market and the withdrawal of existing models, and not to the stepping in and out of firms; of course, sometimes the two types of events coincide.

7. This package was originally written by Charles Manski, later expanded by Bronwyn Hall, and interfaced with SAS by Danny Smith (at the National Bureau of Economic Research in Cambridge, Mass.).

8. Expansions were incorporated as follows: scanners that were in the market in a given year were ranked by month of introduction—τ—so that, disregarding exits, the number of alternatives in the choice set each month would be n_τ, $\tau = 1, 2, \ldots, 12$, $n_\tau \geq n_{\tau-1}$. Each buyer was then assigned a value n_τ, τ corresponding to the month when the scanner was ordered, so that the value of the likelihood function for that individual would be computed for the first n_τ alternatives only. To have an idea of the difficulties in handling exits, suppose that the first scanner in the choice set is withdrawn at time τ; then, for each individual ordering scanners henceforth, all independent variables would have to be redefined so that z_{ij} becomes $z_{i-1,j}$, where i indexes alternatives and j attributes (and price). This is in principle doable, but at too great an effort.

models. Two measures will be reported here: the popular ρ^2 (or "McFadden's R^2"), and the correlation between predicted (π^*) and actual probabilities (π_i), cor(π_i^*, π_i). The first is defined as $\rho^2 = 1 - [L(\beta^*)/L(0)]$, where $L(\beta^*)$ is the maximized value of the log-likelihood function, and $L(0)$ the value of the function when all the coefficients are assumed to be zero, that is, $L(0) = \Sigma\, n_j \ell n(1/m)$, where m is the number of alternatives, and n_j the number of buyers choosing alternative j. In other words, if we knew nothing about the determinants of choice, we would assign equal probabilities to all alternatives (that is, $\pi_j = 1/m$) and therefore $L(0)$ constitutes a natural baseline built on the assumption of total ignorance. Even though $0 \leqslant \rho^2 \leqslant 1$, values of the order of .20 are considered by some authors to represent good fits (see Hensher and Johnson, 1981), but more experience with those models is needed in order to establish well-grounded benchmarks.

The second measure, cor(π_i^*, π_i), is less precise than ρ^2 and more rarely used, but it can still be fairly informative of the performance of the model in the aggregate, namely, in predicting market shares. If the choice sets remained constant all year, then the predicted probabilities would be computed simply as $\pi_i^* = \exp V_i(\beta^*) / \Sigma \exp V_j(\beta^*)$. When entries occur, the probabilities are adjusted as follows:

$$\pi_i^* = \sum_{\tau=1}^{\hat{\tau}} \alpha_\tau \pi_{i\tau}^*, \qquad \hat{\tau} \leqslant 12, \qquad \sum_{\tau=1}^{\hat{\tau}} \alpha_\tau = 1,$$

where α_τ is the proportion of individuals buying scanners in sub-period τ (each sub-period being at least one month long), $\pi_{i\tau}^* = 0$ if i is not in n_τ, and $\pi_{i\tau}^* = \exp V_i(\beta^*) / \Sigma \exp V_j(\beta^*)$ otherwise.

3.4 Head versus Body Scanners

An important issue in formulating the MNL model is how to structure the choice set in view of the existence of these two different scanner types—whether head and body scanners comprise a single choice set or two separate branches of the decision tree, and if the latter proves to be the case, whether or not the two scanner types do actually belong to a common decision tree (see figure 3.2). These questions hinge on the pattern of substitution between the two types, and consequently on the

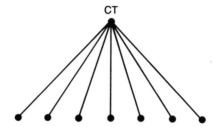

(a) A single market for head and body scanners
(IIA holds for the whole set)

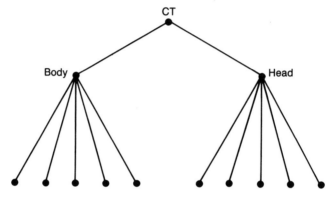

(b) Two sub-markets within a nested structure
(IIA holds within each cluster)

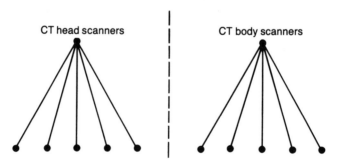

(c) Head and body scanners are unrelated markets

Figure 3.2   Alternative Structures of the Decision Tree

compatibility of the alternative choice structures with the assumption of Independence of Irrelevant Alternatives (IIA) that underlies the MNL. The search for the appropriate specification will begin with estimating the MNL once for the entire set of head and body scanners, and once for a restricted set of body scanners only. On the basis of those results, an appropriate specification test will be conducted. As the null hypothesis that IIA holds for the larger set (fig. 3.2a) is rejected, a nested structure with two branches, one for head and one for body scanners, is specified next, and estimated sequentially (fig. 3.2b). The results indicate that the elasticities of substitution between the two types of scanners are nil, and therefore that head and body scanners constitute in fact unrelated sets from the viewpoint of the choice process (fig. 3.2c). This result, in turn, will critically affect the way of computing the gains from innovation.

3.4.1 A Specification Test

The most distinctive feature of the MNL, accounting for both its advantages (computational and otherwise) and its limitations, is the assumption of IIA. One way of stating it is that, for any pair of choice alternatives i and j in the choice set, the probability ratio π_i/π_j is invariant with respect to the inclusion or exclusion of other alternatives (the famous red bus-blue bus example was meant to illustrate the implausibility of this property in certain choice situations). Similarly, the assumption of IIA implies that the cross-elasticities $\partial \ell n\pi_i / \partial \ell nz_{jk}$ are independent of i, for any k.[9]

The important point is that IIA precludes the possibility of having a flexible pattern of substitution between alternatives. To put it differently, it rules out differential proximity between alternatives in the space of unobserved quality dimensions (this follows directly from the assumption that the error term in the random utility function is independently distributed). Thus, for example, one would expect the cross-price elasticities *within* the sub-set of head (or body) scanners to be higher than those *between* scanners of different types, but IIA constrains them to be

9. Thus, for example, if there are three alternatives in the choice set, with the first two being very similar to each other and the third very different from them, IIA constrains the cross-elasticities between the three of them to be equal, whereas one would expect that $|\partial \ell n\pi_1/\partial \ell nz_{2k}| \gg |\partial \ell n\pi_3/\partial \ell nz_{2k}|$.

equal. The question is how to test for the IIA property and, if necessary, how to override it, that is, how to introduce more flexibility to the model.

Hausman and McFadden (1981) put forward a specification test based upon the comparison between the estimates β_f obtained when applying the MNL to the full choice set, and those arrived at when estimating a restricted set, β_r: if IIA holds, the difference between the two should be statistically insignificant. Formally, the statistic

$$S = (\beta_r - \beta_f)'(\text{Cov}_r - \text{Cov}_f)^{-1}(\beta_r - \beta_f) \sim \chi^2_{(m)}$$

can be used to test the null hypothesis $(\beta_r - \beta_f) = 0$ (m is the rank of the covariance matrix). The problem is that this is in fact an overall test that may fail because of misspecifications other than violations of IIA. Moreover, as McFadden (1982) points out, it is not a powerful test unless deviations from the MNL structure are substantial. Still, it is the only one that does not require a departure from MNL: more sensitive tests call for higher-level models in which IIA obtains as a special case, thus allowing for nested hypothesis testing. That is so, for example, with Hausman and Wise's (1978) "covariance probit"; however, and as is typically the case with discrete choice models other than the MNL, the covariance probit can handle in practice only a handful of choices and hence did not offer a feasible alternative in the present case.

In order to implement the Hausman-McFadden test, one must estimate the MNL for the full set of head and body scanners and for the restricted set of body scanners only. Because strong priors favor the alternative hypothesis, and in order to avoid excessive computations, the test will be conducted only for two years, 1977 and 1981.[10] As shown in table 3.3, the estimated coefficients of the restricted and unrestricted models differ substantially, and indeed the null hypothesis is rejected in both years: the critical χ^2 value at the .99 significance level is 18.5, whereas the values of the test statistic are $S(1977) = 21.83$, and $S(1981) = 27.77$. Thus the data do not support the assumption of IIA for the full choice set, that is, the choice behavior of buyers does not allow for the

10. The years were chosen according to two criteria: first, that they be far apart so that the choice sets would be substantially different, and the results can thus be presumed to hold also in the intervening periods, when the sets overlap. Second, that the ratio of the number of head to body scanners be approximately the same, so that the results will not depend upon the relative number of alternatives deleted when going from the full to the restricted model.

Table 3.3 MNL Estimates of Full and Restricted Models: 1977 and 1981

	1977		1981	
	Restricted	Full	Restricted	Full
Rprice[a]	0.99 (4.8)[b]	1.27 (6.7)	−0.28 (−2.5)	−0.19 (−2.4)
Speed	2.14 (2.8)	−0.77 (−3.6)	−7.50 (−0.5)	11.43 (3.7)
Speed^2	−1.26 (−3.4)	0.12 (2.3)	74.16 (1.4)	−4.33 (−3.3)
Resol	9.11 (2.4)	16.14 (6.8)	32.88 (3.9)	6.71 (3.1)
Resol^2	−2.53 (−1.5)	−5.57 (−5.8)	−24.03 (−4.2)	−6.56 (−4.5)
Rtime	5.08 (7.0)	3.23 (6.6)	−2.59 (−2.8)	−1.64 (−1.8)
Rtime^2	−2.37 (−6.7)	−1.47 (−6.2)	5.56 (3.9)	2.20 (2.6)
$L(\beta^*)/L(\beta^0)$	702/798 = .88	898/1,023 = .88	315/367 = .86	435/475 = .92
# of scanners	15	20	11	14
# of observations	325	367	153	180

[a]Rprice: Residual from hedonic price regression.
[b]Asymptotic *t*-values in parentheses.

symmetric treatment of head and body scanners in the context of a single choice set.

Given the inherent limitations of the Hausman-McFadden test—that it is not difficult to reject the null hypothesis in that type of specification tests—it is worth elaborating further on the qualitative evidence that supports the statistical finding of market segmentation. From a purely technical viewpoint, head scanners are specialized systems (designed only for brain studies), whereas body scanners are multipurpose and can be used to scan any body organ. Thus, the presumption is that "within" substitution effects would indeed be stronger than the "between" effects.[11]

That was not always the case, however. At first, body scanners did not differ much from head scanners, either in terms of their performance characteristics (except of course for the configuration of the gantry), or in their prices. Moreover, given that clinical applications other than for brain studies were highly uncertain in the early years, in practice body scanners were used mostly for head scans. Thus it is reasonable to assume that during the first year of coexistence of the two, 1975, body and head systems were relatively close substitutes.

However, subsequent advances in body scanners (primarily quantum reductions in scan time), and extensive clinical research that proved the efficacy of CT for the study of a widening range of organs and pathologies, rapidly reduced the functional overlap between the two systems. The trend toward simpler and less expensive head scanners that started in 1977–78, exactly opposite to the rapidly increasing sophistication (and higher prices) of body scanners, further widened the gap between them. Thus by 1980 the average body scanner was almost 5 times more expensive than a typical head scanner, and 20 times faster. Not surprisingly, late first-time buyers of CT head systems were mostly small hospitals facing tight budget constraints ("late" means here after 1978). In view of the price gap between the two types, it is reasonable to assume that the relevant choice set for those hospitals was made of head scanners only. In sum, the qualitative evidence suggests that the cross-elasticities between head and body scanners decreased rapidly over time, probably becoming nil by the late seventies.

---

11. That is, "within" the sub-set of head or body scanners, as opposed to "between" the two clusters.

3.5   The Nested Multinomial Logit Model

In light of the above results, a nested MNL (NMNL) model having two branches, one for head (H) and the other for body (B) scanners is discussed next (recall fig. 3.2b).[12] Accordingly, the buyer's decision-making can be conceptually decomposed into two sequential stages: in the first the hospital decides whether to purchase a head or a body scanner, and in the second a specific brand is selected out of the chosen cluster. Formally, the probability of choosing the ith scanner of type h, $h = H, B$, can then be written as $\pi(i,h) = \pi(i \mid h) \, \pi(h)$, where

$$(3.7) \qquad \pi(i \mid h) = \exp V_i / \sum_{j=1}^{n_h} \exp V_j, \text{ and}$$

$$(3.8) \qquad \pi(h) = \exp (\lambda W_h) / [\exp (\lambda W_H) + \exp (\lambda W_B)],$$

n_h being the number of brands in cluster h, and W_h the inclusive value of that cluster, that is,

$$W_h = \ell n \left[\sum_{j=1}^{n_h} \exp (V_j) \right], \qquad h = H, B.$$

3.5.1   The Role of λ

The key parameter in this model is λ, which should be interpreted as a measure of substitutability, proximity or independence among clusters.[13] This can be seen by examining the cross-elasticities among alternatives for the various permutations possible in the context of the NMNL; since

12. Of course, the structure of the choice set may be more complex, with several levels of decision rather than just two as in here (for example, one could add a higher level where the user chooses between different imaging modalities, such as CT versus MRI), and a finer division into more than two clusters at the lowest stage.

13. There has been some confusion in the literature regarding the meaning of λ, which at times has been interpreted as a measure of independence of alternatives *within* rather than *between* clusters.

this will prove to be an issue of prime importance in computing the gains from innovation, those cross-elasticities are carefully derived in appendix 3.1.[14] The limiting cases highlight the above interpretation of λ (normally λ has to lie in the unit interval): $\lambda = 1$ implies that the IIA property holds for the entire choice set, and hence that cross-elasticities do not depend upon the precise location of alternatives. Consequently, the grouping of alternatives into clusters is altogether inconsequential, and the simple MNL applies to the whole set. On the other hand, $\lambda = 0$ means that the cross-elasticities between alternatives belonging to different clusters are zero, and therefore the decision tree should be "sliced down the middle," that is, each cluster ought to be regarded as as separate analytical unit—or market—from the point of view of demand behavior.

Closely related, the value of λ determines also the form of the surplus function $W(\cdot)$: if $0 < \lambda \le 1$, then the form of the function is

$$(3.9) \quad W = \ell n \left[\sum_h \left(\sum_i \exp V_{i,h} \right)^\lambda \right],$$

whereas if $\lambda = 0$, then

$$(3.10) \quad W = \sum_h W_h \pi(h), \qquad W_h = \ell n \left(\sum_{i=1}^{n_h} \exp V_{i,h} \right),$$

where the probabilities $\pi(h)$ no longer depend upon the attributes and prices of the alternatives as captured by the inclusive values in (3.8), but are instead exogenous to the model and can therefore be taken to be simply the observed frequencies in the population.[15]

3.5.2   Estimating the NMNL

The NMNL model will be estimated sequentially: first, eq. (3.7) is estimated separatedly for head and body scanners, then the estimated coef-

---

14. McFadden (1984) does elaborate on these cross-elasticities, but the presentation there is far from transparent. I am not aware of any other source, hence the appendix.

15. In a more general model the $\pi(h)$'s could be made endogenous, that is, they could be estimated as functions of variables pertaining to the different clusters as such (other than their inclusive values), and of individual attributes relevant to the choice of clusters.

ficients are used to compute the inclusive values W_h, and last, these are incorporated in (3.8) to estimate the coefficient λ. This procedure is repeated for every year from 1976 to 1981; 1975 will receive separate treatment. The method of sequential estimation is consistent but not fully efficient, so the second-stage standard errors are not entirely reliable. An alternative would have been to estimate the model using full information-maximum likelihood, a method that could in principle render efficient estimates. However, the procedure is difficult to implement in the case of the NMNL, and the software available to me in the early eighties was not very satisfactory for that purpose.

A rarely noticed limitation of the MNL is that if the independent variables included in the model are "generic," meaning that they vary across alternatives but not across individual observations, then the maximum number allowed is $n-1$, n being the number of alternatives in the choice set. For this reason, and since the vector of individuals attributes was omitted, the small number of different brands of head scanners offered in the market every year imposed some constraints on the first-stage estimation of the head branch. First, only four years (1976–1979) could be estimated: the 1980 and 1981 sets included just three scanners each, and those were very similar in prices and characteristics. Second, V_i had to be specified as linear in the z's (with price), rather than as quadratic with residual price, thus saving three degrees of freedom in the relevant dimension.[16] Third, only three variables could be included in 1979, and therefore RTIME (the least important characteristic) was omitted.

Table 3.4 presents the first-stage MNL estimates for head scanners, and table 3.5 those for body scanners. Without analyzing the results in any detail, I want to point out the following: first, the model fits fairly well, particularly in predicting aggregate shares—that is, in terms of $\text{cor}(\pi_i^*, \pi_i)$—even though individual and firm-specific attributes have been omitted. Second, the estimated coefficients vary substantially from year to year, suggesting that preferences for attributes may have changed over time, as did the CT technology itself. Third, and contrary

---

16. It is worth noting that simple correlations between price and characteristics of head scanners were found to be systematically lower than those for body scanners. This suggests that the multicollinearity problem, which motivated the use of the quadratic in the first place, may be significantly less severe for head scanners. If so, the linear form may actually be an appropriate specification for head scanners. One has to keep in mind, though, that partial correlations may be poor indicators of the magnitude of collinearity in a multivariate context.

Table 3.4 MNL Estimates for Head Scanners: Linear Form

	1976	1977	1978	1979
Price	−0.748 (−1.5)[a]	−0.709 (−1.9)	−0.893 (−5.5)	−0.818 (−2.4)
Speed	0.018 (0.2)	−0.238 (−1.4)	0.303 (1.9)	−0.318 (−0.9)
Resol	−4.706 (−3.6)	−5.565 (−2.9)	−7.756 (−4.8)	−10.307 (−4.7)
Rtime	−0.619 (−2.2)	−0.366 (−1.2)	1.119 (2.7)	
$\rho^2 = 1 - \dfrac{L(\beta^*)}{L(\beta^0)}$	.131	.116	.42	.455
$\mathrm{Cor}(\pi^*,\pi)$	.999	.910	.993	.998
	(.0001)	(.012)	(.0001)	(.0016)
# of scanners	6	6	8	4
# of observations	89	56	69	80

[a]Asymptotic t-values in parentheses.

Table 3.5 MNL Estimates for Body Scanners

	1976	1977	1978	1979	1980	1981
Rprice[a]	11.252	0.993	1.020	0.485	0.695	-0.277
	(6.4)[b]	(4.8)	(4.8)	(1.8)	(2.4)	(-2.5)
Speed	-2.292	2.138	4.624	-8.669	11.347	-7.504
	(-7.3)	(2.8)	(1.0)	(-1.5)	(2.0)	(-0.5)
Speed^2	0.236	-1.264	-8.283	31.292	-34.838	74.161
	(4.0)	(-3.4)	(-0.6)	(1.9)	(-1.6)	(1.4)
Resol	69.107	9.113	-34.126	-15.283	-18.129	32.877
	(7.3)	(2.4)	(-6.3)	(-5.0)	(-3.6)	(3.9)
Resol^2	-23.360	-2.533	15.096	6.291	7.738	-24.028
	(-7.6)	(-1.5)	(5.8)	(3.8)	(2.7)	(-4.2)
Rtime	-3.931	5.082	2.385	3.288	3.161	-2.591
	(-5.3)	(7.0)	(2.0)	(3.3)	(2.8)	(-2.8)
Rtime^2	1.054	-2.370	-1.511	-1.401	-2.093	5.560
	(4.5)	(-6.7)	(-2.0)	(-2.1)	(-2.2)	(3.9)
$\rho^2 = 1 - \dfrac{L(\beta^*)}{L(\beta^0)}$	.29	.12	.16	.16	.20	.14
Cor(π^*,π)	.999	.877	.900	.870	.722	.547
	(.0001)	(.0001)	(.0001)	(.0001)	(.0024)	(.082)
# of scanners	8	15	16	16	15	11
# of observations	285	324	164	177	193	153

[a]Rprice: Residual from hedonic price regression.
[b]Asymptotic *t*-values in parentheses.

to what is normally to be expected, the coefficients of residual price for body scanners are positive (except for 1981); those for head scanners, however, are negative and fairly stable. These findings have important implications for the computations of welfare gains (aside from being of considerable interest in themselves), and will be discussed extensively in coming sections.

As for the second stage of the NMNL, table 3.6 (a and b) presents the computed inclusive values and the estimates of λ for the four years in which the first-stage MNL for head scanners could be estimated. The key result is that the estimates of λ are very close to zero (except for 1978), implying that the cross-elasticities between the two types of scanners are nil, and hence that head and body scanners do not belong to a common decision tree. Lacking the corrected standard errors (recall that the sequential procedure is not fully efficient), the hypothesis that $\lambda = 0$ could not be formally tested, using either a Wald or a Lagrangian test.[17] However, the stated conclusion is not contingent upon the formal acceptance of this hypothesis: even if the λ's had proven to be statistically different from zero, their small magnitude make the "between" cross-elasticities negligible, and that is all that is required. For 1978, the negative value of λ is symptomatic of a local failure of the conditions underlying generalized extreme value models in general, and the NMNL in particular. Although it is difficult to draw any firm conclusion from such a finding, it could be taken as further indication that head and body scanners were not good substitutes for each other (taken at face value, $\lambda < 0$ suggests complementarity, since the cross-elasticities so computed would be positive).

At a more general level, it is worth noting that the procedure followed above, centering on the estimation of λ, may help address the all-pervasive problem of drawing market boundaries in empirical microstudies. Thus starting from a set of priors regarding the appropriate clustering of goods in a differentiated market, the size of λ, as estimated in the NMNL, may indicate the actual degree of segmentation found in the market. In particular, testing the hypothesis $\lambda = 0$ could help decide whether or not the clusters can in fact be treated as separate markets altogether.

---

17. In principle, the correct standard errors could be obtained by further iterations, using the Berndt-Hausman-Hall-Hall (1974) procedure. Unfortunately, the required software was not readily available to me at the time, so I was unable to follow it.

Table 3.6a Nested MNL: Computation of Inclusive Values

Year	Body scanners		Head scanners	
	$\Sigma_i \exp V_i$	$W_B{}^a$	$\Sigma_i \exp V_i$	$W_H{}^a$
1976	5.22E+20	47.704	1.114E-4	−9.102
1977	161,040	11.989	3.012E-5	−10.410
1978	5.42E-7	−14.428	3.231E-5	−10.340
1979	0.00885	−4.728	1.366E-7	−15.806

$^aW_h = \ell n \, (\Sigma_i \exp V_{ih})$.

Table 3.6b Nested MNL: Second-Stage Estimates

Year	Coefficient of W_h:$\hat{\lambda}$	Standard error	ρ^2
1976	0.0205	0.00214	.21
1977	0.0784	0.00646	.40
1978	−0.2120	0.03510	.12
1979	0.0706	0.01211	.10

3.5.3 Estimates for 1975

As already noted, 1975 was the first year in which there was a choice of scanners in the market, and hence the first that could be estimated, albeit in a somewhat special way. Although announcements of new scanners were made in late 1973 and throughout 1974, the only scanner sold in fact during that period was the EMI head scanner. In 1975 the first two body scanners were successfully introduced to the market, as well as an additional head scanner. At that early stage head and body scanners were fairly close substitutes (recall section 3.4.2), so the effective choice set for 1975 comprised both types, totaling four alternatives. That is a very small number for estimation purposes; moreover, since preferences of buyers were still ill-defined because of the newness of the technology, the estimation of the MNL for that year posed a great deal of trouble. After experimenting with several specifications, the model converged and rendered sensible results with the following "hybrid" specification (asymptotic *t*-values in parenthesis; the mean value of RAD was 0.66):

RPRICE	10.18	(4.3)
HEAD × RPRICE	−2.88	(−6.0)
SPEED	−0.17	(−0.8)
RESOL × RAD	−6.34	(−4.8) (RESOL at mean RAD: −4.18)
ρ^2	.24	
No. of scanners	4	
No. of observations	181	

The residual prices, in turn, were obtained from the following hedonic price regression, based on data for just five scanners[18] (the fifth scanner introduced in 1975 had no sales and was not included in the MNL):

$$\text{Price} = 468.3 + 18.4 \text{ HEAD} - 7.7 \text{ } \ell n \text{ SPEED} - 145.6 \text{ } \ell n \text{ RESOL},$$
$$(2.6) \quad (0.5) \quad\quad (-0.2) \quad\quad\quad\quad (-1.0)$$
$$R^2 = 0.55$$

Notice that, since there was room for only three generic variables in the MNL, the quadratic terms as well as reconstruction time were omitted, and resolution was interacted with RAD, an attribute of hospitals.[19] However, in view of the relatively narrow range of values of the included variables, the results are probably not very different from what would have emerged had the quadratic terms been included as well. As will be argued in Chapter 4, there was room to believe that the price response will be different for the two types of scanners, and hence the extra term RPRICE × HEAD, HEAD being a dummy for head scanners. For all its limitations the model performs quite well, at least in that ρ^2 is quite

18. With just one degree of freedom, the results from this regression are clearly open to question (that is clear from the low *t*-values, shown in parenthesis). Note, however, that this is not because of a sampling problem: the five scanners included constituted the whole population.

19. As mentioned in Chapter 2, RAD is defined as $(R1 + R2 + R3)/3$, where the Ri's are dummy variables for the availability of x-ray, cobalt, and radium therapy respectively. The presumption is that hospitals with a wider range of radiation therapy services will tend to put a higher value on the resolution of CT scanners. Since RAD is defined only for hospitals, private clinics were excluded from the 1975 sample. As we recall, interacting a generic variable with an individual attribute (such as RAD) makes the former vary across individuals, thus overcoming the limitation on the number of variables when there are but few alternatives in the choice set.

high and the estimated coefficients lie within the expected range, in light of the results for later years. Still, it is quite clear that the 1975 estimates are less reliable than those for 1976–1981 and should be taken with a great deal of caution.

3.6   Changes in Preferences and Inducement Mechanisms

In the course of reviewing the MNL results, we noted that the estimated coefficients change substantially from year to year,[20] implying that "preferences" for attributes have not been stable, a finding that is usually a source of concern. The questions that arise immediately are, first, how are those changes to be interpreted? And second, are the observed variations in the coefficients purely random, or do they follow some pattern having an economic rationale? These issues are quite complex, and full answers would require a much deeper probe than we can afford at present. The discussion here will be limited to reporting an interesting set of findings having to do with the changes in the coefficients, and to offering a tentative interpretation that will be of relevance in the computation of the gains from innovation.

   In brief, the underlying idea is that changes in preferences for attributes might be related to changes in the attributes themselves, in what could be described as a dual-inducement mechanism. On the one hand, firms presumably respond to the relative intensity of preferences for attributes in designing their products; that is, they will try to enhance attributes that are highly valued and will allocate their R&D efforts accordingly. In that case the observed direction of technical advance in attributes space will be influenced by the relative intensity of preferences for the different attributes. On the other hand, preferences themselves may respond to the changing mix of attributes available in the market: as the set of products offered in one period incorporates innovations that emphasize some attributes more than others, preferences toward the former may weaken relative to the latter. This as yet crude hypothesis will be examined simply by tracing the pattern followed over time

---

20. It is not just that the values of the year-by-year estimates turned out to be different, but that the differences were statistically significant: the MNL model was estimated also by pooling every pair of consecutive years, with time dummies interacted with the attributes, and in most cases the interaction terms were indeed found to be statistically significant.

by "relative preferences" in reference to the gradient of changes in the technology itself.

The empirical analysis will refer to body scanners only, primarily because most of the advances occurred in them rather than in head scanners, and also because the MNL for head scanners could be estimated for four years only. Again, scan time and resolution are the two most important characteristics of CT scanners, not only for users, but also in that they confront firms with crucial technological trade-offs in the design of the systems. Consequently, the analysis will focus on them to the exclusion of reconstruction time (however, the data on the latter will be exhibited as well).

3.6.1   Measures of "Relative Preferences"

The first hurdle is that it is not clear how preferences should be defined and measured in this context, particularly since the indirect utility function V_i was specified as quadratic, and hence the estimated coefficients are not very telling by themselves. One possibility would be to look at the marginal utility of each attribute, though again, that is not uniquely defined (because of the quadratic form), but depends upon the *level* of the attributes. Since the hypothesis outlined above postulates that preferences may influence the optimal configuration of attributes sought by firms, an appropriate magnitude to look at would be the derivative of the choice probabilities,

$$(3.11) \quad \frac{\partial \pi_i}{\partial z_{ij}} = \frac{\partial V_i}{\partial z_{ij}} \pi_i(1 - \pi_i) = (a_j + 2b_j z_{ij})\pi_i(1 - \pi_i),$$

where i is the index of brands, and j of attributes. Averaging over i,

$$(3.12) \quad d\bar{\pi}_j \equiv \sum_i (\partial \pi_i/\partial z_{ij})/n.$$

The use of such measure can be rationalized as follows: consider the highly simplified case whereby price-cost margins are fixed, and the marginal cost of improvements is equal across all attributes. It can be easily shown that the first-order conditions for profit maximization in such a setting entail enhancing each attribute so as to equalize the derivatives $\partial \pi_i/\partial z_{ij}$ to the corresponding Lagrange multiplier. Now, if the parameters a and b in V_i are correctly signed, then π_i will be concave in the z's so the gradient of first derivatives would signal indeed the most profitable direction for the firm to follow in designing the product. To put it differently, if the optimal attributes' mix cannot be attained in one shot, a reasonable rule of thumb for the firms to follow would be to improve the attributes with larger derivatives (as measured by 3.11), as the inducement hypothesis suggests.

Note that (3.12) amounts to a weighted average of the marginal utility of attribute j, with the weights $w_i = \pi_i(1 - \pi_i)$ being a concave function of the market shares ($\partial w_i/\partial \pi_i \lessgtr 0 <=> \pi_i \lessgtr 0.5$). Thus in that respect at least $d\bar{\pi}_j$ is a more reasonable summary estimate than, say, the average elasticity (the other natural candidate in this context)

$$\sum_i (\partial \ln \pi_i/\partial \ln z_{ij})/n = \sum_i [(\partial V_i/\partial z_{ij})z_{ij}(1 - \pi_i)]/n,$$

since the weights in the later are inversely related to market shares.

Table 3.7 shows the average derivatives for scan time, resolution, and reconstruction time computed on the basis of the MNL estimates of table 3.5. Note that, since the three attributes are defined so that less is better, a smaller value of $d\bar{\pi}_j$ implies a stronger preference for attribute j; however, the $d\bar{\pi}_j$'s need not be all negative, since they are averages of a quadratic form. Following the same logic as in traditional inducement models (where relative factor prices are the driving force), the relevant

Table 3.7   Summary MNL Estimates for Body Scanners: Average Derivatives of π_i with Respect to z_{ij}

Year	$d\bar{\pi}$ Speed	$d\bar{\pi}$ Resol	$d\bar{\pi}$ Rtime	($d\bar{\pi}$ Speed $-$ $d\bar{\pi}$ Resol)[a]
1976	-0.166	-0.073	-0.141	-0.093
1977	0.096	0.157	0.123	-0.061
1978	0.131	-0.079	0.039	0.210
1979	-0.117	-0.191	0.091	0.074
1980	0.361	-0.360	0.053	0.721
1981	0.172	-0.138	0.199	0.310

Source: Table 3.5.

[a]This is a measure of "relative preferences", that is, a larger value indicates a stronger preference for resolution vis-à-vis speed.

magnitudes here are the relative preferences for attributes, rather than the values of the average derivatives themselves. Given that the signs of the computed $d\bar{\pi}_j$'s are not uniform, relative preferences will be measured by the differences $d\bar{\pi}_{kj} = d\bar{\pi}_j - d\bar{\pi}_k$ (rather than by the ratio $d\bar{\pi}_k/d\bar{\pi}_j$), as shown in the last column of table 3.7.[21]

The way in which the term "preferences" is used here may have stretched its accepted meaning too far, and therefore ought to be qualified. To begin with, one can never be sure that actual empirical estimates do capture the true structure of preferences. For example, the underlying utility function could in fact be stable, but the observed coefficients might change from year to year because of specification errors. Likewise, as argued before, there is an inherent arbitrariness in choosing a summary measure of the estimated coefficients. Thus it should be kept in mind that whatever one chooses to call preferences is, ultimately, a matter of definition, and its validity is contingent upon the maintained (and untested) hypothesis that the utility function, and the choice model embedding it, are correctly specified.

Finally, it is worth noting that there is in this case some independent evidence supporting the findings on relative preferences as reported in table 3.7: a survey of users of CT scanners conducted in 1975 reveals a strong emphasis on scan time vis-à-vis other attributes (see Buenger and Huckman, 1975), whereas a study conducted in 1978 by the journal *Radiology/Nuclear Medicine and Technology Marketing* indicates that resolution was favored over scan time (the relevant sections of the surveys are reproduced in appendix 3.2). Thus for those two years at least the findings here are upheld.

3.6.2 Measures of the Direction of Technology

The task of devising an appropriate summary measure of the direction of technological advance in characteristics space is relatively simpler, involving some average over the set of products offered each period. The proposed indicator is the rate of change of attributes, defined as

$$(3.13) \quad \%\Delta\bar{z}_{jt} = (\bar{z}_{jt-1} - \bar{z}_{jt})/\bar{z}_{jt},$$

---

21. The two metrics are of course very similar. Note that the difference $d\bar{\pi}_{kj}$ is defined as the average derivate of attribute j minus that of k, that is, the sign is reversed so that the larger $d\bar{\pi}_{kj}$ is, the stronger are the preferences for attribute k relative to j.

where $\bar{z}_{jt}$ stands for the mean value of attribute j in the choice set offered in period t.[22] Note that the $\bar{z}_{jt}$'s are simple averages, so that all scanners in the set are weighted equally, regardless of how many were sold. These were preferred over weighted averages, since the indicator is supposed to capture the *technological choices* made by firms, not their consequences.

Table 3.8 presents the computed values of (3.13) along with the ratio of the rate of change of resolution versus scan time, which is the magnitude that will be related to preferences (for convenience, this ratio will be simply called "technology"). Incidentally, the table shows the staggering pace of technical advance in Computed Tomography: in 1975 it took more than three minutes to perform a scan, whereas by 1982 the average scan time was less than three seconds. Likewise, spatial resolution more than doubled over the same period: from 1.6 mm. at first, to less than 0.7 mm. seven years later.

3.6.3   The Findings

The series of preferences and changes in attributes are plotted in figure 3.3, with the "technology" series moved back one year. Quite clearly, the two move very much in unison (the correlation between them is of 0.8), and the question is how should this close relationship be interpreted. One possibility is to cast those findings in terms of an inducement mechanism: the magnitudes $d\bar{\pi}_{ij}$ signal to the firms the most profitable expansion path in attributes space, and they respond, with a lag, by improving the attributes accordingly. Thus, for example, preferences in 1980 heavily favored resolution over scan time, and the focus of the improvements in the 1981 scanners was indeed on the former attribute. Conversely, a year later demand was more sensitive to scan time, and the scanners offered in 1982 were significantly faster than those in 1981, but not much better in terms of resolution. Note that the indicators of preferences and technology are both expressed as relative magnitudes, and therefore one could explain, at best, the direction of technical advance

---

22. Given that an improvement in an attribute means a smaller average value for it, the rate of change is defined as the average value of the attribute in period $t-1$ minus that in period t, rather than the reverse. Thus, higher values of $\%\Delta\bar{z}_j$ represent larger improvements in that attribute.

Table 3.8 Average Characteristics of Body Scanners and Their Rate of Change

Year	Speed (sec.)	%ΔSpeed[a]	Resol (mm.)	%ΔResol[a]	Rtime (sec.)	%ΔRtime[a]	%ΔResol / %ΔSpeed
1975	195.00	—	1.61	—	8.00	—	—
1976	62.60	2.11	1.55	0.04	82.63	−0.90	0.019
1977	19.24	2.25	1.27	0.22	38.40	1.15	0.097
1978	7.10	1.71	1.15	0.10	30.37	0.26	0.058
1979	6.63	0.07	1.07	0.08	28.56	0.06	1.081
1980	5.54	0.20	0.99	0.08	31.07	−0.08	0.401
1981	4.87	0.14	0.85	0.17	32.36	−0.04	1.241
1982	2.60	0.87	0.69	0.23	27.33	0.18	0.265

[a] $\%\Delta \bar{z}_i = (\bar{z}_{t-1} - \bar{z}_t)/\bar{z}_t$.

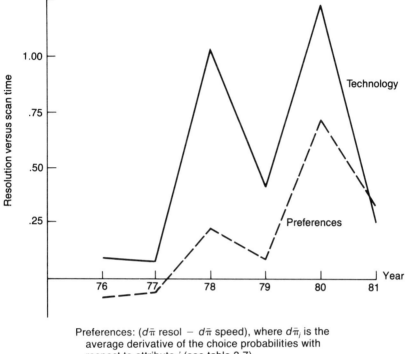

Preferences: $(d\bar{\pi}$ resol $- d\bar{\pi}$ speed), where $d\bar{\pi}_j$ is the average derivative of the choice probabilities with respect to attribute j (see table 3.7).

Technology: $\dfrac{\%\Delta \text{ resol}}{\%\Delta \text{ speed}}$, where $\%\Delta \bar{z}_j$ is the average rate of change of attribute j (see table 3.8).

Figure 3.3   The Dynamics of Preferences and Technology

in attributes space, but by no means its extent: the available analytical tools and data have very little to say on that.[23]

Granting for the moment the inducement hypothesis, the next question is, how long will the lag be? In other words, how long does it take the market signals, embedded in relative preferences, to elicit innovations that would reflect these preferences? In general, this will depend upon two sets of factors: first, the R&D technology itself, that is, the speed at which new scanners incorporating the desired attributes can be

23. See Rosenberg (1976) for an illuminating discussion of the role of "technological imperatives" in determining the rate and direction of technological advance; his is also a well-placed warning against trying to explain too much with inducement theories.

developed; and second, the firms' expectations regarding preferences toward attributes. For example, if technological lead-times were very short, and firms had perfect foresight regarding preferences, then one would expect an almost contemporaneous relation. Clearly, with just six observations at hand, one can do no better than to scrutinize the figures searching for the appropriate lag (if more data were available, one would attempt instead to estimate a lag-structure model, incorporating explicitly expectations and supply factors). The finding of a short lag (one year) would suggest that firms had a good sense of what the market required, and that they were able to move fast in improving the technology in the desired direction.

The other noticeable feature of figure 3.3 is the marked cyclicality of both series: year after year there is a reversal in the relative intensity of preferences, as well as in the focus of improvements in attributes. This seems to suggest a sort of reverse causality: as the set of products offered in one period incorporates innovations that emphasize a particular attribute, preferences for it will subsequently weaken relative to other attributes. Ultimately, the reason for such a phenomenon must be diminishing marginal utility in the relevant dimensions, as well as complementarities between the various attributes of a CT scanner (as is the case with many other systems). Circumstantial evidence for both is plentiful; for example, each discrete increase in the speed of scanners widened the range of organs that could be successfully visualized; however, once that had been achieved, further progress in diagnosing pathologies in those organs depended upon improvements in resolution. Unfortunately, complementarities cannot be detected in the estimated MNL model since, as we recall, the interaction terms were deleted from the quadratic form of V^n when specifying the equation (see 3.5 above). Thus the observed time pattern of "preferences" may be due, at least in part, to a misspecification of the utility function. Likewise, the way the $d\bar{\pi}_j$'s were computed does not allow one to distinguish diminishing marginal utility, in conjunction with changes in the levels of attributes, from changes in the utility function itself. Once again, a careful distinction should be drawn between what is essentially a semantic problem (that is, what the term "preferences" refers to), and the substantive issue of what sort of information is conveyed by the time profile of $d\bar{\pi}_{ij}$, however one may choose to call it. Again, the stand taken here is that the magnitudes $d\bar{\pi}_{ij}$ are indeed very likely to signal the relative valuation of the attributes of the average scanner in the market, and as such are the relevant measures to be used in the context of an inducement hypothesis. Granted that much, the bottom line is that the set of facts summarized in figure 3.3 do lend support to the stated hypothesis.

Finally, it is important to emphasize that even in the best of cases, the inducement mechanism suggested by figure 3.3 constitutes just a partial determinant of the direction of technical change. Thus, for example, the very set of relevant attributes may change over time: some may reach upper limits (either technological or utility-determined) and drop out of sight, whereas new ones may appear, taking precedence in shaping both preferences and innovative efforts. Clearly, that type of changes cannot be dealt with within the narrow mold of figure 3.3. The same can be said of exogenous shocks, such as the appearance of Magnetic Resonance Imaging, or the impact of changes in the regulatory environment.

Appendix 3.1   Derivation of Cross Elasticities in the Nested MNL

Consider a two-level tree:

$$(3.14) \quad \pi(i,h) = \pi(i \mid h)\, \pi(h) \qquad h = H, B$$

$$(3.15) \quad \pi(i \mid h) = e^{\beta' z_{ih}} / \sum_j e^{\beta' z_{jh}}$$

$$(3.16) \quad \pi(h) = \frac{e^{\lambda W_H}}{e^{\lambda W_H} + e^{\lambda W_B}}.$$

Case 1. The two alternatives belong to the same cluster, for example, $i, j \in H$. The cross-elasticity is:

$$(3.17) \quad \eta_{H,H} \equiv \frac{\partial \pi(i,H)}{\partial z_{jH}} \frac{z_{jH}}{\pi(i,H)}$$

$$(3.18) \quad \frac{\partial \pi(i,H)}{\partial z_{jH}} = \frac{\partial \pi(i \mid H)}{\partial z_{jH}} \pi(H) + \frac{\partial \pi(H)}{\partial z_{jH}} \pi(i \mid H)$$

(3.19) $$\frac{\partial \pi(i \mid H)}{\partial z_{jH}} = -\beta\pi(i \mid H)\pi(j \mid H)$$

(3.20) $$\frac{\partial \pi(H)}{\partial z_{jH}} = \lambda\frac{\partial W_H}{\partial z_{jH}}[\pi(H - \pi(H)^2] = \lambda\beta\pi(j \mid H)\pi(H)[1 - \pi(H)]$$

Substituting (3.19) and (3.20) in (3.18),

$$\frac{\partial \pi(i \mid H)}{\partial z_{jH}} = -\beta\pi(i \mid H)\pi(j \mid H)\pi(H)$$

$$+ \lambda\beta\pi(i \mid H)\pi(j \mid H)\pi(H)[1 - \pi(H)] \rightarrow$$

$$\frac{\partial \pi(i \mid H)}{\partial z_{jH}} = -\beta\pi(i,H)\,[\lambda\pi(j,H) + (1 - \lambda)\pi(j \mid H)].$$

Therefore,

(3.21) $$\eta_{H,H} = -\beta z_{jH}[\lambda\pi(j,H) + (1 - \lambda)\pi(j \mid H)].$$

Case 2. The alternatives belong to different clusters, for example, $i \in H$, $j \in B$. The cross-elasticity is then:

(3.22) $$\eta_{H,B} \equiv \frac{\partial \pi(i,H)}{\partial z_{jB}} \frac{z_{jB}}{\pi(i,H)}$$

$$\frac{\partial \pi(i,H)}{\partial z_{jB}} = \frac{\partial \pi(H)}{\partial z_{jB}} = \frac{\partial \pi(H)}{\partial z_{jB}}\pi(i \mid H) = -\lambda\frac{\partial W_B}{\partial z_{jH}}\pi(B)\pi(i \mid H)\pi(H),$$

but $\dfrac{\partial W_B}{\partial z_{jH}} = \beta\pi(j \mid B)$, and therefore

(3.23) $\dfrac{\partial \pi(i,H)}{\partial z_{jB}} = -\lambda\beta\pi(i,H)\pi(j,B).$

Substituting (3.23) in (3.22),

(3.24) $\eta_{H,B} = -\lambda\beta z_{jB}\pi(j,B).$

From (3.21) and (3.24) it is clear that the cross-elasticities depend upon the parameter λ, as follows:[24]

(i) $0 \leqslant \lambda < 1 \rightarrow -\eta_{H,H} > -\eta_{H,B}$

(ii) $\lambda = 1 \rightarrow -\eta_{H,H} = -\eta_{H,B}$

(iii) $\lambda = 0 \rightarrow \eta_{H,B} = 0$

Appendix 3.2   Surveys of Users of CT Scanners

(a) 1975 Survey

Desired advances or improvements	*Frequency*
Shorten scan time	23
Eliminate movements	9
Eliminate water bag	7
Replace polaroid system	6
Eliminate artifacts	5
Better posterior fossa scans	3
Easier chair adjustments	3

24. Note that (i) and (ii) hold only if β, z_{jh}, and $\pi(j, h)$ are the same both for $j \in H$ and $j \in B$. If that is not the case, then some intercluster cross-elasticities may be larger than some of the intracluster ones. For that to happen (assuming still the same β and z), $\pi(j, B) - \pi(j, H) > [(1 - \lambda)/\lambda] \pi(j \mid H)$, that is, the probability of the outside alternative has to be substantially larger than that of the inside alternative. Clearly, the smaller the λ is the less likely it is that the condition will hold.

(b) 1978 Survey

Recognizing that cost considerations are a function of specifications, on a scale of 1 to 4 with 4 the highest, indicate the relative importance of each of the key specification parameters to you and your requirements:

Key specifications	Average Score
Spatial resolution	3.8
Contrast resolution	3.8
Speed of scan	3.4
Speed of reconstruction	3.2
Radiation dose	3.1
Hard copy format	2.9
Simplified operator control	2.8
Data management features	2.7
Automated patient	2.5
positioning	2.3
Remote viewing consoles	

4

Gains from Innovation in CT

The econometric results of the previous chapter constitute the building blocks for the main task of the project: namely, the computation of social gains from innovation in CT, and the analysis of related phenomena with the aid of these figures. A great deal of the effort here is devoted to tackling a series of challenging issues encountered along the way; for example, how to deal with positive price coefficients, which welfare criteria to use given that preferences changed over time, how to interpret the measures in light of the distortions prevalent in the medical sector, and so on. Needless to say, not all the issues have been fully resolved; however, the very attempt to tackle them may prove to be illuminating, or at least thought provoking.

A key stage in the computations is the modeling of the interaction between innovation and diffusion, in order to obtain estimates of the total gains. The numerical results are then used in three applications: the computation of a social rate of return to R&D; a detailed analysis of the time profiles of benefits and costs; and assessing the performance of a real price index devised on the basis of the hedonic technique.

4.1 Preliminary Issues in Computing the Gains

The MNL estimates provide us with the parameters of the utility functions needed to compute the social gains from innovation in CT scanners. Those gains were defined as $\Delta W_t = W(S_t) - W(S_{t-1})$, where S_t is the choice set at time t, and the social surplus function is specified as

$$(4.1) \quad W(S_t) = \ell n \left[\sum_i \exp V_{it} \right] / \alpha.$$

To obtain the gains one needs to compute the functions V_{it} using the estimated MNL coefficients and the observed characteristics and prices of scanners in adjacent years, aggregate them as in (4.1), and take differences. But first, two important issues ought to be considered: one, the price coefficients for body scanners were found to be positive (except for 1981); and two, the estimated coefficients change significantly from year to year, hence the gains ΔW_t are not uniquely defined.

4.1.1 *Upward-Sloping Demand Curves and Welfare Analysis*

As we recall, the price coefficient in the MNL, α, is supposed to estimate the marginal utility of income (MUI), and if correctly measured, it plays the role of conversion factor between utility and money. However, a positive α cannot be regarded as an estimate of MUI,[1] and more generally, one can no longer obtain a measure of consumer surplus by integrating under the observed, upward-sloping demand curve. Likewise, it is no longer clear whether the term $\alpha \bar{p}_i$ should be included as such in the utility function V_i when computing (4.1): that will depend upon the kind of phenomena that give rise to those positive price coefficients.

In the context of a simple model with perfect information, upward-sloping demand curves are readily obtained by having demand depend not only on price but on quality as well, provided that quality and price are positively associated. For an illustration (see, for example, Spence, 1973), take demand to be $x = x(p,q)$, where the quality level q depends in turn on price and quantity, that is, $q = Q(p,x)$. In equilibrium, $x = x[p, Q(p,x)]$, which defines the actual—or observed—demand function, as opposed to the virtual demand function $x(p,q)$ defined for a given q. Totally differentiating $x(\cdot)$, and assuming $Q_x = 0$ (lowered letters indicate partial derivatives), $dx/dp = x_p + x_q Q_p$.

Now, if quality is positively associated with price (in other words, if $Q_p > 0$ and hence $Q(p)$ stands for a sort of inverse hedonic price function), then the slope of the observed demand function will be steeper than that of the virtual demand function, and if $x_q Q_p > -x_p$, it will be positive. In econometric terms, this amounts to having left out quality from the demand equation, thus inducing an upward bias in the price coefficient that may easily overwhelm the pure price effect.

---

1. The corresponding term in the utility function (V_i) is $-\alpha p_i$, so that a positive α means a *negative* marginal utility of income.

At first glance this stylized argument is of no relevance for the case at hand, since quality was presumably included in the estimated model, in the form of the vector z. As mentioned earlier, however, the z's do not exhaust the relevant quality space; moreover, some of the included attributes can be taken only as proxies to the true performance dimensions (for example, spatial resolution vis-à-vis image quality). Thus it may well be that the utility function in the MNL has been misspecified, in that some unobserved quality dimensions (to be denoted z^u) have been omitted from it, and from the hedonic price function as well. If so, the residuals from the hedonic regressions will in fact incorporate those z^u's, and consequently the estimated price coefficient might also pick up the effect of the left-out variables on the choice probabilities. The finding of a positive price coefficient is certainly consistent with such a scenario.

In a more formal statement of the argument, assume that the indirect utility function is additive-separable in the observed and in the unobserved characteristics, $V_i = \phi_1(z_i) + \phi_2(z_i^u) - \alpha p_i$, and that the branch corresponding to the vector of unobserved attributes is a linear function of the residuals from the hedonic regression,[2] that is, $\phi_2(z_i^u) = \beta\, \tilde{p}_i$. Rearranging the terms,

$$(4.2) \qquad V_i = [\phi(z_i) - \alpha p(z_i)] + (\beta - \alpha)\tilde{p}_i.$$

If we recall that the bracketed term in (4.2)—defined as net utility— was approximated by a simple quadratic form on z, and we denote $\delta = (\beta - \alpha)$,

$$(4.3) \qquad V_i = \sum_j (a_j z_{ij} + b_j z_{ij}^2) + \delta \tilde{p}_i,$$

which is the utility function as specified in the estimated model, except that now the price coefficient δ no longer stands for the marginal utility of income, α, because it incorporates also the marginal utility of the unobserved attributes, β (note that now the sign of the estimated δ is not an issue, since $\delta \gtreqless 0 <=> \beta \gtreqless \alpha$). The key implication of (4.2)-(4.3) for the purposes here is that the term $\delta \tilde{p}$ should indeed be included in V_i in

2. The assumption that $\phi_2(\cdot)$ can be expressed as a function of p is simply a reflection of the fact that, as said before, the z^u's have been omitted from the hedonic regression, and hence the residuals there capture those unobserved attributes as well. The further assumption of linearity is much stronger—see next footnote.

order to compute the welfare gains,[3] since that amounts to adding the utility of the unobserved attributes (via $\beta\bar{p}$) and to netting out the residual cost $\alpha\bar{p}$.

This settles the first hurdle, but one still needs to know the true marginal utility of income, α, in order to monetize utility, that is, in order to use α as the denominator in (4.1). Clearly, using the estimated price coefficient δ instead would be like integrating under the upward-sloping demand curve, thus resulting in an altogether meaningless magnitude. Fortunately, the striking differences in the evolution over time of head and body scanners will allow us to decompose δ, and associate α with the price coefficient of head scanners.

Consider the following straightforward proposition: the relative importance of unobserved versus observed quality dimensions will be greater the more technologically complex a product is, the less experience users have with it, and the faster is the pace of technological advance. Conversely, as the basic configuration and range of applications of a product stabilize and as experience with it accumulates, the weight of the unobserved attributes in the utility function will diminish greatly, and probably vanish altogether.

It is clear how this proposition applies to the two types of scanners: head scanners were introduced first, their applications remained unchanged (brain studies) and, after an initial stage of improvements, the dominant trend was toward less expensive, simpler systems. In contrast, the trend in body scanners was all along toward increased sophistication, with quantum technological jumps in the first couple of years, and a slowdown in the pace of change afterward. Thus we would expect, first, that $\phi_2(z^u)$ vanished early on for head scanners so that their estimated price coefficients would be negative and fairly stable after the first few years; and second, that the price coefficients of body scanners would be systematically higher than those of head scanners, but would tend to converge toward the latter as the pace of innovation subsided. And indeed, a look at the estimated price coefficients of the two types of

3. This is exact, however, only under the assumption that $\phi_2(\cdot)$ is linear in p. If the function is not linear, then the estimated δ will still incorporate the impact of the omitted attributes on utility, but not necessarily in a linear fashion with α (as in eq. 4.2, that is, as $\beta - \alpha$). The maintained hypothesis here is that, even if $\phi_2(\cdot)$ is not linear, the difference $(\delta - \alpha)$ is still a good approximation to the marginal utility of z^u, and hence that one is justified in including the term $\delta\bar{p}_i$ *in* V_i when computing the welfare gains as in (4.1).

scanners lends support to those conjectures (these figures are taken from tables 3.4 and 3.5).

	1975	1976	1977	1978	1979	1980	1981
Head scanners	7.31	−0.75	−0.71	−0.89	−0.82	n.a.	n.a.
Body scanners	10.18	11.25	1.00	1.02	0.48	0.69	−0.28

We can thus take the price coefficients of head scanners for 1976–1979 as estimates for the marginal utility of income, α, and hence as the appropriate parameters to be used in computing $W(S_t)$.[4] Likewise, the difference between the price coefficients of body and head scanners provides some idea of the magnitude of the residual uncertainty that buyers of body scanners faced with respect to quality.

Although the foregoing discussion refers to a particular market, there is room to believe that the phenomenon addressed here is fairly widespread, and that the approach used could be widely applied in dealing with quality uncertainty in segmented markets.

4.1.2   The Vector z^u: Whose Ignorance?

I have implicitly assumed above that the vectors z_i^u are known to the agents in the market but not to outside observers such as myself, and therefore that the problem is purely econometric. That is, however, a rather implausible assumption in the case of CT scanners: as suggested in Chapter 2, their performance cannot be fully ascertained prior to purchase (as is generally the case with "experience goods"), and hence the z^u's are, at least in part, unknown also to prospective buyers of CT scanners. For example, radiologists "shopping" for scanners form their expectations regarding image quality on the basis of data provided by the manufacturers (such as spatial resolution), the visual inspection of sample scans, and so on. Clearly, that sort of information is partial and imperfect, and uncertainty remains as to the imaging performance of the systems under different operational conditions, as well as over time. Similarly, as ever faster scanners were being introduced, users could not exactly anticipate the extent of expansion in the range of applications,

4. Since the price coefficient for head scanners could be estimated only for 1976–1979, and in view of the fact that they are fairly stable, the 1976 coefficient will be used as an estimate of α for earlier years, and that for 1979 as the estimate for subsequent years.

or know whether image quality could be maintained at high scanning speeds. Yet as will be argued below, the conclusions of the previous section need not be altered in view of the fact that z^u might be unknown also to users; however, it is important to consider carefully the implications of this observation and to establish the precise conditions under which the stated conclusions would carry through.

The problem is that once the prospective buyers of CT scanners themselves are uncertain of the vector z^u, one can no longer take for granted that residual prices will be highly correlated with the unobserved attributes, and hence that $(\beta - \alpha)\hat{p}$ belongs in V_i in the computation of $W(\cdot)$. To wit, suppose that some firms introduce low-quality scanners in the market, but price them relatively high, taking advantage of users' imperfect knowledge. Eventually the bluff will be called, and those firms will probably be forced to exit the market; until then, however, this fly-by-night behavior garbles the informative content of $\hat{p}$, thus depriving its estimated coefficient of any clear meaning. Conversely, if prices were to serve instead as signals of quality in the context of a "separating equilibrium,"[5] then residual prices would preserve their role in the analysis, exactly as if z^u were known to buyers.

The existence of separating equilibria, with prices signaling quality (in some cases along with conspicuous expenditures such as advertising), has been proved in a variety of theoretical settings (see, for instance, Wolinsky, 1983; Shapiro, 1983; Milgrom and Roberts, 1986). Unfortunately, the empirical implications of that type of analysis are far from clear. More specifically, one can not draw from them a well-defined set of sufficient conditions for the separating equilibria to hold that could be posed as testable hypothesis. Short of that, one can still search for clues indicative of the likelihood of such equilibria in actual cases.

As hinted in Chapter 2, some of the features of the market for CT scanners make it highly unlikely that firms would have followed a fly-by-night strategy, thus preventing a separating equilibrium from emerging. The key to this surmise lies in the following: first, virtually all firms that ever marketed CT scanners were diversified to some extent, many

5. The basic idea underlying this type of equilibria is that the signal succeeds in sorting out (in separating) individuals or products in the market, so that those with higher qualities will indeed cost more, even though their actual qualities are not observed. Thus, for example, workers with higher education are paid higher salaries in a separating equilibrium not because the extra schooling makes them more productive, but because years of schooling truthfully signal higher (inherent) productivity.

offering in fact a whole line of imaging devices. Second, at least some of their other products were aimed at the same users (radiologists and physicians) or at the same decision-makers (hospitals' purchasing departments). Third, reputation plays a crucial role in most markets for healthcare products, in the sense of quality maintenance, credibility as to equipment performance, long-term support, and the like. Fourth, information on the experience of individuals with medical equipment flows rapidly and widely within the medical community. Thus abusing the firm's reputation in one market at one time is very likely to affect badly the performance of the firm in other markets and over a long period of time. In plain words, a hospital that finds a CT scanner to be inferior to its expected quality, having formed its expectations—inter alia—on the basis of price, is not likely to purchase x-ray machines, or intensive care units, or perhaps even pharmaceuticals from the same manufacturer. In sum, the market for CT scanners seems to provide firms with strong incentives to support a separating equilibrium, and therefore residual prices can still be assumed to be highly correlated with z^u, even if users are as ignorant of z^u as outside observers. Consequently, what we had concluded regarding the inclusion of the term $\delta\bar{p}$ in the utility function for the computation of welfare gains does hold in these circumstances as well.

4.1.3   Alternative Measures of Welfare Gains

Because the coefficients estimated in the MNL change substantially from year to year, the welfare measures are not uniquely defined but depend upon the choice of a reference year. There are two alternative ways of assessing the value of a change in the choice set from S_t to S_{t+1}:

(i) ex-ante: $\Delta W^a = W_t(S_{t+1}) - W_t(S_t)$

(ii) ex-post: $\Delta W^p = W_{t+1}(S_{t+1}) - W_{t+1}(S_t)$,

where W_t stands for the surplus function as estimated in year t. That is, the ex-ante or forward-looking measure answers the following question: how much would the consumer be willing to pay for the option of facing next year's choice set rather than the present one, given her preferences today? On the other hand, the question posed by the ex-post criterion is: how much income could be taken away from the consumer so as to leave her indifferent between facing today's and yesterday's choice sets, in light of her present tastes? It is important to emphasize that the ex-ante/ex-post distinction posed here is very different from the traditional distinction between compensating and equivalent variations, or the Laspeyres-Paasche dichotomy: in the latter tastes are held fixed, and the dilemma resides in choosing the reference utility level or consumption bundle, whereas here it is the taste parameters themselves that change.[6]

A word ought to be said about Divisia-like measures, that is, estimating each pair of adjacent years (or more) jointly, and using the resulting "average preferences" to evaluate changes from one period to the next. This is a legitimate and doable procedure, and it has the extra advantage of circumventing the problem altogether, since it results in a unique measure. On the one hand, this very advantage is its weakness, for if tastes are indeed substantially different from year to year, it is hard to see how suppressing those differences (by imposing a common set of coefficients) can render a better measure. On the other hand, if preferences do not vary much, then the ex-ante and ex-post measures would be very similar, and the problem would not be there to begin with.

In general, the ex-ante and ex-post measures will provide different quantitative answers, and a priori it is not clear whether they would differ in a systematic way, or which should be deemed to be more relevant. In the present case, though, the changes in preferences have followed a well-defined pattern, ensuring that the ex-ante measure would be systematically higher than the ex-post. As we recall, the main findings in the last section of Chapter 3 were that the relative valuation of attributes was highly correlated with the relative improvements in those attributes a year later, and that there was a marked cyclicality in both series. Consequently, the value of a change in the choice set will necessarily be larger if judged according to the ex-ante measure, since characteristics that are highly valued in one period will experience a relatively large increase in the next, but that in turn will weaken the preferences for those enhanced attributes then.

The difficult question is how to go about deciding which of the two measures to use in computing the welfare gains. Unfortunately, the the-

---

6. To put it differently, the only source of ambiguity in traditional welfare analysis lies in the existence of income effects: if those were absent, then any two situations would be uniquely comparable. In the present case, however, the hypothetical measure $\Delta W = W_{t+1}(S_{t+1}) - W_t(S_t)$ is meaningless regardless of income effects, for it is tantamount to making interpersonal utility comparisons.

oretical literature on changing tastes cannot provide much guidance, because most of it has to do with proving the existence of time-consistent consumption plans (for example, Peleg and Yaari, 1973; Goldman, 1980), and not with the choice of an evaluation criterion in view of changes in preferences. A related strand of work focuses on endogenous taste changes (von Wëizsacker, 1971) and is somewhat more pertinent to the issue at hand; but again, the problem that arises there from the divergence of short-term and long-term preferences (mirroring the ex-ante/ex-post dilemma here) is inherently inconclusive.

Fisher and Shell (1972) are, to the best of my knowledge, the only ones to grapple with the dilemma explicitly. They do it in the context of tackling the construction of "true" price-of-living indexes when both tastes and qualities change over time.[7] When the choice is of judging a given change (say, in prices) with today's or yesterday's preferences, they contend that the ex-post measure is somewhat more appropriate. Casting their argument in terms of the notions used here, it goes as follows: assume that the choice set at present is S, and that it may undergo alternative innovations A or B, so that in next period the set will be either S^A or S^B. Now, suppose that tastes change in such a way that $\Delta W^a(A) < 0 < \Delta W^p(A)$, but $\Delta W^a(B) > 0 > \Delta W^p(B)$; in words, tastes change so that alternative A looks ex-ante absolutely worse than the present situation and alternative B absolutely better, but the opposite is true if the alternatives are judged ex-post. It is easy to show that in such a case $W_{t+1}(S^A) > W_{t+1}(S^B)$, but $W_t(S^A) < W_t(S^B)$. That is, under today's preferences B looks more attractive than A, but once one gets to the next period A turns out to be preferable to B, and therefore the ex-ante criterion would have led, in that sense, to an inconsistent choice.[8] Fisher and Shell favor the ex-post criterion to avoid that type of potential inconsistency.

In the present case, however, the ex-ante measure is systematically higher than the ex-post, so that both criteria would lead to the same

---

7. Note that the questions addressed by the ex-ante and ex-post measures as specified here are in line with Fisher and Shell's formulations, and do not suffer from the pitfalls they warn against so earnestly. For example, the ex-post measure is, in their words, "a question posed entirely in terms of today's tastes and involves a comparison of present and past constraints, not a comparison of present and past utilities." (Fisher and Shell, 1971, p. 20).

8. However, if both $\Delta W^a(A)$ and $\Delta W^p(B)$ are positive, then $W_{t+1}(S^A) > W_{t+1}(S^B)$ does not necessarily entail $W_t(S^A) < W_t(S^B)$. Moreover, in such a case it can be shown that if $W_t(S^A) > W_t(S^B)$, then $W_{t+1}(S^A) > W_{t+1}(S^B)$. Thus the potential inconsistency upon which Fisher and Shell base their argument applies to rather uncommon cases.

ranking of alternatives, avoiding the sort of inconsistencies just described. Moreover, the same inducement mechanism that lies behind the inequality $\Delta W^a(\cdot) > \Delta W^p(\cdot)$ suggests that the ex-ante measure is more appropriate from a normative viewpoint, since it can be argued that changes should be judged according to the preferences that give rise to them, rather than by hindsight. Consequently, both measures will be computed in the first round, but the ex-ante measure will be the one used in subsequent applications. Note, however, that the rough proportionality between the two measures ensures that the qualitative results will hold equally well for both.

4.2   Incremental Gains from Innovation

4.2.1   *Computing the Gains*

The first step toward the estimation of the welfare gains involves computing numerically the utility function V_{it} for every scanner i in every period t according to (4.3), that is,[9]

$$V_{it} = \sum_j (a_{jt}z_{ijt} + b_{jt}z_{ijt}^2) + \delta_t \hat{p}_{it},$$

and then the function $W(S_t) = \ell n \, [\, \Sigma_i \exp V_{it}]/\alpha$. Note that the residual prices in V_{it} have to be obtained from the hedonic price function of the reference year, since $p(z)$ (the nonstochastic component of the hedonic regression) has to be added back to the quadratic approximation in order to retrieve the original utility function. That is, in computing the ex-ante gains $\Delta W^a = W_t(S_{t+1}) - W_t(S_t)$, the hedonic price function of year t is used to generate the $\hat{p}$'s of both years (t and $t+1$), and likewise, when computing the ex-post gains ΔW^p the residuals are obtained from the hedonic price regression estimated for year $t+1$. Notice also that since I rejected the hypothesis that head and body scanners belong to a common preference tree (from 1976 on), the ΔW's were computed separately for each type of scanners in the period 1976–1982. As for the initial years 1973–1975, the gains correspond to the joint set of head and body scanners because the parameters used are those of 1975, the

---

9. Notice that not only the attributes and residual prices are indexed by t, but also the coefficients a, b, and δ, since I estimated the MNL separately for every year, and those estimates changed from year to year.

Table 4.1 Welfare Gains from Innovation in Body CT Scanners

Year	$\Delta \bar{W}_B =$ $\ell n(\Sigma_i \exp V_i)$ ex-ante	ex-post	$\hat{\alpha}^a$	$\Delta W_B =$ $\Delta \bar{W}_B/\hat{\alpha} \times 100$ ex-ante	ex-post	Price index	ΔW_B in 1982 \$ (thousands) ex-ante	ex-post
1976	14.72[b]	2.93	0.75[c]	1,967.2	391.7	.62	3,173.0	631.8
1977	5.42	0.76	0.75	724.1	107.8	.66	1,097.1	163.3
1978	0.11	−0.42	0.71	15.5	−46.9	.71	21.8	−65.9
1979	1.41	0.35	0.89	158.2	42.7	.77	204.4	55.1
1980	0.68	0.38	0.82	83.3	46.1	.86	97.0	53.7
1981	1.55	−0.07	0.82[d]	189.6	−8.9	.94	200.6	−9.4
1982	1.71	—	0.82[d]	208.9	—	1.00	208.9	—

[a] The coefficient of price as estimated in the MNL for head scanners (absolute value).
[b] Imputed value.
[c] Assumed equal to the 1977 coefficient.
[d] Assumed equal to the 1980 coefficient.

year for which the model was estimated jointly for both types of scanners.[10] For completeness, the 1975–76 ex-ante joint gains are imputed to each type of scanners according to their respective ex-post shares, calculated as follows,

$$s_H = \Delta W_H^p/(\Delta W_H^p + \Delta W_B^p), \qquad s_B = 1 - s_H.$$

Table 4.1 presents the results for body scanners, the calculations being carried out in three stages: first, the following gross differences are computed (see columns 1 and 2):

$$\Delta \bar{W} = \ell n(\sum_i \exp V_{t+1,i}) - \ell n(\sum_i \exp V_{t,i}).$$

Second, I divide $\Delta \bar{W}$ by the "true" price coefficient $\hat{\alpha}$ (the one obtained in the estimation of the MNL for head scanners), as listed in the third

10. In other words, the function $W(\cdot)$ as estimated for 1975 is used to compute the 1973–74 and the 1974–75 ex-post gains, and the 1975–76 ex-ante gains. Note, however, that the 1973 and 1974 sets include only head scanners, one in each year.

Table 4.2   Welfare Gains by Scanner Type and Overall Gains
            (in millions, constant 1982 $)

| | Head scanners | | | Body scanners | | | Overall incremental gains[a] | |
Year	ΔW_H^a	ΔW_H^p	$\pi(H)$	ΔW_B^a	ΔW_B^p	$\pi(B)$	ex-ante	ex-post
1974	—	1.204	1.00	—	1.204	0	8.713[b]	1.204
1975	—	.208	.55	—	.208	.45	1.509[b]	.208
1976	4.776	.319	.24	4.776	.632	.76	4.776	.557
1977	.056	.017	.15	1.097	.163	.85	.940	.141
1978	.361	.225	.28	.022	−.066	.72	.115	.014
1979	−.013	−.047	.30	.204	.055	.70	.140	.025
1980	−.019	—	.20	.097	.054	.80	.074	.010[b]
1981	.007	—	.08	.201	−.009	.92	.184	.026[b]
1982	−.003	—	.06	.209	—	.94	.195	.027[b]

Note: ΔW_h^a: ex-ante gains; ΔW_h^p: ex-post gains.
[a]Overall incremental gains: $\Delta W = \Delta W_H \pi(H) + \Delta W_B \pi(B)$.
[b]Computed using the mean ratio $\Delta W^a / \Delta W^p$ for 1976–1979.

column.[11] Finally, ΔW is deflated by the producer price index for capital equipment (the one most closely related to CT scanners), to obtain the real gains shown in the last two columns. The gains for head scanners for 1976–1982 and for the joint set of head and body scanners (1973–1976) were computed in a similar fashion. Table 4.2 brings all these together, leading to the overall gains $\Delta W = \pi(H) \Delta W_H + \pi(B) \Delta W_B$, where $\pi(h)$ is the percentage of buyers that purchased scanners of type h. Note that an overlapping series of ex-ante and ex-post pairs could be computed only for the four years 1976–1979. As expected, the ex-ante gains ΔW^a were found to be systematically higher than the ex-post gains ΔW^p, and they were so by a relatively constant factor: the mean ratio $\Delta W_t^a / \Delta W_t^p$ for those years was 7.24, with a standard deviation of 1.34. This proportionality factor is used for calculating the 1974 and 1975

11. Since the marginal utility of income, α, was estimated with prices defined in $ hundred thousands, I compute $\Delta W = (\Delta \bar{W}/\alpha) / 100$, so as to present the gains in $ thousands.

ex-ante gains (that is, $\Delta W_t^a = 7.24 \times \Delta W_t^p$, $t = 74,75$), and likewise for the 1980–1982 ex-post measures. As a matter of terminology, ΔW_t is referred to as incremental gains, to be distinguished both from the cumulative gains $CW_t \Sigma_{\tau-1}^t \Delta W_\tau$ (to be used in assessing the impact of innovation on diffusion), and from the total gains to be computed in section 4.3 below.

4.2.2 On the Poor Health of Welfare Measures in the Medical Sector

Although I have referred all along to $W(\cdot)$ as a surplus or welfare function, and to ΔW as welfare or social gains, these notions need to be reexamined and qualified in view of the peculiarities of the medical sector. First, notice that the buyers of CT scanners are not the final consumers, but health-care providers that purchase the systems as a capital input and sell their services to patients. Now, this by itself does not impair the validity of the welfare measures used here (or of any other measure of consumer surplus): it is easy to show that, if markets are perfectly competitive, then it is exactly equivalent to do welfare analysis with reference either to the demand for the final product (as is usually done), or to the derived demand for inputs, as done here.[12] Likewise, government regulations either in the upstream market (the market for CT scanners), or in the market for diagnostic services, can only affect the magnitude of the surpluses actually realized, but the proposed measures will still capture them well (see Bresnahan, 1986, for a detailed discussion of this issue).[13] Thus, for example, the regulatory measures described in Chapter 2 may have affected not only the number of CT scanners purchased, but their type and quality as well; for instance, hospitals fearing future controls may have chosen more advanced—and hence more expensive— scanners than optimal for them at the time. That would have caused a distortion in the observed choice mix (the π_i's), and therefore in the estimated $W(\cdot)$ functions. However, if the behavior of hospitals were other-

12. All this says is that in a perfectly competitive environment the firm is, from a welfare point of view, a redundant entity: all that counts is utility on the one hand, and costs on the other. Thus one could proceed as if hospitals did not exist, and consumers were the ones who purchased inputs (CT scanners) and produced the final product (the diagnostic services).

13. The measures will be adequate except if the marginal regulatory costs are somehow endogenous, in which case the welfare measures will tend to underestimate the true gains, as argued in Bresnahan (1986).

wise "optimal" (see below), the ΔW's would still measure the realized gains correctly, although these would certainly be smaller than the hypothetical optimum that would have obtained in an unconstrained setting.

The problem resides entirely with the behavior of hospitals, both in itself and in relation to the preferences of ill-informed patients. To pinpoint the source of the difficulties, it will be helpful to consider in a very schematic way two ideal types of hospital behavior: in one case the hospital acts as a profit maximizer and a price taker; in the second, the health-care provider maximizes instead a utility function having as an argument the quality of CT scanners, z, the underlying assumption being that the quality of medical services provided is indeed a positive function of the quality of the CT scanner owned. Presumably, the actual behavior of hospitals and clinics approximates one of those two types. To be able to focus exclusively on quality choice, the quantity of medical services, m, is assumed to be exogeneously determined. Since CT scanners are a capital input and what is of interest here is the flow of services, we have a cost function determining the operating costs of a scanner, assumed to be multiplicative, such that $C = C\,[z,\,p(z)]\,m$. Thus

$$\frac{dC}{dz} = m\left(\frac{\partial C}{\partial z} + \frac{\partial C}{\partial p}\frac{\partial p}{\partial z}\right) \equiv mC_z > 0,$$

since more advanced scanners are more expensive to operate ($\partial C/\partial z > 0$), and they cost more ($\partial p/\partial z > 0$). The term $\partial C/\partial p$ involves interest payments or leasing charges, depreciation, insurance premiums, and so on, hence it is also positive. Denoting by $q(z)$ the price of a CT procedure performed with a scanner of quality z, and assuming without loss of generality that $m = 1$, the behavior of the profit maximizing hospital can be described simply as

$$\max_z \Pi = q(z) - C[z,p(z)],$$

rendering the first order condition (FOC) $q_z = C_z$. In the case of a utility maximizer, $q(z)$ is replaced in the objective function of the hospital by the branch of its indirect utility function related to diagnostic medicine, $V^h(z)$ (the underlying utility function is assumed to be additive separable); the first order condition for a maximum is then $V^h_z = C_z$. Likewise, the behavior of the final consumer (the patient) is characterized by the following (the upscript c denotes consumer):

$$\max_{z} V^c = V^c(z) + y^c - q(z), \qquad \text{FOC: } V^c_z = q_z.$$

If the market were perfectly competitive, then the following equalities would obtain:

(4.4) $V^c_z = q_z = C_z = V^h_z.$

Noting that the first order conditions for hospitals ($Q_z = C_z$ and $V^h_z = C_z$) define the demand functions for CT scanners, it is clear that if (4.4) were to hold, the surplus functions $W(\cdot)$ would indeed fully capture the welfare of final consumers. Unfortunately, none of the equalities can be taken for granted; in particular, it is doubtful that $V^h_z = V^c_z$, that is, that the interests and perceptions of the medical profession pertinent to the choice of diagnostic technologies fully coincide with those of patients. If anything, the presumption is that physicians tend to display an upward bias in their valuation of those technologies because of extraneous motives such as rivalry among hospitals, long-range scientific goals that have little to do with the immediate well-being of patients, status and prestige, protection from malpractice suits, and so on. If this is so, the measures ΔW may somewhat overstate the true social gains, the difference being gains accruing at present to hospitals and physicians, which probably will not be entirely passed on, in the long run, to society at large.[14]

A more fundamental problem is that V^c_z is by no means a well-defined construct to begin with, simply because patients are, for the most part, not in a position to evaluate independently the quality and medical value of diagnostic procedures, not to speak of innovations in them. Thus we lack the baseline needed to assess the magnitude of the "principal-agent" problem that may occur in the choice of medical technologies. In other

---

14. Notice, however, that if the divergence between V^h_z and V^c_z resulted primarily from long-term scientific interests (as tends to be the case with the choice of systems by major medical schools), then it is not clear which criteria should be used: taking as a yardstick V^c_z (if it were possible) would be too short-sighted, since it ignores the long-run scientific externalities. So the issue boils down to the choice of an appropriate "social rate of discount" to be applied to a measure based on V^h_z, such as ΔW.

words, we cannot really gauge the extent to which doctors deviate from the choices that consumers would have made, if the latter had the same medical knowledge that their "agents" command. Clearly, though, the problem is not with the method of measurement or the underlying economic reasoning; rather, it is a reflection of a basic fact pertaining to the provision of medical services. All an economist can do, therefore, is to estimate those ΔW's on the assumption that the "extraneous" motives are not the main determinants of hospitals' choices of technologies, and that the bias—presumably upward—in the resulting measures is not too substantial.

4.3   Total Gains, and the Interdependency of Innovation and Diffusion

The ΔW's obtained in the previous section stand for the yearly incremental gains accruing to the representative buyer of CT scanners. I turn now to the computation of the yearly flow of total gains, which are meant to reflect not just the unit value of the innovations, but also the changing size of the market for the products embedding those innovations. The main task in computing the total gains consists in assessing the total number of users of CT who would benefit from the ΔW's, at present as well as into the future. In a static context, and if one were considering the impact of a single innovation, the total gains would simply be $n \cdot \Delta W$, n being the number of buyers of the product embodying the innovation. However, what is being assessed here is a *sequence* of innovations; the ΔW's stand for the per-period *incremental* gains; and the demand for CT scanners is *time-dependent*. These three distinctive features of the problem at hand make the computation of total gains much more complex, and require the careful handling of the dynamic interaction between innovation and diffusion.

4.3.1   The Conceptual Framework

As a first step, consider the problem of delimiting, in time and in technology space, the benefits from innovation accruing to a consumer buying for example a personal computer today. Are such benefits to be identified with the cumulative gains stemming from the long sequence of innovations in computers from the ENIAC on? Or perhaps just from the first Apple onward? Or should we take into account only the latest incremental gains, gauged by contrasting the 1990 versus the 1989 sets of personal computers in the market? Looking at it from a different angle, the same conundrum can be posed in another way: are we to compute the total gains from the innovations embedded in the 1990 set of personal computers simply by multiplying the incremental gains, ΔW_{90} by the number of buyers of PC's in 1990? Or rather, by the projected number of buyers from 1990 onward? And what about buyers of replacement units versus first-time buyers?

In this formulation the problem seems to be the choice of an appropriate baseline—a reference point along the historical path of the technology in question—from which to carry out the computation of benefits. This would indeed be the dominant issue if the question were posed in terms of the cumulative benefits accruing to consumers at a point in time, as they face a set of products that are the end result of a long process of technical advance. In the present case, though, the problem does not arise in this form: first, the benefits are computed year by year, and the natural baseline is, in each case, merely the choice set of the previous year; second, the overall starting point is well defined and not open to controversy, namely, the beginning of Computed Tomography in 1973.[15]

Our problem resides instead in the dynamic aspects of demand and the corresponding treatment of future benefits. To what extent can future buyers of CT be deemed to benefit from the present incremental gains, given that the technology is advancing continuously, and their decision to buy is influenced by those advances? Clearly, the proper way to address the question would be to formulate a dynamic discrete choice model, relying for example on Rust (1987). Such a model would comprise the decision of whether or not to buy in each period, as well as the conditional choice of what product to buy. The upper-level choice primarily concerns the adoption decision (although as time goes by replacements and additions to capacity become the dominant considerations), and would be a function of the evolution of the technology over time, of changes in the relevant aspects of the environment (such as regulatory policies), and of expectations regarding the previous two. If such a mod-

15. The latter issue may eventually pose a problem when assessing other innovations, even if using the same methodology as here (the ΔW's), since in many cases the starting point of a technology is not a discrete event, and therefore the question of how far back to go in the computations will need to be carefully considered.

el were available, then the total gains sought here would be obtained simply by integrating the ensuing intertemporal demand function, over individuals and over time. Unfortunately, the formulation and estimation of such a model posed serious conceptual and technical problems, making it not viable at the time. Short of that, I present here what amounts essentially to a reduced form of the full-fledged dynamic model, that is, a simple diffusion model incorporating the gains from innovation as a determinant of the ceiling.[16]

It will help to grasp the nature of the model if we consider the following polar versions of the diffusion process: in the first, diffusion is due entirely to the workings of the traditional demonstration effect, such as learning, emulation, rivalry, and so on. In other words, the process has to do only with dynamic phenomena occurring within the population of potential adopters, and is not affected by external forces. In this version, the model predicts that if technological change had ceased after the introduction of the first CT scanner, the pattern of diffusion would have been exactly the same as it was in actuality. According to the opposite version, the diffusion path is nothing but a temporal demand curve having only extensive margins, that is, it traces the distribution of some sort of reservation price in the population of potential adopters. Successive innovations that result in what can be thought of as reductions in real (that is, quality-adjusted) prices thus trigger immediate adoption by "inframarginal" consumers.[17] Consequently, if the process of technological advance were to come to a halt, diffusion would stop as well, all future purchases would be for replacement or capacity additions only, and the innovations that took place up to that point would cease to generate further benefits.

The implications of these alternative scenarios for the computation of total gains are immediate. If diffusion corresponds to the second case, the "distribution of reservation prices," then the total gains generated by innovations occurring at time t would simply be

$$(4.5) \quad TW_t = \Delta W_t n_t,$$

16. The ceiling (to be denoted by K) is defined as the maximum number of individuals that will end up adopting the innovation in the long run, expressed as a percentage of the population of potential adopters.

17. "Inframarginal" applies to consumers whose reservation prices are just below the prevalent real market prices (and who thus have not yet adopted the new product), so that a small reduction in the latter would bring them to adopt.

n_t being the number of buyers in period t, and TW_t standing for total gains. On the other hand, if diffusion is due entirely to demonstration effects, then

$$(4.6) \quad TW_t = \Delta W_t N \int_t^\infty f(\tau)e^{-r(\tau - t)}d\tau,$$

where r is an appropriate discount rate, N is the size of the population of potential adopters, and $f(\cdot)$ the marginal distribution of adoption times, corresponding to the cumulative distribution $F(\cdot)$. To make it clearer, let me ignore discounting for a moment and rewrite (4.6) as

$$TW_t = \Delta W_t N[1 - F(t)] = \Delta W_t\{n_t + N[1 - F(t + 1)]\}.$$

Or, if the number of future adopters is defined as $n_t^f \equiv N\,[1 - F(t+1)]$,

$$(4.7) \quad TW_t = \Delta W_t(n_t + n_t^f).$$

When (4.7) is compared to (4.5), it is easy to see that the total gains would be larger in the "demonstration effects" model, since they include also the benefits of current innovations to future buyers (with discounting, n_t^f will be somewhat smaller).

4.3.2 Diffusion and the Computation of Total Gains

Actual diffusion processes may correspond to either of the models outlined above or, most likely, to a combination of both, and it is of course an empirical matter to uncover the appropriate characterization. My next step is thus to estimate the aggregate diffusion process as a function of time and of the cumulative gains from innovation, $CW_t = \Sigma_{\tau=1}^t \Delta W_\tau$. As in traditional diffusion models, time is meant to capture the forces associated with demonstration effects, whereas CW_t can be thought of as tracing the cumulative changes in a quality-adjusted index, thus bringing in the scenario associated with the distribution of reservation prices. In particular, it is assumed that the diffusion path corresponds to a logistic distribution,[18] and that innovation impacts the process by shifting the ceiling K (see note 16), so that $K = K(CW_t)$. As to the functional form of $K(\cdot)$, both a linear and a concave specification were considered, corresponding to an underlying uniform and exponential distribution of "reservation prices" respectively. Since the two yielded very similar results, only those obtained with the linear form, $K(CW_t) = K_0 + kCW_t$, are shown here. The estimated equation is thus[19]

$$(4.8) \quad F(t) = (K_0 + kCW_t)/[1 + \exp(\alpha - \beta t)].$$

The data consist of the monthly number of adopters of CT scanners in the United States, with t defined in months and covering the period from November 1972 to July 1981. The dependent variable is $F(t) = n_t/N$, where n_t is the number of first-time buyers in month t, and $N = 3{,}457$ is the total population of potential adopters;[20] the figures for CW_t were computed from table 4.2. As a benchmark I estimate also a logistic equation without the term $k \cdot CW_t$, but with a free ceiling. The results are as follows (the numbers in parenthesis are asymptotic standard errors):[21]

	$\hat{K}_0$	$\hat{k}$	$\hat{\alpha}$	$\hat{\beta}$	residual sum of squares
(i)	0.459		4.053	0.071	0.013
	(.004)		(.076)	(.002)	
(ii)	0.074	0.025	3.443	0.06	0.006
	(.003)	(.002)	(.07)	(.001)	

18. The assumption of a logistic distribution is by no means an innocent one, particularly when the goal is to estimate correctly the speed of diffusion (see Trajtenberg and Yitzhaki, 1989). For our purposes, however, the particular functional form of the estimated distribution is not of much consequence.

19. Note that eq. (4.8) cannot be linearized by taking the log of the odds ratio (as is usually done in diffusion studies), but has to be estimated with nonlinear methods instead.

20. This includes 3,078 community hospitals with more than 100 beds, plus 379 private clinics that purchased CT scanners by July 1981. For more details see Trajtenberg and Yitzhaki (1989).

21. I also experimented with ΔW_t affecting the rate of diffusion, β, that is, $F(t) = K(CW_t) / [1 + \exp(\alpha - \beta t - \beta' t \Delta W_t)]$. The coefficient β' turned out to be statistically significant, but of a very small magnitude; because its effect on subsequent computations would have been nil, I chose to ignore this extra term.

First, note that diffusion was strongly influenced both by demonstration effects (embedded in *t*) and by technological advance (as revealed by the high significance of the estimates of β and *k*). Moreover, the fit improves greatly when going from (i) to (ii), implying that the traditional diffusion model (one that ignores innovation) would have been widely off the mark. To put it in quantitative terms, $k = 0.025$ means that for every million $ worth of improvements in CT, the number of adopters increased by 2.5 percent. Thus if innovation had ceased just after the introduction of the first CT scanner, only 7.4 percent of the total population would have adopted throughout the period (since $K_0 = 0.074$). In reality, the ceiling had climbed to 49 percent by 1982, as a result of the flow of innovations from 1974 on (that is, $CW_{82} = 16.6$, and hence $K_{82} = 0.074 + 0.025 \times 16.6 = 0.49$).

The estimated equation can also be used to obtain, albeit in an indirect way, a measure of the initial gains from innovation—those associated with the introduction of the first CT scanner (recall the limitations of ΔW discussed in Chapter 1). The question can be formulated as follows: what would those first gains (ΔW_{73}) have to be to give rise to the initial ceiling K_0, given the estimated function $K(CW_t) = K_0 + kCW_t$? The answer is simply $\Delta W_{73} = K_0/k = 0.074/0.025 = 2.99$, that is, to put it carefully, (ii) above is equivalent to an equation in which K_0 is deleted, and ΔW_{73} is set equal to 2.99 rather than to zero. In other words, if the behavior underlying equation (ii) is stable, then the introduction of the first CT scanner had to be worth about $3 million, so as to induce 7.4 percent of hospitals and clinics to adopt it. Even though ΔW_{73} will be used below along with the other ΔW's, it should be borne in mind that this figure has been computed in a very different, and probably less reliable fashion.

The yearly total gains can now be computed as follows (note that n_t includes also second scanners and replacements):[22]

$$(4.9) \qquad TW_t = \Delta W_t[n_t + N(K_0 + kCW_t)\int_{t+1}^{\infty} f(\tau)e^{-r(\tau - t - 1)}d\tau],$$

---

22. The assignment of benefits to purchases for replacement and additions to capacity can be properly dealt with, once again, only in the context of a full-fledged dynamic model, incorporating explicitly a capital accumulation process. Short of that, and to avoid the risk of overstating the total gains, I proceed on the assumption that the benefits accruing to repeat purchases at time *t* are only the incremental gains ΔW_t (see the next section for further discussion of this issue).

Gains from Innovation in CT

where the values of the parameters K_0, k, and $f(\cdot)$ are taken from the diffusion equation estimated above, and the yearly discount rate is assumed to be .05 (since $f(\tau)$ is defined in months, the rate actually used is .0041). The integral in (4.9) does not have a closed-form solution (because of discounting), so it had to be solved numerically. The computations are presented in table 4.3, which is largely self-explanatory. Notice that the total gains are computed on the basis of the ex-ante measures only: given that those were found to be systematically higher than the ex-post, the two sorts would be roughly proportional to each other and hence there is no point in computing the total gains for both (the qualitative results are invariant with respect to the type of measure used).

4.3.3 Possible Biases in the Measures of Total Gains

There are at least three potential sources of bias in the computation of total gains as carried out above. First, purchases of additional scanners,

Table 4.3   Computation of Total Ex-Ante Gains (in millions, constant 1982 $)

Year	ΔW_t	$K(CW_t)$	$1-F(t)$	$1-F(t)$ discounted	n_t^f	$\tilde{n}_t^f$	n_t	$n_t + \tilde{n}_t^f$	TW_t
1973	2.990	.074	.938	.772	240	197	16	213	638
1974	8.713	.290	.878	.751	879	752	43	795	6,926
1975	1.509	.327	.777	.685	879	775	221	996	1,503
1976	4.776	.445	.628	.568	967	874	374	1,428	5,959
1977	.940	.469	.451	.414	731	671	390	1,061	997
1978	.115	.471	.285	.265	465	431	250	681	79
1979	.140	.475	.162	.151	267	249	275	524	73
1980	.074	.477	.086	.081	142	133	271	404	30
1981	.184	.481	.024	.023	41	38	392	430	79
1982	.195	.486	.012	.011	20	19	428	447	87

Note: ΔW_t = incremental gains; $K(CW_t) = K_0 + kCW_t = 0.074 + 0.025CW_t$; $1 - F(t) = \Sigma_{t+1}^\infty f(\tau)d\tau$; $1\text{-}F(t)$ discounted $= \Sigma_{t+1}^\infty f(\tau) \exp - r(\tau - t - 1)d\tau$; $n_t^f = K(CW_t) \times [1 - F(t)] \times N$, $N = 3,457$; $\tilde{n}_t^f = K(CW_t) \times [1 - F(t)]$ discounted $\times N$; n_t = number of scanners sold in year t; $n_t + \tilde{n}_t^f$ = number of current and future discounted beneficiaries from the incremental gains at t; and TW_t = total gains.

both for replacement and as additions to capacity, are assumed to confer only the incremental gains at the time of purchase, that being quite probably an understatement. Moreover, the assumption implies that second-time buyers from 1983 on would not benefit at all from the stream of innovations up to 1982: the gains are assumed to accrue only to future new adopters. Considering that the share of repeat purchases in total sales has been increasing steadily over time, the potential downward bias becomes more significant the farther we look into the future.

Second, I have ignored altogether the gains stemming from upgrades—from the retrofitting of older units (usually at a low cost to the user), a strategy widely followed by the manufacturers in this field.[23] These upgrades amount to the substitution of new scanner models for old ones at a discount, and hence the gains generated by them are at least as large as those associated with replacements. Given that about 25 percent of all scanners sold up to 1981 have been upgraded, leaving them out could result in a significant undercounting of total gains.

The only possible source of upward bias lies in the implicit assumption that the underlying distribution of reservation prices is a step function, that is, that inframarginal users are indeed just at the margin prior to purchase so that as the latest innovations trigger adoption, they receive the full extent of the incremental gains ΔW_t. Clearly, if that is not the case, then only a fraction of the gains would actually be realized. On the other hand, users may delay adoption even when they have already gone over their threshold price because of expectations regarding future improvements in the technology. In that case the actual gains at the time of adoption would exceed the latest incremental gains, thus reducing—and perhaps even reversing—the potential upward bias just mentioned.

It is very difficult to assess the extent of the potential biases and, in particular, of the first two vis-à-vis the third. Some preliminary computations based on very conservative assumptions indicate that the two downward biases easily outweigh the latter one, resulting in a net down-

---

23. Given the rapid pace of technical change in CT, users were wary of locking themselves in with equipment that might be rapidly superseded. To counteract these fears, many of the firms in the market offered to upgrade the systems at low cost as the technology evolved, thus protecting the consumer against "premature technological obsolescence."

ward bias of small magnitude.[24] The tentative conclusion is thus that the total gains as computed here quite probably underestimate the true gains and can therefore be taken at least as a lower bound.

4.4　R&D Expenditures and Social Returns

After calculating the stream of social benefits from innovations in CT, the natural next step would be to relate the gains to the costs of bringing them about and compute some version of a rate of return. The costs refer of course to R&D expenditures in CT. Hence the immediate concern is how to obtain project-specific R&D figures, as virtually all firms had diversified research portfolios. This is part of a more general and pervasive problem in empirical microstudies, namely, the difficulties in obtaining data on specific, well-defined industries or markets—the level of disaggregation usually prescribed by theory. R&D is particularly troublesome in that respect, since the allocation of such expenditures across projects within firms is usually regarded as highly confidential information, and in most cases there is little external evidence of such allocation. Furthermore, even if that kind of information were available, it is not clear how to go about distributing overheads among the firm's various research fields, not to mention the problem of accounting for externalities across R&D projects. Not surprisingly, studies using product-specific R&D are extremely rare.

4.4.1　Computing a Rate of Return to R&D

In spite of these difficulties, I succeeded in gathering fairly complete data on the R&D devoted specifically to CT scanners by almost all firms that have been active in this field. The sources used vary substantially in their reliability and extent of coverage (see appendix 4.1 for a detailed account of those sources), but there is a fair amount of independent

---

24. The assumptions were: the distribution of reservation prices is uniform (and continuous), and hence new adopters get only *half* of the incremental gains; second-time buyers benefit from the incremental gains generated in the previous year as well (that is, their gains are $\Delta W_t + \Delta W_{t-1}$); and upgrades confer the average incremental gains, amounting to $1.85 million. The net effect on total gains is a downward bias of just $30 million. Notice that replacements, second scanners, and upgrades beyond 1983 are still omitted, and so is the restraining role of technological expectations.

Table 4.4   R&D Expenditures in CT Scanners (in millions, constant 1982 $)

Year	R&D by U.S. firms	Total R&D[a]	Number of firms	R&D per firm[b]
1968–1971	—	6.22	1	1.55[c]
1972	.22	5.42	2	2.71
1973	.82	9.00	3	3.00
1974	7.79	22.62	8	2.83
1975	28.63	59.68	12	4.97
1976	58.18	96.08	13	7.39
1977	46.64	79.68	14	5.69
1978	37.03	64.33	11	5.85
1979	33.70	56.05	9	6.23
1980	29.58	46.40	8	5.80
1981	22.58	37.94	8	4.74
Total	265.17	483.42	—	—
Mean (1974–1981)	33.02	57.85	10	5.44

Note: The R&D deflator used is taken from Cummins and Hall (1982).
[a]CGR, Hitachi, and Philips are not included.
[b]Col. 2/Col. 3
[c]Average for the 1968–1971 period.

evidence indicating that at least the orders of magnitude are correct. The yearly figures for total and U.S.-only R&D expenditures are shown in table 4.4[25] (the breakdown by firms cannot be exhibited because of a pledge of confidentiality).

The question now is which R&D should be used in computing a social rate of return: that performed both in the United States and abroad, or in the United States alone? The source of ambiguity is that the estimated

25. A note of caution: at least three out of the four foreign firms included in table 4.4 (Elscint, EMI, and Siemens) conducted part of their research on CT in the United States; however, there is no evidence available on the percentage of the work done here and abroad, so they are treated as if all the R&D were done in their home country.

Gains from Innovation in CT

benefits are those accruing to U.S. users only, whereas the market for CT is global, both in terms of the origin of innovations and the spread of their benefits. For example, if one were to use just the R&D performed by U.S. firms, the resulting rate of return could be seen as an overstatement, since the measured gains are due in part to foreign innovations (embedded in imported scanners) whose costs are not counted.[26] Given the inconclusive nature of the issue, I shall compute rates of return to total and to U.S.-only R&D and loosely interpret them as lower and upper bounds to the true rate.

One perennial problem of trying to obtain rates of return is that there is no unique way of computing those rates; likewise, the relative merits of the commonly used procedures are not clear-cut. The method chosen here is the capitalized benefit/cost ratio, to be denoted by ρ (see, for example, Griliches, 1958);[27] in the present case it takes the form

$$\rho = rB/C = r\left[\sum_{\tau=73}^{82} TW_\tau\gamma^{(\tau-73)}/\sum_{\tau=68}^{81} R\&D_\tau\gamma^{(\tau-73)}\right],$$

where $\gamma = 1/(1 + r)$. Assuming the interest rate to be $r = 0.05$, and applying the formula to the two alternative R&D series,

(i) U.S. R&D: $\rho = .05(14,813/214) = 3.46$

(ii) total R&D: $\rho = .05(14,813/397) = 1.87;$

that is, a dollar of R&D expenditures in CT scanners resulted in $3.5 of annual returns in perpetuity when only local R&D is considered, and in

---

26. Notice that even if estimates of worldwide gains were available, it is not clear whether a global cost/benefit analysis would be a meaningful procedure: the implicit goal of any such analysis is to help find the optimal allocation of resources in the economy. However, the group of countries where firms working in CT happen to be located can hardly be seen as comprising an economic entity facing a common allocation problem. This problem is not simply a peculiarity of the case at hand, but would probably arise whenever the industry extended beyond national boundaries.

27. The principal contender was the internal rate of return. Aside from the fact that this method cannot render a unique solution, its main drawback (for the case here) is that the results are very sensitive to the costs and benefits in the first two to three years of the period under consideration: small changes (or errors) in the magnitude or timing of those initial figures may drastically alter the rates obtained. Since in the present case the figures for the first years are in fact the least reliable, the internal rate of return was discarded in favor of the capitalized benefit/cost ratio (the latter does not suffer from the problem just mentioned).

$1.9 when foreign R&D is included as well. Taking their average as a summary figure (since (i) and (ii) may be interpreted loosely as upper and lower bounds), one arrives at a rate of about 270 percent.

4.4.2 Significance of the Computed Rate

The figure of 270 percent may be taken as the best available estimate of the social rate of return to R&D in the field of CT, but only with a grain (or two) of salt, and subject to certain qualifications. First, the computations of both benefits and costs involve some inherent ambiguities, such as the ex-ante/ex-post dilemma as to the benefits, and the total versus U.S.-only R&D as to the costs. Consequently, it is impossible to rid the end figures of an element of arbitrariness, regardless of how persuasive the arguments voiced to support this or that choice might be. Clearly, one has to be particularly careful when it comes to applications based on *absolute* magnitudes, and rates of returns are certainly a case in point. But inferences made on the basis of relative figures can be made with much more confidence, since in most cases the alternative calculations led to results roughly proportional to each other.[28] Second, the interpretation of gains as social is contingent upon the motives that govern the behavior of hospitals when choosing medical technologies (see section 4.2). Third, profits have not been included in the measure of benefits because of lack of accurate data. However, even if profits amounted to, say, a staggering 50 percent of revenues over the whole period,[29] their impact on the computed rate of return would be negligible, simply because the total gains are larger by a few orders of magnitude.

What can be learned from this result? Clearly, a rate of 270 percent indicates, once more, that at least some segments of R&D turn out to be highly rewarding for society as a whole (keep in mind, though, that the *private* returns varied a great deal: about half the firms in CT realized *negative* returns on their R&D investments). This is hardly news, but the sparseness of solid quantitative results of this kind, and the traumatic impression left by the recent productivity slowdown seem to have fostered the (mistaken) perception that we may be exhausting the technology frontier. True, our ability to produce ever larger quantities of *existing*

28. That will be the case, for example, when analyzing the time profile of benefits and costs, and other applications involving correlations.

29. This exceeds the profit rates of any firm in any particular period; moreover, a few actually incurred substantial losses.

goods may not be increasing as fast as it once did, but the economy can and does generate new and better products with a vengeance.

Unfortunately, there are very few studies of the returns to R&D for individual innovations, making it difficult to assess the significance of the particular figure arrived at here (clearly, that can be done only in a comparative context). Although it refers to a process rather than a product innovation, the main study in this context is still Griliches (1958):[30] he estimated the social returns to R&D in hybrid corn to be about 700 percent, much higher than my estimates for CT scanners. Although there is no reason to expect that the social, ex-post rates of return for unrelated innovations will be of a similar order of magnitude, a closer look reveals a key methodological difference between the two studies that, at least technically, may account for most of the disparity in results. This has to do with the treatment of future benefits.[31] In Griliches's study the flow of benefits increases over time following the diffusion path, and then continues indefinitely at the level determined by the ceiling of the diffusion curve. In other words, whenever hybrid corn is planted, now as well as in the future, society reaps the benefits of its superior yield vis-à-vis conventional corn. By contrast, in the present study the benefits cease as the diffusion process dies off, since the purchase of additional—or replacement—scanners in the future is assumed to confer no further gains.[32] If the rate of return on hybrid corn is calculated anew omitting future benefits (those accruing after 1955, Griliches's cutoff date),[33] one gets $\rho = .05(4,405/63) = 3.5$, almost the

30. The other important study of the kind is by Mansfield and coauthors (1977). They found that the median social rate of return in a set of 17 innovations was 56 percent, the highest being 307 percent. Unfortunately, their results are not directly comparable to those here, since they used internal rates of return rather than benefit/cost ratios.

31. Of course, the computation of incremental gains is entirely different, but that is of no consequence for the issue at hand: Griliches's per-unit extra yield brought about by hybrid corn can be thought of as analogous to the average ΔW here.

32. The questions asked in the two studies are thus quite different: in Griliches's context the question is, how much is gained by growing hybrid rather than conventional corn? Having thus fixed the baseline (conventional corn), we realize the benefits stemming from the superior yield of hybrid corn whenever hybrid seeds are planted, however far in the future. By contrast, in the present case the question is not how much better off we are as a result of taking CT scans than, say, conventional x rays, but rather how much we benefit from successive improvements over time in the CT technology itself.

33. This calculation was done using the figures for cumulated social net returns and cumulated research expenditures, as they appear in Griliches (1958), table 2.

same as the upper bound of 346 percent for CT. This similarity of results is somewhat suggestive and mildly reassuring, but in order to go any further in assessing the social returns to R&D more generally, one would need a much better understanding of the determinants of those returns, and many more empirical studies of this kind.

4.5 The Time Profile of Benefits and Costs

Moving beyond the summary view provided by rates of return, it is time to examine in detail the chronological evolution of both social gains and R&D expenditures in the hope that this will shed some light on the dynamics of the innovative process itself. To that end, figure 4.1 presents the time path of incremental gains, both the actual figures and a three-year moving average,[34] and figure 4.2 the profiles of total gains and total R&D expenditures, in logs.[35] The incremental gains, we recall, reflect advances in the technology itself (that is, the social valuation of those advances), whereas total gains incorporate also the effect of market size.

The first notable feature is that the gains generated in the first half of the period are far larger than those in the second half. In fact, the smoothed-out profile resembles a sort of log-normal distribution: it starts high, rises still further during the initial period, and then declines rapidly, carrying a low-level tail into the future.[36] Such a pattern is certainly highly plausible, and may be accounted for by a generalization of a common feature of economic processes, namely, an initial phase of scale economies, promptly followed by the onset of sharply diminishing returns. What is peculiar in the context of innovation is that these non-

34. There is always an element of randomness in the precise timing of specific innovations. Given the arbitrariness of any discrete partition of the time dimension (for example, in calendar years), a moving average may better capture the essence of the underlying process.

35. The use of logs in plotting figure 4.2 is due simply to the enormous differences in the order of magnitude of the various figures: total gains in the 1973–1977 period are of *billions* of dollars, whereas later on they dip below $100 million, and R&D expenditures are well under that mark throughout.

36. Even though the gains actually measured extend up to 1982 only, the available qualitative information indicates that no major technical advances in CT have occurred since (aside from Cine CT, but those systems have had very few sales so far). However, relatively minor improvements have been introduced, so it is reasonable to assume that the tail does indeed extend well beyond 1982.

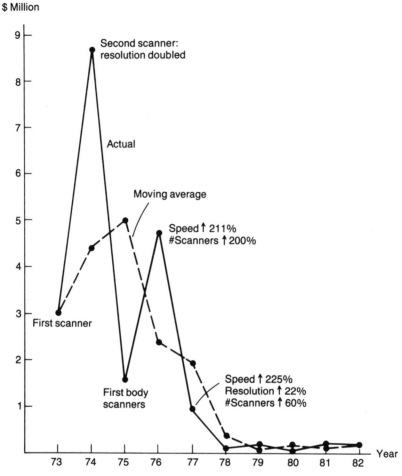

Figure 4.1   The Time Profile of Incremental Gains (yearly figures and
             3-year moving averages)

linearities appear to take place simultaneously in three different dimensions: in the production of innovations (the R&D technology), in the utility or value generated by them, and in determining the size of the market for them.

With respect to R&D, usually it is relatively easy to improve the performance of a technology during its initial stages, both from the viewpoint of the resources needed, and of the enabling scientific and tech-

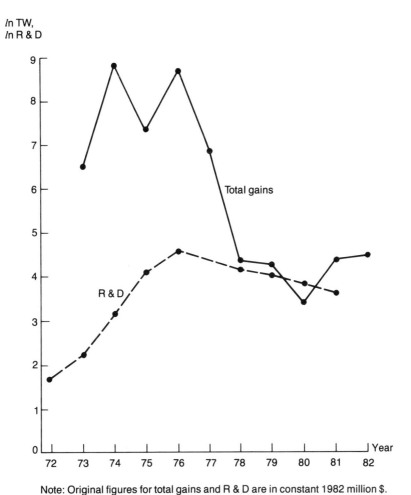

Figure 4.2   Total Gains and Total R&D Expenditures (logarithmic scale)

nological principles. Later on, as the obvious advances are no longer there to be made and the technology is pushed to its limits, the marginal cost of further improvements rises and the rate of innovation tends to abate. As to the utility derived from the characteristics of new products, there often is a "threshold effect" in the sense that the product is virtually worthless below a certain level of performance (for example, minimal resolution in CT scanners). That would account for an initial phase of increasing returns in the valuation of technical improvements, but soon diminishing marginal utility prevails: thus, for example, increasing the speed of CT scanners from 12 to 2 seconds was not nearly as valuable as going from 60 to 10 seconds. As to the third dimension, market size, consider how n_t^f evolves over time (n_t^f stands for the number of users that benefit from the incremental gains ΔW_t as the diffusion process unfolds): from (4.7)-(4.9), and assuming for simplicity that the initial ceiling K_0 is 0,

$$\frac{d \ln n_t^f}{dt} = \frac{d \ln CW_t}{dt} - h(t), \qquad h(t) = \frac{f(t)}{1 - F(t)},$$

that is, the behavior of n_t^f over time depends upon the rate of technological improvement, $d \ln CW_t/dt$, vis-à-vis the hazard rate of the diffusion process, $h(t)$. As argued above, one would expect the former not to increase over time, whereas if diffusion follows for example a logistic pattern, then $h(t) = \beta F(t)$, and hence it increases monotonically. Thus n_t^f will be in general a concave function and have a maximum; that is, even if innovation proceeds at a constant pace, total gains will eventually decrease because the diffusion process exhausts itself faster than the rate at which the market expands as a result of technical advance.

A convenient illustration of these effects is the innovation that generated the largest benefits in the history of CT, namely, the introduction of the second CT scanner (the EMI 1000) in 1974: this system was very similar to the original EMI Mark I but had much better resolution, which greatly improved the ability to visualize brain pathologies. The first scanner proved the feasibility of Computed Tomography; the second transformed it into a useful diagnostic tool that could be widely applied. This seems to be a fairly general phenomenon in product innovations: the first models of a new product are rarely more than the embodiment of a potentially useful idea. The real leap forward (and the concomitant benefits) comes with the advent of a model in which some key attributes are greatly improved, turning it into a practical product that commands wide appeal, rather than being just an ingenious device. Examples abound: the Ford Model T in cars, the DC-3 in aircraft, the UNIVAC I in computers, and so on.

The early emergence of a "big winner" that brings about the most gains can thus be seen as the realization of increasing returns that operate simultaneously along the three dimensions mentioned above.[37] Likewise, the rather dramatic drop in the flow of gains from innovation occurring later on can be attributed to diminishing returns setting in at the same time in those same dimensions. As a result, ΔW_t displays a definite wave-like pattern over time. It is tempting to venture a step further and relate this finding to the many theories asserting that the process of technological change at large follows a cyclical pattern (see Schumpeter, 1939). However, within the confines of this case study, all that can be said is that the evidence presented, and its underlying rationale, may be seen as enhancing the *plausibility* of technology-driven cycles.

A few remarks about the time profile of R&D: as figure 4.2 reveals, the flow of R&D outlays is not correlated with either incremental or total gains, reflecting the increasing/decreasing returns sequence in the technology dimension. Moreover, the ratio of gains to R&D for the period 1968–1977 was a staggering 80 to 1, whereas for 1978–1982 it was a bare 1.4 (in 1980, R&D actually exceeded the benefits). A straightforward implication is that average social rates of return to R&D are not very informative, certainly not as guides for policy. The question is not so much whether public support to R&D is warranted (it is not too difficult to make a case for it), but rather how long should such support be provided in the course of the innovation cycle.

In the case of CT it may have been socially desirable at first to promote research (on hindsight, and using as a criterion the gap between gains from innovation and R&D costs), but that was certainly not the case after 1976. The British government did in fact support the development of the first CT scanner at EMI, and it is quite possible that the project would have not been carried out, or at least would have been seriously delayed, had that support not been forthcoming. In line with that presumption, it is worth noting that W. H. Oldendorf, an American radiologist, had independently developed a tomographic device similar to the EMI scanner, but was unable to pursue the project for lack of support in the United States, either from the government or from private

37. Typically, not one but a few such discrete jumps are observed along the technological history of a product; in CT, for example, an additional major leap in 1976 was primarily due to a threefold increase in speed, which made it possible to scan a wide range of body organs. Note, however, that it is not possible to determine what constitutes a leap just by observing the rates of improvements in attributes: rather, it is the valuation of those changes, as captured in the ΔW's, that counts.

firms.[38] The problem is that, if one waits for hard evidence on returns to R&D to decide what fields to support, the support may no longer be necessary once the evidence is available. Thus learning more about time profiles of innovations may substantially contribute to the design of public policy in this area.

These observations highlight one of the key features of the present study, namely, that it looks into the very emergence of a new, high-technology market. The results, if typical, suggest that most of the innovative action takes place very early on. Thus studies focusing mostly on well-established or mature sectors are likely to be missing a great deal. Moreover, since innovation plays a vital role in the dynamics of technologically advanced sectors, it is crucial to have a better grasp of their initial stages to understand how they evolve into their long-term equilibria, and what are the normative aspects of those equilibria.

4.6   The Construction of Real Price Indices

One of the leading concerns driving this project is the suspicion that commonly used indicators of economic performance (such as real GNP) may fail to account properly for product innovations, and hence be quite misleading. Moreover, simple quality adjustments—such as those based on hedonic price indices—are not likely to overcome these deficiencies. The measurement of the gains from innovation with the ΔW's allows us to compute real price indices that would faithfully reflect those innovations, and thus to assess how far off the mark a hedonic-based price index would have been in this case. In this way we can get a sense for the extent of distortions that might be prevalent in indicators pertaining to high-technology sectors.

As shown in Chapter 1, the real price reduction equivalent to innovations worth ΔW_t can be computed as $\delta'_t \equiv \phi_t/(1+\phi_t) = \Delta W_t/(\Delta W_t + \bar{p}_t)$ (this is for the second index developed in section 1.5; the first index is not applicable in the present case). That is, we can think of consumers as having benefited from a real price reduction of δ'_t as a consequence

38. The only instance in the United States of direct public support to research in CT was the grant given by DHEW to AS&E in 1975–76 to develop a fast, fourth-generation scanner. This project was technologically successful, generating significant social gains (the 1976 pike in figure 4.1 was partly due to the AS&E scanner).

of the innovations valued ΔW_t, vis-à-vis their notional reservation price of $(1 + \phi_t)\, \bar{p}_t$. Thus one can build a real, or quality-adjusted price index on the basis of the series δ'_t that can be used *inter alia* to judge the performance of indices derived from hedonic price regressions.

Table 4.5 brings together the estimates of ΔW_t, the mean prices, and the index δ' for all CT scanners and for each scanner type separately (since prices are nominal the ΔW_t's are in current dollars, not in constant 1982 dollars as they were in tables 4.2 and 4.3). Notice that ΔW_t exceeds $\bar{p}_t$ during the first three or four years of CT, that is, there were drastic technical advances in CT during its initial period (as reflected in the large values of ΔW_t relative to prices), and hence the first index, requiring $\Delta W_t < \bar{p}_{t-1}$, cannot be implemented. Notice also that the index δ' indicates the occurrence of "negative innovations" (that is, increases in real prices) in head scanners in 1979, 1980, and 1982, in spite of a downward trend in nominal prices. This finding has to do with the decrease in the number of head scanners offered in the market, as body scanners gained dominance.

The computation of hedonic indices can be done in various ways, of

Table 4.5 Computation of the ΔW-Based Price Indices for CT Scanners

Year	Head scanners			Body scanners			All scanners		
	ΔW	$\bar{p}$	$-\delta'$	ΔW	$\bar{p}$	$-\delta'$	ΔW	$\bar{p}$	$-\delta'$
1974	—	—	—	—	—	—	4,391	370	−0.92
1975	—	—	—	—	—	—	875	372	−0.70
1976	994[a]	374	−0.73	1,967[a]	471	−0.81	2,961	448	−0.87
1977	37	354	−0.09	724	573	−0.56	620	541	−0.53
1978	257	167	−0.61	15	620	−0.02	82	494	−0.14
1979	−10	154	+0.07	158	667	−0.19	108	515	−0.17
1980	−16	154	+0.12	83	739	−0.10	64	626	−0.09
1981	7	150	−0.04	190	827	−0.19	174	770	−0.18
1982	−3	150	+0.02	209	850	−0.19	195	804	−0.19

Note: ΔW is in current dollars; $\bar{p}$ is weighted mean price (weights: annual unit sales); and $-\delta'_t = -\Delta W_t/(\Delta W_t + \bar{p}_t)$ (the index is written as minus δ' since a positive ΔW means a real price reduction).

[a] Imputed figures.

Table 4.6 Hedonic Price Regressions: Double-Log

	All scanners[a]		Body scanners		Head scanners	
	Weighted	Unweigh.	Weighted	Unweigh.	Weighted	Unweigh.
Constant	8.12 (28.1)[a]	7.99 (27.7)	6.73 (21.1)	6.9 (53.2)	6.25 (10.4)	6.78 (9.8)
Head dummy[b]	-.22 (-3.1)	-0.26 (-3.7)	—	—	—	—
Speed	-0.22 (-9.0)	-0.19 (-8.6)	-0.14 (-13)	-0.15 (-8.8)	-0.04 (-0.7)	-0.10 (-1.7)
Resolution	-0.53 (-5.4)	-0.44 (-4.7)	-0.30 (-7.7)	-0.44 (-7.4)	0.35 (0.9)	0.11 (0.30)
Recon. time	-0.05 (-2.2)	-0.06 (-3.5)	-0.03 (-3.5)	-0.05 (-3.7)	-0.12 (-2.3)	-0.10 (-2.5)
D74	0.07 (0.3)	-0.43 (-1.5)	—	—	0.15 (0.7)	0.09 (0.2)
D75	-0.49 (-2.0)	-0.54 (-2.0)	0.06 (0.2)	0.04 (0.3)	0.15 (0.5)	-0.24 (-0.6)

	(1)	(2)	(3)	(4)	(5)	(6)
D76	−0.78	−0.67	0.13	0.13	0.06	−0.16
	(−3.2)	(−2.6)	(0.42)	(1.1)	(0.2)	(−0.4)
D77	−0.95	−0.84	0.11	0.03	−0.005	−0.28
	(−3.9)	(−3.2)	(0.34)	(0.3)	(−0.0)	(−0.7)
D78	−1.19	−0.96	0.10	−0.01	−0.73	−0.52
	(−4.7)	(−3.6)	(0.30)	(−0.1)	(−2.1)	(−1.2)
D79	−1.28	−1.05	0.07	−0.03	−0.82	−0.88
	(−5.0)	(−3.9)	(0.21)	(−0.2)	(−2.3)	(−1.9)
D80	−1.26	−1.12	0.10	−0.08	−0.79	−1.01
	(−4.8)	(−4.1)	(0.31)	(−0.7)	(−2.2)	(−2.2)
D81	−1.20	−1.06	0.18	0.02	−0.83	−1.03
	(−4.4)	(−3.9)	(0.56)	(0.16)	(−2.2)	(−2.2)
D82	−1.30	−1.11	0.09	−0.04	—	−0.98
	(−2.2)	(−4.0)	(0.24)	(−0.3)		(−2.1)
Obs.	115	136	81	96	33	39
R²	0.84	0.81	0.94	0.83	0.89	0.69

Note: Annual unit sales are used as weights; there are fewer observations in the weighted regressions, since some of the CT scanners had zero sales.

[a]The values in parentheses are *t*-values.

[b]"Head" is a dummy variable for head scanners.

Table 4.7 Quality-Adjusted Price Changes: Hedonic versus ΔW-Based Indices (All Scanners)

Year	Hedonic-pooled		Hedonic-adjacent		$-\delta_t'$
	Unweighted	Weighted	Unweighted	Weighted	
1974	-0.43	$+0.07$	—	—	-0.92
1975	-0.11	-0.34^a	$+0.03$	$+0.01$	-0.70
1976	-0.12	-0.25^a	$+0.13$	$+0.03$	-0.87
1977	-0.16	-0.16^a	-0.05	$+0.01$	-0.53
1978	-0.11	-0.21^a	-0.09	-0.17^a	-0.14
1979	-0.09	-0.09	-0.08	-0.04	-0.17
1980	-0.07	$+0.02$	-0.08	$+0.02$	-0.09
1981	$+0.06$	$+0.06$	$+0.06$	$+0.05$	-0.18
1982	-0.05	-0.10	-0.08	-0.14	-0.19

[a]Difference from previous year statistically significant ($\alpha = 0.05$ or better) (applies only to hedonic index).

which the following were considered here: (a) weighted versus unweighted regressions (the weights being annual unit sales of each brand); (b) pooled regressions with dummy variables for each year, versus separate regressions for each pair of adjacent years (see Griliches, 1971, for a discussion of the relative merits of each method). Table 4.6 presents the estimated hedonic equations pooling all years, weighted and unweighted (the regressions for adjacent years are not reported since there are too many of them); the corresponding hedonic-based indices are computed in tables 4.7 and 4.8. The functional form used in all cases is the double-log,[39] and hence the coefficients of the yearly dummies, properly adjusted, can be taken as the "pure" (or "quality-adjusted") price change, in percentage terms.[40]

39. In Chapter 3 we found that the linear-log and the double-log specifications performed very well (in terms of MSE), with a slight advantage to the former. Clearly, though, the double-log is more convenient for the purpose at hand.

40. Denote the coefficient of the dummy for year t in a pooled hedonic regression as β_t; the "pure" price change between year $t-1$ and t (in percentages) is computed as $\exp(\beta_t - \beta_{t-1})$. Recall that for small β's, $\exp \beta \cong \beta$, hence the common practice of taking just the differences $\beta_t - \beta_{t-1}$. In the present case, though, those differences are often quite large, and for that reason one should indeed take the exponent.

The results of all four hedonic specifications considered are quite similar when contrasted with the ΔW-based index: the real price reductions that occurred in CT were much larger than what the hedonic method is able to uncover, particularly during the first few years. Table 4.9 shows that in a condensed way: if no correction were made at all, one would

Table 4.8   Quality-Adjusted Price Changes: Hedonic versus ΔW-Based Indices (Separate Figures for Head and Body Scanners)

	Hedonic-pooled		Hedonic-adjacent		
Year	Unweighted	Weighted	Unweighted	Weighted	$-\delta_i'$
		Head Scanners			
1974	+0.09	+0.15	—	—	—
1975	−0.28	0.00	−0.09	—	—
1976	+0.08	−0.09	+0.10	+0.04	−0.73
1977	−0.11	−0.06	−0.10	−0.05	−0.09
1978	−0.21	−0.51[a]	−0.26	−0.43[a]	−0.61
1979	−0.30	−0.09	−0.17	−0.03	+0.07
1980	−0.12	+0.03	−0.19	+0.09[a]	+0.12
1981	−0.02	−0.03	−0.02	−0.04	−0.04
1982	+0.06	—	+0.06[a]	—	+0.02
		Body Scanners			
1975	+0.04	+0.06	+0.04	n.a.	n.a.
1976	+0.07	+0.05	+0.05[a]	+0.04[a]	−0.81
1977	−0.09	−0.03	−0.02	+0.02	−0.56
1978	−0.03	−0.01	−0.00	+0.01	−0.02
1979	−0.03	−0.03	−0.01	−0.03	−0.19
1980	−0.05	+0.03	−0.06	+0.01	−0.10
1981	+0.09[a]	+0.08[a]	+0.08	+0.07	−0.19
1982	−0.05	−0.09	−0.12	−0.14	−0.19

[a]Yearly differences are statistically significant ($\alpha = 0.05$ or better).

Table 4.9   Comparing Various Price Indices: All CT Scanners

Year	Nominal index[a]	Hedonic[b]	ΔW-based
1973	10,000	10,000	10,000
1974	11,940	10,770	800
1975	12,000	6,130	240
1976	14,450	4,600	31
1977	17,450 *100*[c]	3,850 *100*	15 *100*
1978	15,940 *91*	3,050 *79*	13 *87*
1979	16,610 *95*	2,780 *72*	11 *73*
1980	20,190 *116*	2,840 *74*	10 *67*
1981	24,840 *142*	3,020 *78*	8 *53*
1982	25,940 *149*	2,730 *71*	7 *47*

[a] $\bar{p}_t / \bar{p}_{73}$, where $\bar{p}_t$ is the weighted mean price in year t.
[b] The hedonic index is based on the weighted pooled hedonic regression.
[c] Figures in italics are the same indices, using 1977 = 100.

conclude that CT scanners were about 2.5 times more expensive in 1982 than a decade earlier, and hence that we are significantly worse off on that account. Using the hedonic technique significantly alters that initial assessment: the quality-adjusted hedonic index goes down from 100 to 27, implying an average annual price decrease of 13 percent. Still, that is a far cry from the actual pace of technical advance that took place in CT: the ΔW-based index goes down from *10,000 to 7,* implying a staggering real price reduction of 55 percent per year on average! It is important to note that, if one were to start the measurements say, in 1977, the extent of the discrepancies would be greatly attenuated, as can be inferred from the figures in italics in table 4.9. However, rather than finding comfort in those figures, they should serve as a warning: even though the hedonic method may not do so badly when it comes to technologically mature industries, it seems to be completely off the mark early on, when it is needed most.

Going back to table 4.8, it is interesting to contrast the relative performance of the hedonic index for head versus body scanners. Notice that, starting in 1977, the hedonic indices for head scanners based on weighted regressions do not diverge significantly from δ'. On the other hand, those for body scanners do extremely poorly, except for two years (1978 and 1982). This is no coincidence: even though there were some improvements in the attributes of head scanners after 1977, most of the "action" in that segment of the market took the form of downward displacements of the hedonic price function, that is, price reductions for only slightly altered systems. As argued in section 1.5, the hedonic technique is indeed quite appropriate in that case. Body scanners, on the other hand, kept getting better and more expensive, a phenomenon that completely eludes the hedonic method.

Appendix 4.1   Sources of Data on R&D Expenditures on CT

1. Four companies (Elscint, Omnimedical, Technicare, and Varian) provided yearly figures of R&D expenditures on CT in response to the questionnaire (data given in strict confidentiality).

2. AS&E openly disclosed this information in its annual reports and 10K forms, since the bulk of its research on CT was done under contract with the National Cancer Institute and DHEW.

3. A case study on CT prepared by the Harvard Business School in 1978 contains information on the R&D expenditures of EMI, GE, Pfizer, and Technicare. The figures for the latter coincide with those provided by Technicare itself, so there is reason to believe that the data are indeed reliable. Furthermore, a study by the American Hospital Association (AHA, 1977) provided almost identical figures for those companies.

4. Further data on GE and estimates for Picker are included in a confidential report prepared by one of the companies on its rivals (I am precluded from naming the company).

5. Syntex's annual reports give indications of the order of magnitude of its annual R&D outlays on CT.

6. Scattered evidence suggests that Siemens's R&D effort was of a similar order of magnitude as that of GE, at least in terms of the size of the R&D team.

7. The figures for Interad were inferred from the size of its research team (recall that Interad entered in 1981, and that its sole product was CT).

8. The figures for Artronix, Searle, and Toshiba are tentative estimates based on the size of their CT operation, number of scanners

designed, length of stay in the field, and their similarities in these aspects with companies for which precise data are available.

9. An NSF study (NSF, 1981) concluded that cumulative total R&D outlays in CT amounted to half a billion dollars by 1981. This figure corresponds quite closely to the total arrived here.

In most cases the data for 1975–1978 are more reliable than those for 1973–74 or 1979–1981, simply because a number of independent studies focused on that intermediate period in response to the keen public interest in the field at the time. In fact, the 1979–1981 figures for a number of companies (EMI, GE, Pfizer, Picker, Siemens, and Toshiba) were not directly available and had to be extrapolated from earlier data, with due attention paid to known changes in the commitment of those firms to CT (for example, reduced R&D efforts in the period preceding exit—recall that EMI exited in 1980 and Pfizer in 1981).

R&D performed by Philips and CGR is not included in the data: the first company was excluded from the study altogether, and there was no information whatever regarding R&D expenditures by the latter (CGR marketed just one scanner in the United States during the period studied, without much success.)

5

Patents as Indicators of Innovation

Patents have long exerted a compelling attraction on economists dealing with technical change, particularly since Jacob Schmookler's seminal work in this area (1966). The reason is quite clear: patents are the only observable manifestation of inventive activity having a well-grounded claim for universality. They cover virtually every field of innovation according to more or less uniform standards, and they have been doing that in many countries—certainly in all industrialized economies—for a very long time (about two centuries in the United States).

The wealth of information thus assembled is in fact quite extraordinary, with some four million patents issued in the United States (about 70,000 new patents are granted annually), and over 25 million worldwide; each of these patents is, in turn, a rather elaborate document, containing extensive quantifiable as well as literary (qualitative) data. Moreover, in contrast to some other massive data collections, this one is not the result of the seemingly boundless appetite of governments for official documents and figures, but is meant to serve a well-defined and desirable economic purpose.[1] There is nothing like it in the area of technical change, and actually it is hard to think of any other data file related to economic phenomena of such vast dimensions and potential.

Yet it is quite apparent that patents have not lived up to expectations: their use in economic research has been sparse and the results rather

1. It could readily be argued that the legitimacy and appropriateness of using patent-based data in economic research are greatly enhanced by the fact that patenting is a voluntary act that responds to clear economic incentives. In contrast, respondents perceive government's gathering of data by the force of law or regulation as a bothersome imposition, to be avoided if possible.

disappointing, and they have failed to become a standard data source feeding run-of-the-mill empirical research. The reasons are to be found in two fundamental problems that to this day, a generation after Schmookler's valiant efforts, remain largely unsolved: first, the enormous variation in the importance or value of patents, and second, the lack of a satisfactory match between the patent classification system and any set of meaningful economic categories. The first casts a heavy shadow on the use of patent counts (the measure commonly used), because if patents vary so much in their worth, their numbers cannot be informative of the extent of innovation that has taken place, which is what we are after. The second means that it is exceedingly difficult to assign patents correctly to whatever happens to be the relevant unit of analysis (industries, markets, products), and consequently to construct any accurate patent-based indicator (including simple counts).

It is the aim of this chapter to address these basic issues once again, albeit in a modest and limited fashion. The usefulness of patent data will be probed here by bringing a particular innovation under sharp focus, rather than doing that in a comparative (cross-sectional) context. The advantages of this approach lie in the clear demarcation of the boundaries of the innovation, in the completeness and accuracy of the data pertinent to it (including of course patents) and, more important, in the availability of the measures of gains from innovation ΔW, which offer a well-defined—and unique—yardstick with which to assess the performance of patent-based indicators. Clearly, though, the sharp focus comes at the expense of generality, and hence the conclusions can only be regarded as suggestive and tentative.

Following a general discussion of the value of patents, section 5.2 addresses the main problems encountered when using patent data in economic research (the large variance in the value of patents, and the classification problem), and outlines the proposed solutions. Narrowing the focus, section 5.3 lays out and examines the patent data in CT. Statistical tests of the main hypothesis and the existence of "supply-push" effects are probed subsequently. Appendix 5.2 presents a detailed statistical procedure to test for "age" versus "importance" and for truncation effects; those tests were called for by the finding that the average number of citations per patent decreases drastically over time, thus raising the suspicion that citations might be determined simply by age and have little to do with importance.

5.1 The Value of Patents

At the outmost level of generality, the value of a patent is but the value of the segment of innovative outcomes documented in it. This in turn comprises three concentric aspects: first, the value of the property rights conferred by the patent (to be denoted *VPR*), which is that fraction of the profits generated by the innovation exclusively attributable to the extra monopoly power traceable to the legal exclusion of potential competitors. Second is the private value of the innovation/patent (*PV*), which is the present discounted value of the stream of additional profits to the assignee, brought about by the innovation disclosed in the patent (if, for example, the assignee is a publicly held firm, this may show up as increments in the market value of the firm). Clearly, the private value of a patent is inclusive of the value of the property rights, and may actually be much larger than that.[2] The third aspect is the social value (*SV*) of the innovation/patent, which consists, as repeatedly stated, of the extra surplus the innovation generates in the form of incremental consumer surplus and profits. In sum, $VPR \subset PV \subset SV$; and recalling that ΔW comprises as measured only the incremental consumer surplus, $SV = \Delta W + (PV - VPR) + VPR$.

Unfortunately, many of the references to the value of patents that one encounters in the literature are vague and do not specify which of the three components are included in the measures used. This is clearly a matter of consequence, since these components are likely to be of very different orders of magnitude, and it is not clear a priori whether or not they are highly correlated. In the discussion below, unless stated otherwise, the value of patents will refer to their social value. However, the empirical analysis will proceed as if the social value consisted only of the incremental consumer surplus as captured by ΔW, since in the case of CT scanners that happened to be by far the dominant component.

It is worth noting that conceptions regarding the nature of innovation translate logically into implicit priors about the distribution of patent values. The "heroic" view alluded to in Chapter 1, for example, sees the

---

2. In the first place, some of the private gains from innovations do not stem from enhanced monopoly power but from other advantages, such as costs savings associated with process innovations in an otherwise competitive environment. Furthermore, enhanced monopoly power need not be associated with legal exclusion, but is often due to lead time advantages, improved technological capabilities, and so forth.

innovative process largely as a sequence of well-defined, sizable events to which various tags might be attached, such as the name of *the* inventor and of *the* new product, the time and place of *the* innovation, and so forth. Accordingly, this view presupposes a one-to-one correspondence among those singular innovations and patents: each innovation so conceived is expected to be spelled out in a patent, and conversely, each patent is thought to stand for a distinct, clearly delimited segment of technical advance.

By contrast, the view taken here regards innovation by and large as a continuous process in time, predominantly incremental in nature, and punctuated by occasional breakthroughs that redirect the innovative efforts into novel channels. Accordingly, to use a movie metaphor, most patents can be thought of as individual frames in a film that document slightly different aspects of the ongoing innovative action, in the context of a few central motifs and themes. Each frame is of course somewhat different from the others, and yet within any given scene what is striking are the similarities and concomitant incrementalism, not the differences. That is the case for most patents, but not for all, the exceptions being of course those few associated with the first formulation of important innovations. The implications of these opposing views of the innovative process for the distribution of patent values are immediate: the "heroic" view would suggest that the distribution of patent values is symmetric and has a sizable mean,[3] whereas the second clearly implies skewness and a large variance, with no hint as to the expected value (the available empirical evidence clearly favors the latter).

5.2 Using Patent Data

5.2.1 *The Problem of a Large Variance in the Value of Patents*

Given that patents vary enormously in their technological and economic importance and value, merely counting them at any level of aggregation cannot be regarded a priori as a good indicator of the magnitude of innovation.

Griliches and coauthors (1988) provide some quantitative indication of how badly simple patent counts would perform if used in lieu of true

---

3. Symmetry is assumed simply by default, as is commonly done whenever there is no prior information suggesting otherwise.

patent values. They do that in the wider context of assessing the extent to which various patent measures can contribute to the explanation of changes in the market value of firms, over and above what can be accounted for by R&D expenditures. The results are not very encouraging: in the best of cases, the variance in patent values could account for about 1 percent of the variance in market values. More important for the purposes here, patent counts could be expected to explain less than *one tenth of one percent* of that same variance.[4] Not surprisingly, as the authors show, that percentage depends inversely on the size of the variance of the distribution of patent values (actually, on the coefficient of variation); the large variance in those values thus deprives patent counts of much of their informational content.

Furthermore, substantial evidence indicates that the distribution of patent values is highly skewed toward the low end, with a long and thin tail into the high-value side. As Scherer (1965) notes, these Pareto-like distributions might not have finite moments and, in particular, they might not have a finite variance (for example, if $\alpha < 2$ in the Pareto distribution). That would make the use of patent counts as proxies even more problematic: their inclusion in a regression, for example, would cause the residuals to be non-normal and have an infinite variance as well; hence the least-squares estimators would lose their minimum-variance linear unbiaseness property (see Maddala, 1977, p. 308).

It is important to emphasize that the problem just outlined is inherent to the patent system as such,[5] and therefore definite solutions can hardly be expected. Yet the importance of the matter warrants the search for some corrective measures, even if they turn out to be only partially successful.

5.2.2   The Use of Patent Citations

An idea that has often been suggested is to use patent *citations* as an index of the importance of patents, that is, to count the number of times

4. The value of patents in Griliches and coauthors (1988) refers to their *private* value; moreover, some of the figures they use in the calculations build upon estimates that refer solely to the value of the property rights. It is quite likely that the disparity in the explanatory power of patent counts versus patent values would be greatly exacerbated if it referred to social values instead.

5. This is so because the importance of a patent—however defined—can hardly be assessed ex-ante, and because it is not the task of patent examiners to make sure that the patents granted are of comparable worth.

that each patent has been cited in subsequent patents and compute with it weighted patent counts (the intention of course is to use those weighted counts as indicators of innovation further down the line). This idea can be traced directly to the widespread use of citations in the study of various aspects of the scientific enterprise. Indeed, numerous studies in the discipline of scientometrics (or "evaluative bibliometrics") have shown that a citation-based index can serve as good indicator of the impact of scientific contributions, of the influence of scientific journals, and so on.[6] But contrary to the somewhat arbitrary nature of citations in scientific publications,[7] those in patents are grounded in the Patent Law and are ultimately decided by a supposedly objective third party, namely, the patent examiner:

> During the examination process, the examiner searches the pertinent portion of the "classified" patent file. His purpose is to identify any prior disclosures of technology . . . which might anticipate the claimed invention and preclude the issuance of a patent; which might be similar to the claimed invention and limit the scope of patent protection . . . or which, generally, reveal the state of the technology to which the invention is directed . . . If such documents are found they are made known to the inventor and are "cited" in any patent which matures from the application. . . . The citations contained in a patent, therefore, can be regarded as pertinent to the technology disclosed in that patent. Consequently, if a single document is cited in numerous patents, the technology revealed in that document is apparently involved in many developmental efforts. Thus, the number of times a patent document is cited may be a measure of its technology significance.   (Office of Technology Assessment and Forecast, 1976, p. 167).

Moreover, as Campbell and Nieves (1979) argue at length, there is an important legal dimension to patent citations, since they represent a limitation on the scope of the property rights established by a patent's claims that carry weight in court. Equally important, the process of arriving at the final list of references, involving also the applicant and his attorney, apparently does generate the right incentives to have *all* truly

---

6. Classic works in this field are those of Derek de Solla Price (Price, 1963 and 1975), and of Cole and Cole (1973). See also Narin (1976) for an extensive review of scores of studies on the subject.

7. The authors of scientific articles decide by themselves which publications to cite, and such decisions might be influenced by a variety of extraneous motives (such as "politics," fashion, personal feelings toward other scientists, and so on) that obviously have little to do with scientific merit.

relevant patents cited, and *only* those (see Campbell and Nieves, 1979, Appendix II). The presumption that citation counts are potentially informative of the "importance" of patents is thus well-grounded.[8]

Still, the question remains as to whether citations counts may be indicative also of the *economic* value of the innovations disclosed in the cited patents, not just of *technological* importance. Obviously, this can only be answered empirically, but one can advance some further arguments that would strengthen the prior. Most patents cited are referenced in subsequent patents disclosing innovations within the same narrowly defined field as the earlier patents. Now, the very existence of those later patents attests to the fact that the earlier patents opened the way to a technologically successful line of innovation. More important, they presumably attest to *economic* success as well (at least in expected value terms), for those patents are the result of subsequent costly innovational efforts undertaken mostly by profit-seeking agents. Given that citations to a patent are counted over a period of a few years following its issuance, there should be enough time for the uncertainty regarding the economic value of the innovation to resolve itself. If citations keep coming, it must be that the innovation originating in the cited patent had indeed proved to be valuable.

Whatever their presumed merits, in practice patent citations have rarely been used in economic research primarily because of two serious obstacles: first, until not long ago it was quite difficult to retrieve the frequency of citations for each patent considered. Second, in the absence of independent evidence of the value of the innovations disclosed in patents, it is virtually impossible to ascertain the merits of a citations-based index or, for that matter, of any alternative indicator of the outcome of innovative activities.

Nowadays the problem of data availability can be easily overcome with the aid of computerized search techniques: once the relevant set of patents has been identified, the number of citations each of them received can be obtained by searching in the "references cited" field of these same patents (so called "within referencing") or of all subsequent patents. Better still, some of the patent dababases available through DIALOG (one

---

8. I am referring here only to the citations appearing in Item 56 on the front page of each patent, under "References Cited" (see figure 5.1), not to ones that may be mentioned in the text of the patent. To the best of my knowledge the latter play only a descriptive role and do not carry legal weight.

United States Patent [19]

Hounsfield

[11] **4,118,629**

[45] * **Oct. 3, 1978**

[54] **RADIOLOGY**

[75] Inventor: **Godfrey Newbold Hounsfield, Winthorpe, England**

[73] Assignee: **EMI Limited, Hayes, England**

[*] Notice: The portion of the term of this patent subsequent to Jun. 7, 1994, has been disclaimed.

[21] Appl. No.: **776,661**

[22] Filed: **Mar. 11, 1977**

Related U.S. Application Data

[63] Continuation of Ser. No. 584,172, Jun. 5, 1975, Pat. No. 4,028,554.

[30] **Foreign Application Priority Data**

Jun. 7, 1974 [GB] United Kingdom 25361/74

[51] Int. Cl.^{2} G01N 23/00
[52] U.S. Cl. .... 250/445 T
[58] Field of Search .... 250/445 T, 505, 363 S, 250/252, 510

[56] **References Cited**

U.S. PATENT DOCUMENTS

3,486,022	12/1969	Matuda et al.	.... 250/445 T
3,778,614	12/1973	Hounsfield	.... 250/445
3,881,110	4/1975	Hounsfield	.... 250/445 T
3,965,358	6/1976	Macouski	.... 250/445 T
3,996,467	12/1976	Froggatt et al.	.... 250/445 T
4,028,554	6/1977	Hounsfield	.... 250/445 T

Primary Examiner—Alfred E. Smith
Assistant Examiner—B. C. Anderson
Attorney, Agent, or Firm—Cooper, Dunham, Clark, Griffin & Moran

[57] **ABSTRACT**

Computerized tomographic apparatus is capable of producing representations which show, with high accuracy, the absorption coefficients, with respect to x-radiation, at various locations distributed over one or more selected cross-sectional slices of a patient's body. The evaluation of the absorption coefficients is effected by determining the absorption suffered by the radiation on traversing each of many substantially linear paths, the paths traversing the body slice. The invention resides in compensating for changes in the energy spectrum of the radiation as projected through the body along different ones of said paths, which changes could otherwise impair the accuracy of said representations.

12 Claims, 4 Drawing Figures

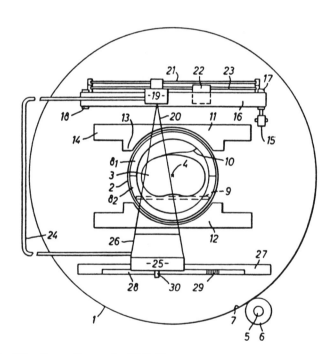

Figure 5.1   The Front Page of a U.S. Patent

of the largest providers of computerized search services) already include citation counts as a standard information item in each patent.

The second obstacle, judging the merits of a citation-based index, is much more difficult to overcome, since it hinges on the availability of self-justifiable measures of the value of innovations that could help validate citations-weighted patent counts. Without such validation the claim that citations are indicative of importance will remain just an untested hypothesis, and no conclusions can be drawn from citations-based statistical findings.[9] At the same time, however, there are hardly any value measures of innovations to be found in the literature that could be of help in the present context. Here, therefore, the advantage of having the ΔW figures for CT scanners proves to be crucial, since they make it possible to assess directly the performance of the citations-weighting scheme. A further advantage in this case is that both the patent counts and the measures used to validate them refer precisely to the same "stretch" of innovative activity: advances in a carefully circumscribed product class and time period. Thus the usual problems that arise when trying to match information belonging to disparate units (as often happens in this context) are altogether absent here.

Granted the use of citations, the question is how to go about constructing with them a sensible weighting scheme. A straightforward possibility is to weight each patent i by the actual number of citations that it subsequently received, to be denoted C_i. Thus if we were to compute an index of weighted patent counts (*WPC*) for, say, a given product class in a given year t, we would have

$$WPC_t = \sum_{i=1}^{n_t} (1 + C_i),$$

where n_t is the number of patents issued during year t in that product class. This linear weighting scheme assigns then the same "value" of one to all citations and all patents. Lacking more information on the citation process, this is clearly a natural starting point, but certainly not the only

9. Some time ago a series of articles in the press proclaimed loudly that Japanese outpace Americans in innovation, because of findings showing that Japanese patents have been cited more often than U.S. patents (see *New York Times*, March 7, 1988, and *Time*, March 21, 1988; the study cited was conducted by Computer Horizons for the National Science Foundation). Although the conclusion may be correct, a higher frequency of citations does not and cannot prove anything by itself.

possibility. In fact, in section 5.4.3 I will compute also a nonlinear index that allows for the possible existence of "returns to scale" in the informational content of citations.

The literature on this subject contains up to now just a handful of studies using patent citations, and all but one (Lieberman, 1987) are outside the realm of economics proper.[10] Lieberman (1987) looked at the impact of patent counts on price changes (as proxies for costs) for a sample of chemical products. He finds that own-patents are positively correlated with prices and become statistically insignificant when weighted by citations. Lieberman provides plausible explanations for these negative results based on the nature of *process* innovations in those sectors. Carpenter and coauthors (1981) show that 100 important patents received more than twice as many citations as a matching sample of randomly chosen patents. They took "important" to mean patents associated with products that received the IR100 Award of the *Journal of Industrial R&D* in 1969 and 1970. Ellis and coauthors (1978) use citation "networks" to map the technological history of selected fields. Thus, for example, starting from a handful of patents issued in the 1970s for semi-synthetic penicillin, they were able to trace back the key patents in the development of the field. They make use of conventional historical material to validate the "historiographs" thus constructed. Campbell and Nieves (1979) also emphasize the importance of tracing the evolution of a technology and propose for that purpose a variety of patent-based indicators. In sum, bits and pieces of evidence exist to support the contention that patent citations may be indicative of something like importance, but the issue remains wide open.

5.2.3   The Problem of Classification

The use of patents in economic research for any purpose requires that they be related to economic categories of interest, such as products, industries, countries, and so on. However, the enormous size of the U.S. Patent File, which contains millions of patents, turns this seemingly simple task into an extremely problematic endeavor. There is of course a

---

10. Beside those reviewed here, additional (unpublished) studies putting forward the use of patent citations include Narin and Wolf (1983), and Narin (1983). However, the intended use of patent data in the last two is for business consulting, rather than academic research.

very elaborate Patent Classification System (PCS) comprising more than 110,000 patent categories (called subclasses), aggregated into some 400 patent classes, with no well-defined intermediate layers of aggregation.[11] The problem is that this vast classification scheme has not been designed according to a clear set of criteria (scientific or other) that could be mapped into an economic system. Instead, the PCS has evolved first and foremost according to operational convenience, and with good reason: after all, its main goal is to assist patent examiners in establishing the patentability of new applications by facilitating the search for related patents. Thus it is inherently very difficult to create a satisfactory matching between those 110,000 patent subclasses and any set of economic categories. For instance, in the mid-1970s the Patent Office constructed a concordance between the US-PCS and the Standard Industrial Classification (SIC) at the request of the National Science Foundation, but the results have been so far quite disappointing, primarily because most patent subclasses were assigned to multiple industries (see Office of Technology Assessment and Forecast, 1975).[12]

Aside from various ad-hoc solutions proposed in the literature, there have been just two attempts in recent years to tackle the classification problem on a large scale: one by Griliches (1984), and one by Scherer (1984). Griliches and his associates at the National Bureau of Economic Research sought to overcome the problem by using *firms* as the unit of analysis, rather than industry-type categories. Since one of the data items on the patent document is the name of the legal entity to whom the patent was issued (see figure 5.1), the problem was confined to counting the patents that each assignee received in each period.[13] The main drawback of this approach is that firms are not the most appro-

11. Mirroring the rapid pace of technological advance, the U.S.-PCS is changing and updating continuously, primarily by the creation of new patent subclasses. When Schmookler was engaged in his massive classification effort in the early 1960s, there were just about *half* the number of subclasses that we have today. There is also an international PCS of similar size and complexity.

12. Lately, a group at Yale University lead by Robert Evenson has been attempting to create an estimated concordance on the basis of the classification of patents into industries by the Canadian Patent Office. Their approach seems promising, but it remains to be seen how well it will perform.

13. Even that tally proved to be a formidable task: firms appeared under a variety of different names, patents awarded to subsidiaries had to be reassigned to the parent companies, and mergers and takeovers had to be properly accounted for.

priate units for many purposes, and the grouping of firms by SIC is unsatisfactory.[14]

Scherer took a different track, more reminiscent of Schmookler's: he actually classified a sample of over 15,000 patents according to industry of origin and industry of use by having a team of experts examine the contents of each patent. Quite clearly, though, such a massive and team-dependent enterprise cannot be put forward as an universal research strategy and has to be regarded as a one-time event. Thus although both projects made big strides in this area, the classification problem remained essentially unsolved.

The solution proposed here is more modest in nature and relies upon the recent availability of powerful techniques for computerized search in large dababases. These techniques allow one to identify quite easily all the patents issued in predetermined economic categories (as narrowly defined as wanted) and retrieve them for further analysis (see appendix 5.1). With the aid of properly classified patents one can conduct in-depth studies of innovation in single sectors, or comparative studies involving, as of now, a not-too-large number of industries.[15] Clearly, this does not provide for an all-out solution to the classification problem, but it does open up a promising, more narrowly focused avenue of research, whereas the feasibility of universal solutions of any sort remains dubious.

5.3 Patents in Computed Tomography

The complete set of patents granted in Computed Tomography was located and retrieved by using the search method described in appendix 5.1, from the first entry in the field in 1971[16] up to the end of 1986, for

14. Keep in mind that this method does not allow the researcher to select directly from the patent file patents issued in predetermined product classes or industries.

15. There is nothing in the nature of the approach that precludes the undertaking of more ambitious projects (large panels, for example). However, in addition to requiring generous research budgets, more experience in searching by industries is needed before larger studies can be contemplated and eventually conducted on a routine basis.

16. In this case it was very easy to identify the first patent: the origin of Computed Tomography is unequivocally associated with the invention by G. Hounsfield of EMI, England, as described in his U.S. patent # 3778614, applied for in December 1971. Since there were no patents in CT in 1972, I shall treat this first patent as if it had been

a total of 456 patents.[17] To appreciate the extent to which the search techniques used here represent a major leap in our ability to identify patents in a given field, consider that the 456 patents in CT are spread over 75 patent subclasses, the leading one comprising 43 percent of the patents, the next largest four, 26 percent, the remaining 31 percent of the patents being scattered over 70 categories, each of them with no more than 1 percent of the patents. Had I tried to locate the patents in CT by going over the Patent Classification System, I would have probably succeeded in identifying no more than 70 percent of the total. Moreover, even in the subclasses with the largest numbers of patents in CT, the latter represent only a fraction of the total in those categories (except for the leading subclass, where 90 percent of the patents belong to CT); thus the percentage of patents wrongly selected could have been quite large. Decidedly, a "clean" set of patents and "clean" patent-based indicators are crucial for assessing the usefulness of those indicators: otherwise it would be impossible to tell the extent to which the results (whatever they may be) reflect real phenomena rather than errors of measurement.

As is by now standard practice, patents will be dated according to their application rather than granting date, since the latter depends entirely upon the examination procedure at the Patent Office and has nothing to do with the innovation process itself. However, since the availability of patents at the time of the search obviously reflects granting rather than application dates, there is a question as to how well the data cover the period under consideration, particularly the more recent years. To answer it we just need to look at the distribution of lags between application and granting:[18]

---

applied for in January of 1972 rather than in December of 1971, so as to avoid an unnecessary discontinuity in the data points.

17. The computerized search actually produced 501 patents, but 45 of them were eliminated after a careful examination of their abstracts. Thus I am certain that all the patents included do belong to CT, but obviously one cannot be equally sure that they constitute all the relevant patents. Still, in this case one can be quite confident in that respect as well, since it was possible to cross-check with other sources, including listings of patents from manufacturers of CT scanners.

18. The lag is computed as the difference (year granted – year applied); thus, the second row, for example, means that 76 percent of the patents applied for in any given year were granted within the following two calendar years. The distribution is virtually identical if the 1982–1986 patents are excluded.

Lag (in years)	No. of patents	Cumulative percent
1	105	23.2
2	243	76.3
3	91	96.3
4	11	98.7
5	4	99.6
6	1	99.8
7	1	100.0

Assuming that the distribution is stable, and recalling that the search was conducted in December 1986 (so the set includes all patents granted in CT up to that date), I conclude that the data comprise virtually all patents applied for up to (including) 1982, about 96 percent of the patents applied for in 1983, 76 percent of those applied in 1984, and a mere 23 percent of the 1985 patents. The analysis will thus be restricted to the period 1972–1982, although the citations appearing in the patents for 1983–1986 will be taken into account.

With regard to citations, counts can be done in two different ways, namely, counting all citations, or just those appearing in the set of patents belonging to the same field. Each procedure has its own merits and leads to a different interpretation of the resulting weighted patent counts: in the "within" referencing case the weighted counts will be associated with the value of the patents for—and in the terms of the specific technological field to which they belong. On the other hand, an all-inclusive index will presumably capture the value that has spilled over to other areas as well. Given that the measures of innovation to be used in conjunction with the patent data refer to the gains from advances in CT as such, with no attempt to account for spillovers, the citations are taken just from the references appearing in patents in CT.[19]

The first two columns of table 5.1, graphically displayed in figure 5.2, show the basic patent data to be used throughout. Note the smooth, cycle-like path followed by the yearly count of patents: it rises quite fast after 1973, peaks in 1977, and then declines steadily, carrying forward a long and thin tail (presumably extending into the indefinite future).

---

19. In this case it would not have mattered much which count was used: in a sample of 30 patents in CT the correlation between the two counts was found to be 0.99. Similarly, Campbell and Nieves (1979) report a correlation of 0.73 between what they called "in-set" and total citations, for some 800 patents in the field of catalytic converters.

Table 5.1 Patents in CT: Counts and Citations by Year

	Patents		Citations		
				% of patents with:	
Year	Simple counts	Weighted by[a] citations	Average # per patent	0	5+
1972	1	73	72.0	0.0	100.0
1973	3	50	15.7	0.0	100.0
1974	21	199	8.5	4.8	76.2
1975	48	242	4.0	12.5	47.9
1976	66	235	2.6	21.2	22.7
1977	115	260	1.3	45.2	11.3
1978	71	126	0.8	54.9	4.2
1979	59	88	0.5	66.1	0.0
1980	26	33[b]	0.3	84.6	0.0
1981	15	18[b]	0.2	86.7	0.0
1982	12	13[b]	0.1	91.7	0.0
1983[c]	13	14	—	—	—
1984[c]	6	6	—	—	—
All	456	1,357	2.1[d]	45.1[d]	16.2[d]

[a]The weighted patent counts are computed as $\sum_{i=1}^{n_t}(1 + C_i) = n_t + \sum_{i=1}^{n_t}C_i$, where C_i is the number of citations received by patent i, and n_t is the number of patents in year t (the simple patent count).
[b]These figures are slightly biased downward (see appendix 5.2).
[c]Partial figures.
[d]Averages.

Notice also that the weighting scheme strongly influences the shape of the time distribution, shifting it back toward the earlier period. In fact, the mean of the distribution of simple counts is 70.6 (in number of months elapsed since 1/72, the date of the first patent), whereas that of weighted counts is 54.0. That is, the weighting scheme moves the bulk of the innovative action back seventeen months, centering it on mid-1976, rather than late 1977. Given the very fast pace at which the CT

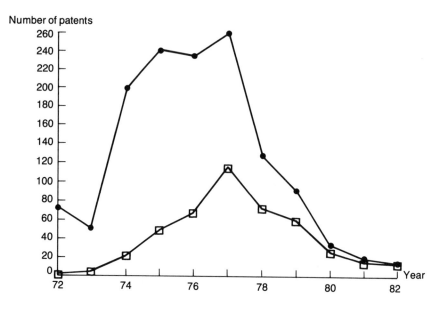

□ Simple patent count (*source:* table 5.1, column 1).

● Count weighted by citations (*source:* table 5.1, column 2).

Figure 5.2   Patents in CT: Simple Counts and Counts Weighted
by Citations

technology evolved, and considering that the period is just eleven years long, a difference of one-and-a-half years in the means is certainly very significant. Clearly, the reason for it has to be that earlier patents were cited more frequently than later ones. And indeed, table 5.1 proves that to be the case: the average number of citations per patent goes down dramatically over time (from 72 to below 1), the percentage of patents with no citations increases from 0 to 92 percent, and so on.

The crucial question is whether the observed citation frequency is to be regarded as a real phenomenon, presumably reflecting something like the importance of patents, or as a statistical artifact, induced primarily by the mere passage of time. Two main concerns arise in this context: first, it could be that older patents are cited more often simply because they have been around longer; in other words, they have had more opportunities to be cited because they precede a larger number of patents that could cite them. Second, given that CT is an ongoing technology, it is quite certain that additional patents have been—and will be—issued since the end of my search time (December 1986). The data set is thus necessarily truncated, and that might bias downward the citation counts of *recent* patents, since the probability of being cited is likely to decline over time. In that case the observed phenomenon could just be the result of the arbitrariness of the cut-off point.

These are serious a priori objections for anyone trying to attach any meaning to citations data, and deserve careful scrutiny.[20] Appendix 5.2 analyzes them in detail and shows that neither age nor truncation can account for the observed distribution of citation counts. The issue of age is tackled by constructing an hypothetical "iso-important" distribution of citations, and testing it against the observed distribution with the aid of a χ^2 test: the null hypothesis that older patents received more citations just because of the passage of time is rejected by a wide margin. As to the effect of truncation, the magnitude of the biases is estimated by extrapolating from the observed distribution of citation lags, and of the application-granting lags. The main finding is that a bias does exist, but the absolute expected number of missing citations to recent patents is so small that they could not possibly affect the statistical analysis to be performed.

5.4   The Statistical Evidence

The question is, then, to what extent can patent-based indices (denote them in general by P) serve as "indicators" of the value of innovations as measured by ΔW (or TW). By indicators I formally mean here *predictors*, and hence the criterion for a good indicator will be the mean squared prediction error: $MSE = E(\Delta W - P)^2$. However, since little is known about the links between those measures, I confine myself just to *linear* predictors. Assuming that the regression function of ΔW on P is in fact linear (that would be the case if the distribution of $[\Delta W, P]$ is for example bivariate normal), then the MSE of the (best) linear predictor is just $\sigma^2(1 - \rho^2)$, where σ^2 stands for the variance of ΔW, and ρ^2 for the

---

20. In fact, the issue of age versus importance (closely related to de Solla Price's "immediacy factor") has commanded a great deal of attention in the scientometric literature; to the best of my knowledge, however, so far it has not been addressed with rigorous statistical tests (see for example Line, 1970, and Campbell and Nieves, 1979).

Table 5.2   Measures of Innovation and Other Data on CT Scanners

Year	ΔW	TW	R&D	# of firms	# of new brands	# of new adopters
1973	2.99	638	20.6[a]	3	1	16
1974	8.71	6,926	22.6	8	1	74
1975	1.51	1,503	59.7	12	4	216
1976	4.78	5,959	96.1	13	11	317
1977	0.94	997	79.7	14	14	328
1978	0.12	79	64.3	11	6	211
1979	0.14	73	56.1	9	5	209
1980	0.07	30	46.4	8	2	177
1981	0.18	79	37.9	8	3	101
1982	0.20	87	37.9	8	8	—

Note: The figures for ΔW, *TW*, and R&D are in constant 1982 $ millions.
[a]This figure refers to total R&D expenditures from 1968 through 1973.

correlation coefficient between ΔW and P (see Lindgren, 1976, pp. 476–77). Thus in probing the adequacy of alternative patent-based indicators, I shall use the size of the correlation coefficient as the sole criterion.[21]

The main hypotheses to be tested (note that they refer to a given technological field—or product class—as it evolves over time) are:

H1: Patent counts weighted by citations (*WPC*) are good indicators of the *value* of innovations as measured by ΔW (or *TW*), but simple counts (*SPC*) are not.

H2: Simple patent counts are good indicators of the *inputs* to the innovative process, as measured by R&D expenditures.

Table 5.2 presents the summary data (other than patents) to be used in testing these hypotheses; as we recall, ΔW stands for the incremental

21. A less formal way of presenting this is to say that since the maintained hypothesis is that the measures (ΔW, *TW*) accurately capture the value of innovations, the only remaining question is whether patents (which could be at best just an indirect manifestation of the same) closely follow the path of those variables over time. More pragmatically, with the small number of observations available it would have been very hard to estimate anything but simple correlations.

gains from innovation accruing to the representative buyer of CT, whereas *TW* refers to the total gains (all figures are taken from Chapters 2 and 4). For purposes of the statistical analysis the hypotheses have to be formulated in more detail, defining more precisely the scope of the patents counts and the time structure of their links with the measures of innovation. Regarding scope, should all patents in CT be included in the count, or just those granted to firms that were active in the market for CT scanners (the latter accounted for 66 percent of all patents and for 80 percent of all citations)? Since ΔW and *TW* were computed on the basis of the CT scanners actually marketed in the United States, we would expect those measures to be more highly correlated with the patents granted to manufacturers of CT. This assumption would not hold only if the "appropriability" of the patents issued to the other assignees were extremely low, that is, only if the manufacturers of CT scanners benefited from the innovations done by other inventors as much as they did from their own. The issue of timing is much more complex, and will be discussed in detail in the coming section.

5.4.1 *Application Date, Foreign Priority, and the Lag Structure*

Even if all agree that patents should be dated according to their application dates, it is still far from clear what sort of information those dates convey. This is because innovation is obviously not a single event but a continuous time process, starting from the formulation of a novel idea and ending with the introduction in the market of the product embedding that idea (hence with ΔW). Sometime along the way the inventor files for a patent application, presumably before the development stage is completed, but how much earlier, and what determines the length of the lag? Two of the main forces at work have to do, first, with the stringency of the application requirements set by the Patent Office, and second, with the technological characteristics and the competitive structure of the industry. The more stringent the requirements and the more intense the technological rivalry in the field, the shorter will be the lag between patent counts and ΔW. Beyond that, however, no general prior can be put forward regarding the expected lag. In principle the patent might be filed just before the innovation reaches the market or much before that; notice also that there is no reason for the lag to be constant over time.

There is, however, further information on dates that may shed light on the lag structure: in addition to the application date in the United States, many patents have a "foreign priority application date," and some make reference to earlier "Related U.S. Application Data."[22] To quote the Office of Technology Assessment and Forecast in relation to the former, "It is common to seek patent protection on a single invention in several countries . . . International multiple patenting has been facilitated by a treaty which permits applications filed in a foreign country within a year of filing in the home country to be accorded the home country filing date. However, the treaty requires that . . . the initially filed patent application must be identified by country, serial number and filing date, and that the 'priority' of this filing be claimed" (1977, p. 17).

Thus, for example, according to OTAF (1977) 30 percent of all patents granted in the United States in 1975 contain foreign priority data. In the case of patents in CT, 56 percent of them mention a foreign application date, with an average lag between it and the application date in the United States of fourteen months (see table 5.3).[23] Such a lag implies, quite simply, that the innovation process underlying the patents stretches back at least fourteen months longer than what could be inferred from the American application date. The lag is also consistent with the observation that patenting requirements are more exacting in the United States than in foreign countries, since it is often the case that the innovations had not been developed enough at the time of the foreign application for them to meet U.S. standards. Notice also from table 5.3 that the foreign-U.S. application lag was much longer in the initial years of CT: it took three-and-a-half years in 1973, dropping to one-and-a-half in 1974, and hovering around seven months from then on (those figures refer to patents to firms in CT). Figure 5.3, tracing the "genealogical tree" of the first patents taken by G. Hounsfield, the inventor of CT, throws light on those initial long lags and confirms

22. Sixteen percent of the patents in CT make reference to an earlier "related U.S. application," that is, they are designated as continuations of previous applications, which may have failed or given rise to other (related) patents. Unfortunately, I do not have the actual dates of those earlier applications, only the fact of a reference to them.

23. According to the regulations, the application in the foreign country has to be made *within* a year of the home country's filing date; indeed, some 80 percent of the patents with foreign priority were filed in the United States just before a year elapsed. The rest have a bridging "related U.S. application," meaning that within a year of the filing abroad a patent was indeed applied for in the United States, but it either failed or gave rise to another patent; in either case, the present patent, by being designated as a continuation of the related U.S. application, can still claim the foreign priority date.

Table 5.3   Lags between Foreign and American Patent Applications in CT, by Years

Year	% of patents with foreign priority	Mean lag (months)		
		All patents	Patents to firms in CT	Patents with foreign priority
1972	1.00	41.0	41.0	41.0
1973	1.00	41.3	41.3	41.3
1974	0.76	17.1	21.0	22.4
1975	0.48	6.0	5.8	12.6
1976	0.56	7.7	8.1	13.7
1977	0.64	6.8	7.2	12.6
1978	0.56	8.4	8.9	14.9
1979	0.54	7.1	4.9	13.1
1980	0.65	8.0	9.8	12.2
1981	0.60	8.1	6.6	13.6
1982	0.42	3.2	3.0	7.6
Average	0.56	7.8	8.2	14.1
Weighted[a] average	0.63	11.5	12.7	14.1

[a]Weighted by the number of citations of each patent.

the stringency of the American application requirements vis-à-vis those in the United Kingdom.[24] Figure 5.3 implies also that the innovations contained in those first patents were more general (hence indeed more important), in the sense that it took longer to embed them in demonstrably working—and useful—systems that could comply with the U.S. requirements for patentability.

24. The first U.S. application actually failed, even though it was filed one year *after* the first application in the United Kingdom. It then took Hounsfield more than two years of further development (in the course of which a first working prototype of a CT scanner was installed in a London hospital), before he could win a U.S. patent.

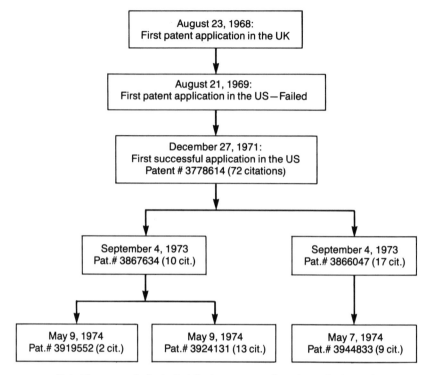

Note: The arrows indicate that the lower patents have been designated as continuations of the preceding patent document.

Figure 5.3 The First Patents in CT, by G. Hounsfield

Because the patenting requirements differ across countries, and because the array of the foreign-priority countries changed significantly over the period studied (the United Kingdom ceding its initial dominant place to Germany and Japan), it does not make sense to date all patents according to the *earliest* date appearing on them. Instead, I will still date them according to the American application date, so as to be able to interpret consistently whatever lag is found between patent counts and ΔW in light of the implied (uniform) standard. I can then superimpose on it the foreign-U.S. application lag (which, as table 5.3 reveals, varies by year), gaining some notion of the *minimal overall span* of the innovation process in CT.

Finally, it should be clear that the most serious limitation in this procedure is that the period studied is very short and does not allow for the estimation of any sort of lag structure, let alone of a changing lag. Thus the findings referring to the lag between patents and ΔW, obtained by maximizing pairwise correlations over the time dimension, should be regarded as tentative.

5.4.2 Testing the First Hypothesis

Table 5.4 presents the correlations between alternative versions of simple and weighted patent counts, and $\{\Delta W, TW\}$,[25] with the former variables lagged between 0 and 6 months.[26] The first and most important finding is that in all the cases considered, weighted patent counts are in effect correlated with the value measures of innovation whereas simple counts are not. Thus the first hypothesis is confirmed, and decisively so. Moreover, the correlations increase substantially as we narrow down the scope of the (weighted) counts to the patents granted to firms in CT. This supports the stated priors and implies, as suggested, that the patents awarded to other assignees did not quite become a "public good" (that is, appropriability was not nil).

The correlations peak when the patent counts are lagged just one quarter, declining monotonically as the lag increases (this is true for lags far beyond the six months shown in table 5.4).[27] Superimposing on this finding the mean foreign-U.S. application lag of 12.7 months found earlier (for patents to firms in CT, weighted by citations; see table 5.3), one obtains an overall innovation span, or lead time, of 16 months. This may strike us as rather short (although it is not clear against what standard one ought to judge it), but if so it would certainly be consistent with the intense technological rivalry that characterized the evolution of CT scanners.[28]

---

25. If we recall that ΔW refers to the incremental gains whereas TW stands for total gains, it is not clear a priori which of them is more relevant in the present context.

26. Although the variables refer to yearly figures, the lag can be varied by *monthly* increments because the patent data is virtually continuous in time. It is also important to note that since the ΔW series begins in 1973, I just added the 1972 (first) patent to the patent count of 1973; in other words, given that the ΔW figure for 1973 refers to the first CT scanner marketed, it obviously corresponds to the initial patents in the field, including the very first.

27. Because we simply added the 1972 patent to the 1973 patents in computing the correlations, the first lag was actually longer (about one year long), and the overall lag would increase from three to four months if one averaged that first lag with the rest.

28. The foreign-U.S. application lag declined from three-and-a-half years in 1973 to about seven months later on, so effective lead times were much longer at first.

Table 5.4   Correlations of Simple and Weighted Patent Counts with ΔW, *TW*

Lags	All patents		Patents to firms in CT	
	ΔW	*TW*	ΔW	*TW*
	Weighted counts			
Contemporary	0.509	0.587	0.616	0.626
	(0.13)[a]	(0.07)	(0.06)	(0.05)
3 months	0.513	0.635	*0.685*	*0.755*
	(0.13)	(0.05)	(0.03)	(0.01)
4 months	0.480	0.600	0.677	0.744
	(0.16)	(0.07)	(0.03)	(0.01)
6 months	0.317	0.466	0.495	0.605
	(0.37)	(0.17)	(0.15)	(0.006)
	Simple Counts			
Contemporary	−0.162	0.032	0.087	0.093
	(0.65)	(0.93)	(0.81)	(0.80)
3 months	−0.198	0.006	−0.076	0.131
	(0.58)	(0.99)	(0.83)	(0.72)
6 months	−0.283	−0.090	−0.175	0.027
	(0.43)	(0.81)	(0.63)	(0.94)

[a]Significance levels in parentheses.

Returning to the basic finding of this section (that weighted patent counts are highly correlated with ΔW), we can now (re)interpret the distribution of citation counts across patents as an implied distribution of the value of innovations. As shown in table 5.5, the observed distribution fits well with the received wisdom on this matter (see for example Pakes and Shankerman, 1984, and Pakes, 1986): it is very skewed, with almost half the patents never cited (hence of little ex-post value), and a lucky few being worth a great deal.[29] Thus, contrary to Scherer's pessimistic

29. Campbell and Nieves (1979) present the distribution of citations for all US patents issued from 1971 to 1978 (over 4 million patents), and Narin (1983) shows the distribution corresponding to 13,264 chemical and allied product patents issued in1975. Both look remarkably similar to the one for CT scanners. Unfortunately, the citation values in Campbell and Nieves (1979) go only up to 13+, and therefore I cannot be sure whether or not the distribution for CT is typical in its upper tail.

Table 5.5   Distribution of Patents According to Number of Citations

Number of citations	Number of patents	Percent of patents	Cumulative percent
0	215	47.1	47.1
1	78	17.1	64.3
2	54	11.8	76.1
3	35	7.7	83.8
4	21	4.6	88.4
5	10	2.2	90.6
6	15	3.3	93.9
7	8	1.8	95.6
8	3	0.7	96.3
9	3	0.7	96.9
10	2	0.4	97.4
12	1	0.2	97.6
13	2	0.4	98.0
14	1	0.2	98.2
16	1	0.2	98.5
17	2	0.4	98.9
19	1	0.2	99.1
20	1	0.2	99.3
21	1	0.2	99.6
25	1	0.2	99.8
72	1	0.2	100.0

observation that economists cannot expect to capture important innovations with patent data,[30] the results here show that citation counts can in fact span the whole range of innovations.

30. According to Scherer (1965), "patent statistics are likely to measure run-of-the-mill industrial inventive output much more accurately than they reflect the occasional strategic inventions which open up new markets and new technologies. The latter must probably remain the domain of economic historians." Of course he was absolutely right at the time, given the kind of data available then.

5.4.3 Nonlinearities in Citations

In constructing the weighting index I have implicitly assumed so far that a citation is worth as much as a patent; that is, the weights are linear in the number of citations. There may be, however, increasing or decreasing returns to the informational content of citations, in which case the weighting scheme would be nonlinear. This is of course an open empirical matter, to be decided by the closeness of association between the patent index and the benchmark values of ΔW and TW. Thus consider the more general specification

$$WPC_t(\alpha) = \sum_{i=1}^{n_t} (C_i^\alpha + 1) = n_t + \sum_{i=1}^{n_t} C_i^\alpha, \qquad \alpha > 0,$$

where WPC stands as before for weighted patent count and C_i for the number of citations to patent i. I want now to find α_1^* and α_2^* such that[31]

$$\alpha_1^* = \arg\max_\alpha \text{cor } [WPC_t(\alpha), \Delta W_t], \quad \text{and}$$

$$\alpha_2^* = \arg\max_\alpha \text{cor } [WPC_t(\alpha), TW_t].$$

The answers emerge clearly from table 5.6: $\alpha_1^* = 1.30$, and $\alpha_2^* = 1.10$, which means that there are in fact "increasing returns" to citations, and they manifest themselves more strongly in the context of the relationship of patent counts with ΔW, rather than with TW. Note that these results are robust, in that they obtain also in the absence of a lag, and when using counts of all patents rather than counts of patents to firms dealing in CT.[32] Moreover, as figure 5.4 shows, the highest correlations arrived at can indeed be taken as global maxima. In other words, the WPC's based upon patents to firms in CT, lagged one quarter, and using as exponents $\alpha_1 = 1.30$ and $\alpha_2 = 1.10$ dominate all other cases along the three dimensions considered here.

---

31. One could not have estimated these exponents by, say, running a regression in the logs, since the nonlinearity occurs in the citations to *each* patent, and not in the aggregate (weighted) patent count.

32. The actual maximized values of the exponents are somewhat higher in the latter case: $\alpha_1^* = 1.40$, and $\alpha_2^* = 1.30$. This may be related to the fact that the patents of firms in CT received more than their proportional share of citations.

Table 5.6 Correlations of WPC with ΔW and *TW*: Searching for Nonlinearities

| | Patents to firms in CT | | | | All patents | |
| | Contemporary | | Lagged 3 months | | Lagged 3 months | |
Exponent α	ΔW	*TW*	ΔW	*TW*	ΔW	*TW*
0.80	0.455	0.543	0.512	0.653	0.329	0.503
	(0.19)[a]	(0.10)	(0.13)	(0.04)	(0.35)	(0.14)
0.90	0.538	0.590	0.601	0.711	0.419	0.570
	(0.11)	(0.07)	(0.07)	(0.02)	(0.23)	(0.09)
1.00	0.616	0.626	0.685	0.755	0.513	0.635
	(0.06)	(0.05)	(0.03)	(0.01)	(0.13)	(0.05)
1.10	0.680	0.642	0.754	*0.777*	0.605	0.687
	(0.03)	(0.05)	(0.01)	(0.008)	(0.06)	(0.03)
1.20	0.721	0.635	0.798	0.770	0.684	0.719
	(0.02)	(0.05)	(0.006)	(0.009)	(0.03)	(0.02)
1.30	0.738	0.607	*0.813*	0.736	0.738	0.720
	(0.01)	(0.06)	(0.004)	(0.02)	(0.02)	(0.02)
1.40	0.730	0.560	0.800	0.677	0.760	0.689
	(0.02)	(0.09)	(0.006)	(0.03)	(0.01)	(0.03)
1.50	0.703	0.501	0.766	0.606	0.751	0.634
	(0.02)	(0.14)	(0.01)	(0.06)	(0.01)	(0.05)
1.60	0.663	0.436	0.718	0.527	0.719	0.562
	(0.04)	(0.21)	(0.02)	(0.11)	(0.02)	(0.09)

[a]Significance levels in parentheses.

The finding that $\alpha_i^* > 1$ is in itself important, and it provides further support to the claim that *WPC*'s convey a great deal of information on the value of innovations disclosed in patents[33]; in particular, it means that the marginal informational content of the *WPC*'s increases with the number of citations. The finding also implies that the variance in the value of patents is larger, and the distribution of those values more skewed, than could have been inferred from the simple count of citations (recall table 5.5).

33. This was a rather surprising result: originally I thought that there might be *diminishing* returns to citations—that citations may be given too generously and hence that their marginal informative value would be low and declining. Had that been the case, the role of *WPC*'s as indicators of innovations would have been weakened.

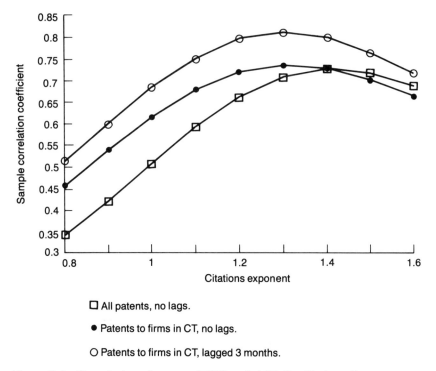

Figure 5.4   Correlations between WPC and $\triangle W$, for Various Exponents

As for the finding that $\alpha_1^* > \alpha_2^*$, we will recall that $\triangle W$ is a measure of the gains to the representative consumer from improvements in the set of available products, and therefore it amounts to a snapshot valuation of the innovations underlying those improvements, while TW multiplies $\triangle W$ by the number of consumers that benefit from the innovation at present and in the future. Thus the fact that $\alpha_1^* > \alpha_2^*$, and that cor $[WPC(\alpha_1^*), \triangle W] > \text{cor } [WPC(\alpha_2^*), TW]$, means that citations are more informative of the value of innovations as such than of the size of the market for the products embedding those innovations. This is a reassuring result, since we do expect that factors related to the technology itself (rather than to the market) will be dominant in the citing process.

5.4.4   The Second Hypothesis

This hypothesis, as we recall, states that simple patent counts would be good indicators of the inputs into the innovative process in a field, as reflected in R&D expenditures. The relationship between patents and R&D has been intensively scrutinized in past research,[34] and the results appear to be quite uniform, centering on the following "stylized facts": there is a strong statistical association between patents and R&D expenditures; this association appears to be mostly contemporaneous; and R&D explains a great deal of the *cross-sectional* variance in patenting, but not much of the variation in time. Much of this research has used short panels of firms' data, leading Griliches to conclude, in summing up, that "patents are a good indicator of differences in inventive activity across firms, but that short-term fluctuations in their numbers within firms have a large noise component in them". (Griliches, 1984, p. 3)

The second hypothesis can be seen as extending those results to the time dimension, that is, it also postulates a close association between patents and R&D, but within a given field along time, rather than across firms or industries. I resort again to simple correlations, and explore in detail the possible existence of lags. The main findings, summarized on table 5.7, are: first, there is indeed a high correlation between yearly patent counts and R&D, and a much weaker one between R&D and patents weighted by citations; thus the second hypothesis is amply confirmed. Second, the degree of association peaks when R&D is lagged just five months, supporting previous findings of short gestation lags. Third, the correlations are slightly higher for counts of all patents than for patents to firms in CT, suggesting some degree of spillover from the R&D done by manufacturers of CT to other asignees.

It is also worth reporting the following correlations, indicating that simple patent counts (*SPC*) tend to move together not just with R&D, but also with other manifestations of the "innovative action" taking place in a given field over time (all are contemporaneous; the data are taken from table 5.2):

cor (*SPC*, no. of firms in the CT market) = 0.858

cor (*SPC*, no. of new scanners introduced in the market) = 0.813

cor (*SPC*, no. of new adopters) = 0.913

The first two confirm that competition in this technologically progressive market was driven primarily by rivalry in innovation; the third reflects the impact of innovation on diffusion, that is, it indicates that the market expanded as the technology improved.

---

34. Many of the papers in Griliches (1984) have to do in one way or another with this issue; extensive references to previous works can also be found there.

Table 5.7 Correlations between Patent Counts and R&D

Lag	All patents		Patents to firms in CT	
	SPC[a]	WPC[b]	SPC	WPC
None	0.869	0.609	0.843	0.525
	(0.0002)[c]	(0.05)	(0.001)	(0.097)
3 months	0.919	0.591	0.912	0.495
	(0.0001)	(0.04)	(0.0001)	(0.102)
4 months	0.924	0.582	0.914	0.491
	(0.0001)	(0.05)	(0.0001)	(0.105)
5 months	*0.933*	0.577	*0.918*	0.483
	(0.0001)	(0.05)	(0.0001)	(0.112)
6 months	0.921	0.543	0.903	0.450
	(0.0001)	(0.07)	(0.0001)	(0.142)
1 year	0.831	0.248	0.794	0.152
	(0.0008)	(0.44)	(0.002)	(0.638)

[a]SPC: Simple Patent Counts.
[b]WPC: Weighted Patent Counts.
[c]Significance levels in parentheses.

5.5 The Patents-R&D-Patents Connection, and Other Extensions

Although hard evidence for this is difficult to come by, it has been widely observed that important innovations often generate a flurry of further innovative activity, which brings in turn a host of minor improvements. In fact, new products embedding truly novel technologies are usually crude and lacking at first, but improve gradually as a result of further research efforts.[35] In the present context this would imply the existence of a unidirectional link going from weighted patent counts (*WPC*) to R&D, probably with a substantial lag. Moreover, since we already know that simple patent counts (*SPC*) follow R&D after a five-month lag, we would also expect to observe a link between *WPC* and *SPC*, the lag between them being the sum of the lag between *WPC* and R&D, and

---

35. Indirect support for this contention can be found in the often noted claim that consumers are well aware of this process, and their ensuing technological expectations appear to play a key role in their decision of when to purchase a new or rapidly advancing product.

that between R&D and *SPC*. In other words, I have in mind a sort of self-propelling innovative cycle, in which important innovations (as reflected in high *WPC*) bring about further R&D aimed at implementing and perfecting them, and this in turn results in further patents. Some of the latter may prove to be important innovations (and thus collect many citations), opening up a new phase in the cycle.

Table 5.8 shows the correlations between *WPC*, R&D and *SPC*, allowing for various lags. First, notice that there is indeed a strong correlation between lagged *WPC* and R&D, peaking with a lag of nine months. Second, the correlation between *WPC* and *SPC* is highest when the two are

Table 5.8   The Patents-R&D-Patents Chain

Lag	Correlation of R&D with:		Correlation of SPC with:	
	WPC	SPC	WPC	SPC
+ 3 months	0.591 (0.04)[a]	0.919 (0.0001)	—	—
None	0.609 (0.05)	0.855 (0.0008)	0.701 (0.02)	1.00
− 4 months	0.711 (0.01)	0.834 (0.001)	0.784 (0.004)	0.969 (0.0001)
− 6 months	0.796 (0.003)	0.820 (0.002)	0.835 (0.001)	0.922 (0.0001)
− 7 months	0.819 (0.002)	0.810 (0.0025)	0.870 (0.0005)	0.917 (0.0001)
− 8 months	0.861 (0.0007)	0.806 (0.003)	0.854 (0.0008)	0.872 (0.0005)
− 9 months	*0.866* (0.0006)	0.772 (0.005)	0.853 (0.0009)	0.843 (0.001)
− 12 months	0.854 (0.0008)	0.674 (0.02)	0.875 (0.0004)	0.727 (0.01)
− 14 months	0.774 (0.005)	0.611 (0.05)	*0.935* (0.0001)	0.706 (0.02)
− 16 months	0.697 (0.02)	0.543 (0.08)	0.903 (0.0001)	0.649 (0.03)

[a]Significance levels in parentheses.

fourteen months apart, this corresponding exactly to the sum of the
$WPC \rightarrow$ R&D nine-month lag, and the R&D $\rightarrow$ *SPC* five-month gestation
lag. Notice also that the correlations between lagged *WPC* and R&D are
systematically higher than those between *SPC* and R&D, and hence the
chain of events is clearly of the form $WPC \rightarrow$ R&D $\rightarrow$ *SPC*, not *SPC* $\rightarrow$
R&D $\rightarrow$ *SPC*.

These findings have a strong "supply-push" flavor and evoke Schum-
peterian notions of innovation-induced cycles.[36] However, the short span
of the history of innovation in CT does not really allow one to make
causal inferences from the statistical associations that have been found,
as supply-push theories would imply. Still, it would be fair to say that
these results are at least consistent with the sort of self-propelling process
(or chain of events) sketched above.

As far as the intended extensions are concerned, the first has to do
with the question of whether patent data are also informative at a more
disaggregated level (for example, firms within a product class), and the
extent to which they may be indicative also of the private value of innovations (recall that ΔW refers to their social value). The idea is to have a
panel of sales by firms over time, with their own patents and patents by
everybody else as independent variables (I do have all the data needed
in the context of CT scanners). The basic model would be that of Spence
(1984), and one of the interesting issues that could be investigated in
such context is the degree of appropriability (the coefficient of others
firms' patents) prevalent in the industry. The second extension refers to
spillovers across sectors: a possible source to study this elusive issue may
be in cross-sectoral citations, that is, references to patents in the source
sector, appearing in patents belonging to the field that benefits from the
spillovers. In the case of CT scanners, for example, one would look into
citations to CT patents made in patents belonging to more recent imaging technologies, such as MRI, ultrasound, and positron emission
tomography.

5.6   The Usefulness of Patent Data: Concluding Remarks

Aside from the interest that the results presented in this chapter hold in
themselves, I hope that they will also serve to enhance the appeal of

36. Recent papers dealing with the supply-push hypothesis are Beggs (1984), Gort
and Wall (1986), and Griliches et al. (1988).

patent data as a research tool of vast potential. From a purely technical viewpoint, it is clear that the search techniques used here are the key to the realization of that potential: with their help one can overcome the classification problem and thus begin to unlock the wealth of information contained in the patent file.

The focus on narrowly defined product classes (very close to the economist's notion of markets), rather than on firms or industries as defined in the Standard Industrial Classification, entails a major advantage: patent counts by product classes appear to be good indicators in the *time* dimension, not only cross-sectionally as is the case with counts of firms' patents.[37] This may be of great significance because innovation is in essence a dynamic—hence a time-dependent—phenomenon. A closely related advantage is that patent data can be easily obtained all the way to the very beginning of a product class, whereas the gathering of conventional industry data usually starts only when a sector is well established. Thus patent counts and citations may play an important role in studying the very emergence of new markets, which seems to be the period when most of the innovative activity takes place (quite clearly, studies focused on mature industries are very likely to miss the bulk of the innovative segment). Moreover, the whys and hows of cross-sectional results regarding the structural characteristics of mature sectors (such as concentration, entry barriers, and so on) cannot really be understood except in light of how those sectors evolved into their observed equilibrium; again, the type of patent data used here seems to be particularly well suited to trace that process.

The results relating to lag structure (from patents to ΔW) underscore the importance of dating patents correctly and call for extra caution in interpreting such findings. The relatively long lags between foreign and U.S. applications suggest that the filing of patents in the United States occurs fairly late along the innovation process; this fact may help explain the pervasive finding of a contemporaneous relationship between patents and other indicators, such as R&D and the value of firms.

The close association of patents with R&D raises once again some questions as to the proper use (and interpretation) of either variable in empirical research. In accordance with the prevailing view, the results

---

37. As Griliches and coauthors (1988) point out in summing up previous research, both the fact that the R&D budgets of firms are typically stable over time, and that most firms take a small but highly variable number of patents per year, make it very difficult to trace innovative activity over time on the basis of firms' data.

here show that simple patent counts are certainly not to be regarded as a measure of innovative *output:* that requires the weighting by citations. Yet patents are not quite akin to an input either (as R&D is), since they also reflect, to some extent, "effort" and a modicum of technological success.

To understand the role of patents it may be helpful to think of them as working papers in economics (the analogy translates firms into economic departments, and industries into fields in economics). These papers are produced roughly in proportion to the number of faculty,[38] as patents are with respect to R&D. The fact is that it does not take much to get a patent, once the firm has an established R&D facility going, as it does not take much to write a working paper. Still, a larger number of patents presumably indicates more research effort by the R&D staff (as more papers would suggest that the faculty is working harder). Patent counts can thus be regarded as a more "refined" measure of innovative activity than R&D, in the sense that they incorporate at last part of the differences in effort, and filter out the influence of luck in the first round of the innovative process. On the pragmatic side, good R&D data are more difficult to obtain than patent data, and the latter have a wider coverage. Moreover, patent data are richer and finer, in that they are practically continuous in time and can be further classified by a variety of criteria. So there is plenty of room to expand the use of patent counts, while lowering at the same time the dependency upon hard-to-get R&D data.

The results that hold the greatest promise are those related to the use of citations, since they offer a quantitative indicator for a key variable that had virtually none, namely, the value of innovations. The marked skewness in the distribution of those values appears to be no longer an impediment to the use of patent data, but rather the main source of their usefulness. At the same time, this and all previous conclusions must remain tentative for the obvious reason that they are based upon the findings from a case study; future research may bring in more supportive evidence and further demonstrate the attractiveness of the proposed indicators.

---

38. Of course, as also happens with patents, that does not say much about the importance of the working papers: for that one would need information on whether and where they get published, the number of citations that they receive over time, and so on.

Appendix 5.1   Online Search and Retrieval of Patent Data from Large Databases

During the last decade or so we have witnessed the emergence and proliferation of a whole new field of sophisticated information services, consisting basically of: (1) very large computerized databases on a wide range of topics, to which one can gain easy access through a communications network (Telenet, Unitet) and vendor (DIALOG, BRS), using just a personal computer equipped with a modem; (2) online search facilities, that is, making use of the vendor's software search package to identify the desired documents (the packages consist essentially of basic boolean operators such as "and," "or,' "not," and a set of rules governing the use of key words, fields of search, and the like); (3) online retrieval capabilities that allow one to unload the selected data into the personal computer. Today there are thousands of databases containing millions of documents, and their use is spreading extremely fast, both in business and in the academic world (although economists appear to be particularly slow in taking advantage of those services).

For this work I have used the PATDATA database, through BRS. This database includes all patents issued in the United States from July 1975 to the present, it is updated weekly, and its current size is in the order of 800,000 patents. Each patent document consists of fifteen fields, such as application and issue dates, classification codes, assignee, a descriptive abstract of about 10 to 30 lines long, and so on. It is worth pointing out that DIALOG offers access to about ten databases on patents, covering most countries and going back in some areas to the 1960s.

The search for patents in a particular product field or industry can be done in a variety of ways: using key words pertaining to the product in question that may appear in the title or in the abstract, identifying a small set of relevant patent classification codes, locating assignees (typically firms) that are known to operate in the field, and so on. Needless to say, there is no single, well-defined method that would deliver with certainty all the patents in a given field, and only those. With much trial and error, the search process consists of sampling by a given set of initial criteria, examining the abstracts to determine whether the sampled patents do belong to the desired category, searching anew according to an updated set of criteria, and so forth. Since it is always possible to reexamine patents, the dominant concern early on is to minimize the probability of overlooking patents that may belong to the desired field. Once the desired set of patents has been identified and retrieved, it can yield the required data with the aid of a specially designed computer program (patents come in the form of full-text documents). At this point the actual analysis can begin.[39]

Appendix 5.2   A Statistical Analysis of Truncation and Age Effects

Testing age versus importance. The starting point is the specification of a hypothetical citation process by which all patents are of equal importance and hence the only differentiating factor is age. The distribution of citations thus generated could then be compared to the actual one, and the maintained hypothesis that all patents are equally important tested with the aid of a χ^2 test.

As a first step, patents are ordered chronologically according to their application date, and indexed with $i = 1, \ldots, N$ (N=456); note that i thus indicates the cumulative number of patents in CT applied for up to patent i. Denoting by p_{ij} the probability that patent i will be cited in patent j (for $i<j$), and by r_j the number of references to previous patents in CT appearing in patent j, one can now define all patents $1 \leqslant i < j$ to be iso-important if

$$(5.1) \quad p_{ij} = \frac{r_j}{j - 1} = p_j \quad j = 1, \ldots, N.$$

Thus equal importance is taken to mean that all patents applied for up to a point in time have the same probability of being cited by a subsequent patent. In other words, (5.1) means that the citations appearing in patent j are the result of r_j random drawings (without replacement) from a pool containing the $j-1$ patents that preceded it.[40] Because (5.1)

39. Narin (1983) suggested a similar search procedure, but one that relied upon proprietory search techniques and data, whereas part of the appeal of the approach here is easy access and widespread availability.

40. Clearly, this is not the only possible way of designing a citation process that would render patents of equal importance. But by defining p_{ij} to be independent of the time interval $(j-i)$, I implicitly favor the earlier patents, thus increasing the power of the test. That is, any plausible departure from (5.1) would have the probabilities decrease with $(j-i)$, making the distribution of expected citation more uniform, hence making it easier to reject the null hypothesis.

implies also time independence (for any $i < j < k$, p_{ik} is independent of p_{ij}), the expected number of citations of patent i can be computed simply as

$$(5.2) \quad C_i^e = E(C_i) = \sum_{j=i+1}^{N} p_j.$$

Obviously, $C_i^e > C_j^e$ for any $i < j$, meaning that older patents will get on average more citations than recent ones, just by virtue of their age. Notice also that p_j has to decrease eventually with j,[41] thus reinforcing the pure age effect. In other words, not only do later patents miss the earlier p_j's, but these probabilities tend to be the large ones, a fact that further reduces the expected number of citations of recent patents vis-à-vis older ones.

For purpose of performing the χ^2 test the data are aggregated by months, since it would be unreasonable to attach any significance (in the sense of differences in C_i^e) to the precise day of application. Indexing by τ and t the number of months elapsed since January 1972, the observed (or actual) number of citations is $C_t^0 = \sum_{i=1}^{n_t} C_i$, where n_t is the number of patents in month t. Similarly, and redefining (5.1) in monthly terms,

$$(5.1)' \quad p_\tau = \frac{\displaystyle\sum_{i=1}^{n_\tau} r_i}{\displaystyle\sum_{j=1}^{\tau-1} n_j}$$

and, accordingly,

$$(5.2)' \quad C_t^e = n_t \sum_{\tau=t+1}^{T} p_\tau$$

Table 5.9 presents the annualized values of the various variables needed for the test (the actual test, however, will be carried out with monthly, rather than the annual data). To illustrate, take for example the row

41. The assumption would not hold if r_j were to increase indefinitely over time, which is highly unlikely; in fact, in the case of CT scanners, r_j was quite stable over the entire period.

Table 5.9 Expected and Actual Number of Citations under the Iso-Importance Hypothesis

Year	Number of patents	Number of references	Pool of previous patents[a]	Prob. of being cited[b]	Total		Number of citations[c] Average	
					expected	actual	expected	actual
1972	1	0	0	0.00	6	72	5.96	72.00
1973	3	0	2	0.00	18	47	5.96	15.67
1974	21	8	15	0.67	116	178	5.52	8.48
1975	48	72	40	1.69	202	194	4.21	4.04
1976	66	104	102	1.05	196	169	2.97	2.56
1977	115	190	195	1.01	228	145	1.98	1.26
1978	71	181	287	0.64	84	55	1.18	0.77
1979	59	174	350	0.50	37	29	0.63	0.49
1980	26	65	397	0.16	8	7	0.31	0.27
1981	15	34	416	0.08	3	3	0.20	0.20
1982	12	23	429	0.05	2	1	0.17	0.08
1983	13	38	442	0.09	1	1	0.08	0.08
1984	6	12	452	0.03	1	0	0.17	0.00
Total	456	901		5.96	901	901	1.98	1.98

[a]Average over the year of the cumulative number of patents, computed on a monthly basis and lagged one month (rounded to the closest integer).
[b]Sum over the year of the monthly probabilities, calculated according to eq. (5.1)'.
[c]Rounded to the closest integer.

corresponding to 1975: the figure in column 4 means that under the iso-importance hypothesis, previous patents can be expected to get an average of 1.7 citations in the course of 1975. On the other hand, each of the patents applied for in 1975 can be expected to get from then on 4.21 citations under the same hypothesis (see column 7), whereas in fact they gathered an average of 4.04 citations. Since the average number of references is quite stable over time (that can be seen by dividing column 2 by column 1), the ever increasing pool of patents competing for citations (see column 3) becomes early on the dominant factor, bringing about a steady decline in the probability of being cited. Turning now to the test itself,

$$(5.3) \quad \chi^2 = \sum_{t=1}^{155} \frac{(C_t^e - C_t^0)^2}{C_t^e} = 1025 >> 148 = \chi^2_{(111)} \quad \alpha = 0.01.$$

Thus the hypothesis that the observed distribution of citations is due to age alone is strongly rejected. As is to be expected, the largest discrepancies between actual and expected values occur at the very beginning of the period. In particular, the values for the first patent are $C_1^0 = 72$, $C_1^e = 5.96$, and hence $(C_1^e - C_1^0)^2/C_1^e = 731$, which amounts to 3/4 of the computed χ^2. Since this first patent can be regarded in many ways as an exception, the test was redone after deleting it, and again the null hypothesis is rejected by a wide margin.

Assessing the truncation bias. The other potential problem in this context is that the unavoidable truncation of the data might induce a bias in the citation counts. Of course, the further back in the past the period studied, the less reason for concern. For a given distance in time, though, the extent of the bias will be determined by the behavior of citation lags and by the rate of new patent arrivals after the date of search. Citation lags refer to the time elapsed between the dates of the citing and of the cited patent: the shorter the interval, the less severe the problem will be. Table 5.10 presents the distribution of citation lags by year of the cited patents: for example, the 1975–1977 patents were subsequently cited 508 times, 12.6 percent of those citations occurring during the first year following the application date, 37.4 percent in the course of the second year, and so forth, the mean lag being of almost three years. Note that the frequency distribution of citation lags for all patents is very skewed to the left, most citations occurring within the first three to four years

Table 5.10   Frequency Distribution of Citations Lags, by Year of Cited Patent

Lag (years)[a]	1972–74	1975–77	1978–80	1981–82	All patents
1	2.0	12.6	7.7	25.5	8.7
2	15.8	35.6	37.4	75.0	29.4
3	23.2	25.4	19.8	0	24.0
4	22.6	15.2	12.1	0	17.2
5	18.2	4.5	13.2	0	9.9
6	9.1	3.1	6.6	0	5.4
7	4.4	2.0	3.3	0	2.9
8	3.0	1.4	0	0	1.8
9	1.0	0.2	0	0	0.4
10	0.7	0	0	0	0.2
Number of citations	297	508	91	4	900
Mean lag (years)	4.1	2.9	3.2	1.8	3.3

[a]The lags have been computed on the basis of monthly data, so that a one-year lag means the interval 0–11 months, a three-year lag, 24–35 months, and so on.

after a patent has been applied for, and the process dwindling down to a trickle after five to six years.[42] In particular, this is true for the distribution of lags of the 1975–1977 patents, which is arguably the most representative period in this context. As for the maximum lag, it seems quite certain that it does not exceed ten years, judging from the evidence of the initial years (1972–1974), for which the maximum lag could have been significantly longer (eleven to fourteen years).

So far the qualitative evidence seems to indicate that the truncation problem is not too severe; still, we need actual estimates of the biases in order to make a final judgment. Denote by f_τ the frequency distribution

42. Campbell and Nieves (1979) report longer lags for the case of catalytic converters, but theirs refer to all citations (which would indeed have longer lags) rather than to "within citations" only, as is the case here.

of citation lags; then if year t patents are to receive (on average) C_t citations per patent, f_τ stands for the percentage of those citations to be received after τ years (obviously, $\sum\limits_{\tau=t}^{\infty} f_\tau = 1$). Likewise, define $c_{t\tau} = f_\tau C_t$ and $g_{t\tau} = c_{t\tau}/n_\tau$, where n_τ is as before the total number of patents in year τ. Now, suppose that because of truncation one can actually obtain only a fraction h_τ of them; then, assuming that $g_{t\tau}$ is invariant with respect to h_τ (that is, that citations to year t patents are randomly distributed among the n_τ patents), the observed average number of citations to year t patents will be: $c^0_{t\tau} = g_{t\tau}h_\tau n_\tau = h_\tau f_\tau C_t$. Thus given the sequences $\{h_\tau, f_\tau\}$, one can compute for each year the fraction $v_t = \sum\limits_{\tau=t}^{\infty} h_\tau f_\tau$, that is, v_t stands for the percentage of citations that patents in year t can be expected to receive, out of the total that they would have received had it not been for the truncation of the data.

The figures for h_τ are obtained from the granting-application lags shown in section 5.3; for example, $h_{83} = 0.76$, $h_{85} = 0.23$, and so on (obviously, for $\tau \leqslant 81$, $h_\tau = 1.00$, and for $\tau > 86$, $h_\tau = 0$); those for f_τ are a slight variation of the citation lags displayed in table 5.10.[43] The results are as follows:

Year of cited patents	v_t	Actual citations	Citations missing (rounded)	Citations, fraction missing
up to 1975	1.000	491	0	0.00
1976	0.998	169	0	0.00
1977	0.990	145	1	0.01
1978	0.969	55	2	0.04
1979	0.930	29	2	0.07
1980	0.861	7	1	0.14
1981	0.732	3	1	0.33
1982	0.527	1	1	1.00

43. The citation lags were computed here as: year of citing patent − year of cited patent, rather than according to their respective months, as in table 5.10. The figures for v_t shown in the table are the averages of two values, one computed on the basis of the distribution f_τ corresponding to the 1975–1977 patents, and a second on the basis of the f_τ's for all patents.

We do miss a few citations because of the truncation of the data; more important, there is the expected truncation *bias,* in the sense that the fraction of missing citations to later patents is much larger than to earlier ones. Notice, however, that the absolute expected number of missing citations is very small and that, even if the bias was somehow underestimated in those calculations by a factor of 2, the true citations count would still differ only slightly from the count used here. Thus it is clear that the truncation problem is mostly inconsequential for the computations and findings presented above.

Finally, to press the truncation issue further, I asked the following question: given that the above calculations are done on the basis of averages, could it not be that one or more of the patents applied for in, say, 1982, actually turned out to be very important, but went undetected because only four years of granted patents had elapsed? To be sure, one cannot rule it out altogether, but as the following exercise indicates, such possibility is very unlikely. I took the three patents applied for in 1973 (each of which received a large number of citations) and counted the number of citations that they would have been given if only the patents granted up to the end of 1977 had been available, thus replicating the present situation vis-à-vis the 1982 patents. The partial count for the first patent was of 7 citations versus a true count of 11, of 5 versus 18 for the second, and of 8 versus 21 for the third, meaning that the importance of those patents would have been recognized right away. I repeated the exercise with the latest two patents to receive more than 10 citations each (both were applied for in 1976), obtaining similar results: the restricted count was of 16 citations versus a total of 20 for one, and of 6 versus 13 for the other. These findings are important not so much for the statistical analysis, but rather in that they confirm that we get an accurate description of the evolution of the CT scanners over time. In other words, it is very unlikely that some major innovation occurred in the field of CT in the early 1980s, and the patent data failed to detect it because of truncation. Instead, the field seems to be lingering on, as figure 5.2 shows, giving way to MRI and other rising technologies.

References

Alexander, Arthur J., and Bridger M. Mitchell. 1985. "Measuring Technological Change of Heterogeneous Products." *Technological Forecasting and Social Change* 27(2/3):161–195.

American Hospital Association. 1977. *CT Scanners—A Technical Report.* Chicago: American Hospital Association.

Beggs, J. J. 1984. "Long-Run Trends in Patenting." In *R&D, Patents, and Productivity,* ed. Z. Griliches. Chicago: University of Chicago Press.

Berggren, Ulf. 1985. "CT Scanning and Ultrasonography: A Comparison of Two Lines of Development and Dissemination." *Research Policy* 14(4):213–223.

Berndt, E., J. Hausman, B. Hall, and R. Hall. 1974. "Estimation and Inference in Non-Linear Structural Models." *Annals of Economic and Social Measurement* 3(4):653–665.

Bradford, D. F., and C. G. Hildebrandt. 1977. "Observable Preferences for Public Goods." *Journal of Public Economics* 8(2):111–131.

Bresnahan, Timothy. 1986. "Measuring the Spillovers from Technical Advance: Mainframe Computers in Financial Services." *American Economic Review* 76(4):742–755.

Brooks, R. A., and G. DiChiro. 1976. "Principles of Computer Assisted Tomography (CAT) in Radiographic and Radioisotopic Imaging." *Physics in Medical Biology* 21(5):689–732.

Brown, James N., and Harvey S. Rosen. 1982. "On the Estimation of Structural Hedonic Price Models." *Econometrica* 50(3):765–768.

Buenger, Richard E., and Michael S. Huckman. 1975. "Computed Tomography Survey." Chicago: Rush-Presbyterian-St. Luke's Medical Center. Unpublished.

Campbell, R. S., and A. L. Nieves. 1979. "Technology Indicators Based on Patent Data: The Case of Catalytic Converters. Phase I Report: Design and Demonstration." Battelle, Pacific Northwest Laboratories.

Carpenter, M. P., F. Narin, and P. Woolf. 1981. "Citation Rates to Technologically Important Patents." *World Patent Information* 3(4):160–163.

Cole, J. R., and S. Cole. 1973. *Social Stratification in Science.* Chicago: University of Chicago Press.

Cormack, A. M. 1963. "Representation of a Function by Its Line Integrals, with Some Radiological Applications." *Journal of Applied Physics* 34(9):2722–2727.

——— 1964. "Representation of a Function by Its Line Integrals, with Some Radiological Applications, II." *Journal of Applied Physics* 35(10):2908–2913.

Cowling, K., and A. J. Rayner. 1970. "Price, Quality, and Market Share." *Journal of Political Economy* 78(6):1292–1309.

Cummins, Clint, and Bronwyn Hall. 1982. "The R&D Master File Documentation." Cambridge, Mass.: National Bureau of Economic Research, unpublished manuscript.

Deaton, Angus, and John Muellbauer. 1980. *Economics and Consumer Behavior.* Cambridge: Cambridge University Press.

Dhrymes, Phoebus J. 1971. "Price and Quality Changes in Consumer Capital Goods: An Empirical Study." In *Price Indexes and Quality Change,* ed. Z. Griliches. Cambridge, Mass.: Harvard University Press.

Diewert, Erwin W. 1987. "Index Numbers." In *The New Palgrave: A Dictionary of Economics,* vol. 2, ed. J. Eatwell, M. Milgate, and P. Newman. London, Macmillan, 767–780.

Dodson, E. N. 1985. "Measurement of State of the Art and Technological Advance." *Technological Forecasting and Social Change* 27(2/3):129–146.

Ellis, P., G. Hepburn, and C. Oppenheim. 1978. "Studies on Patent Citation Networks." *Journal of Documentation* 34:12–20.

Epple, Dennis. 1987. "Hedonic Prices and Implicit Markets: Estimating Demand and Supply Functions for Differentiated Products." *Journal of Political Economy* 95(1):59–80.

Evaluation of the Effects of Certificate of Need Programs. 1981. Vols. I, II, and III. Report prepared for the Department of Health and Human Services, Public Health Service, Health Resources Administration. Brookline, Mass.: Policy Analysis; Cambridge, Mass.: Urban Systems Research and Engineering.

Fisher, Franklin M., and Karl Shell. 1972. *The Economic Theory of Price Indices: Two Essays on the Effects of Taste, Quality, and Technological Change.* New York: Academic Press.

Goldman, Steven M. 1980. "Consistent Plans." *Review of Economic Studies* 47(3):533–537.

Gorman, W. M. 1959. "Separable Utility and Aggregation." *Econometrica* 27(3):469–481.

Gort, M., and R. A. Wall. 1986. "The Evolution of Technologies and Investment in Innovation." *Economic Journal* 96:741–757.

Griliches, Zvi. 1958. "Research Costs and Social Returns: Hybrid Corn and Related Innovations." *Journal of Political Economy* 66(5):419–431.

——— ed. 1971. *Price Indexes and Quality Change*. Cambridge, Mass.: Harvard University Press.

——— 1979. "Issues in Assessing the Contribution of Research and Development to Productivity Growth." *Bell Journal of Economics* 10(1):92–116.

——— 1984. *R&D, Patents, and Productivity* (ed.) Chicago: University of Chicago Press.

Griliches, Zvi, Bronwyn H. Hall, and Ariel Pakes. 1988. "R&D, Patents, and Market Value Revisited: Is There a Second Technological Opportunity Factor?" Cambridge, Mass.: National Bureau of Economic Research, Working Paper No. 2624.

Hanemann, W. M. 1984. "Discrete/Continuous Models of Consumer Demand." *Econometrica* 52(3):541–561.

Hausman, Jerry, and Daniel McFadden. 1981. "Specification Tests for the Multinomial Logit Model." Cambridge, Mass.: M.I.T., Working Paper #292.

Hausman, Jerry, and David A. Wise. 1978. "A Conditional Probit Model for Qualitative Choice: Discrete Decisions Recognizing Interdependence and Heterogeneous Preferences." *Econometrica* 46(2):403–426.

A Health Planning Document: CT Scanning Systems. 1975. Report prepared for the Health Resources Administration. Cambridge, Mass.: Arthur D. Little.

Heckman, J. 1981. 'Statistical Models for the Analysis of Discrete Panel Data." In *Structural Analysis of Discrete Data*, ed. C. Manski and D. McFadden. Cambridge, Mass.: M.I.T. Press.

Hensher, David A., and Lester W. Johnson. 1981. *Applied Discrete Choice Modelling*. New York: Wiley.

Krantz, D., D. Luce, P. Suppes, and A. Tversky. 1971. *Foundations of Measurement*, vol. 1. New York: Academic Press.

Kuznets, Simon. 1962. "Inventive Activity: Problems of Definition and Measurement." In *The Rate and Direction of Inventive Activity: Economic and Social Factors* (Universities-National Bureau Conference Series No. 13). Princeton, N.J.: Princeton University Press.

Lancaster, Kelvin J. 1971. *Consumer Demand: A New Approach*. New York: Columbia University Press.

———— 1979. *Variety, Equity, and Efficiency.* New York: Columbia University Press.

Lieberman, M. B. 1987. "Patents, Learning by Doing, and Market Structure in the Chemical Processing Industries." *International Journal of Industrial Organization* 5(3):257–276.

Lindgren, B. W. 1976. *Statistical Theory.* New York: Macmillan.

Line, M. B. 1970. "The Half-Life of Periodical Literature: Apparent and Real Obsolescence." *Journal of Documentation* 26:46–52.

Maddala, G. S. 1977. *Econometrics.* New York: McGraw-Hill.

Mansfield, E., J. Rapoport, A. Romeo, S. Wagner, and G. Beardsley. 1977. "Social and Private Rates of Return from Industrial Innovation." *Quarterly Journal of Economics* 91(2):221–240.

Mansfield, Edwin. 1968. *Industrial Research and Technological Innovation: An Econometric Analysis.* New York: Norton.

McFadden, Daniel. 1981. "Econometric Models of Probabilistic Choice." In *Structural Analysis of Discrete Data with Econometric Applications,* ed. C. Manski and D. McFadden. Cambridge, Mass.: M.I.T. Press.

———— 1984. "Econometric Analysis of Qualitative Response Models." In *Handbook of Econometrics,* vol. II, ed. Z. Griliches and M. D. Intrilligator. New York: North Holland.

Menger, Carl. 1950. *Principles of Economics.* Glencoe, Ill.: Free Press.

Milgrom, Paul, and John Roberts. 1986. "Price and Advertising Signals of Product Quality." *Journal of Political Economy* 94(4):796–821.

Muellbauer, John. 1974. "Household Production Theory, Quality and the 'Hedonic Technique'." *American Economic Review* 64:977–994.

Narin, F. 1976. "Evaluative Bibliometrics: The Use of Publication and Citation Analysis in the Evaluation of Scientific Activity." Cherry Hill, New Jersey: *Computer Horizons, Inc.*

———— 1983. "Patent Citation Analysis as an Analytical Tool in Marketing Research." CHI Research / Computer Horizons, Inc.

Narin, F., and P. Wolf. 1983. "Technological Performance Assessments Based on Patents and Patent Citations." CHI Research / Computer Horizons, Inc.

National Academy of Sciences, Institute of Medicine. 1977. *Computed Tomographic Scanning, A Policy Statement.* Washington, D.C.: IOM.

National Science Foundation. 1981. *Only One Science.* 12th Annual Report of the National Science Board. Washington, D.C.: U.S. Government Printing Office.

Office of Technology Assessment and Forecast, U.S. Department of Commerce, Patent and Trademark Office. 1975. *Fifth Report.* Washington D.C.: U.S. Government Printing Office.

———— 1976. *Sixth Report.* Washington D.C.: U.S. Government Printing Office.

———— 1977. *Seventh Report.* Washington D.C.: U.S. Government Printing Office.

Office of Technology Assessment, U.S. Congress. 1976. *Development of Medical Technology: Opportunities for Assessment.* Washington, D.C.: U.S. Government Printing Office.

———— 1978. *Policy Implications of the Computed Tomography (CT) Scanner.* Washington, D.C.: U.S. Government Printing Office.

———— 1981. *Policy Implications of the Computed Tomography (CT) Scanner: An Update.* Washington, D.C.: U.S. Government Printing Office.

Otha, Makoto, and Zvi Griliches. 1976. "Automobile Prices Revisited: Extensions of the Hedonic Hypothesis." In *Household Production and Consumption,* ed. N. E. Terleckyj. New York: N.B.E.R.

Pakes, A. 1986. "Patents as Options: Some Estimates of the Value of Holding European Patent Stocks." *Econometrica* 54(4):755–784.

Pakes, A., and M. Schankerman. 1984. "The Rate of Obsolescence of Patents, Research Gestation Lags, and the Private Rate of Return to Research Resources." In *R&D, Patents, and Productivity,* ed. Z. Griliches. Chicago: University of Chicago Press.

Palmquist, 1984. "Estimating the Demand for the Characteristics of Housing." *The Review of Economics and Statistics* 66(3):394–404.

Peleg, Bezalel, and Menahem E. Yaari. 1973. "On the Existence of a Consistent Course of Action when Tastes Are Changing." *Review of Economic Studies* 40:391–401.

Price, D. J. de Solla. 1963. *Little Science, Big Science.* New Haven, Conn.: Yale University Press.

———— 1975. *Science since Babylon.* New Haven, Conn.: Yale University Press.

"React Forum: Special Report on the CT Forum Study." 1978. *Radiology/Nuclear Medicine Magazine.*

Rosen, Sherwin. 1974. "Hedonic Prices and Implicit Markets: Product Differentiation in Pure Competition." *Journal of Political Economy* 82(1):34–55.

Rosenberg, Nathan. 1976. *Perspectives on Technology.* Cambridge: Cambridge University Press.

———— 1982. *Inside the Black Box: Technology and Economics.* Cambridge: Cambridge University Press.

Russell, Louise B. 1979. *Technology in Hospitals: Medical Advances and Their Diffusion.* Washington D.C.: The Brookings Institution.

Rust, John. 1987. "Optimal Replacement of GMC Bus Engines: An Empirical Model of Harold Zurcher." *Econometrica* 55:999–1035.

References

Scherer, F. 1965. "Firm Size, Market Structure, Opportunity, and the Output of Patented Innovations." *American Economic Review* 55:1097–1123.

——— 1984. "Using Linked Patent and R&D Data to Measure Interindustry Technology Flows." In *R&D, Patents, and Productivity*, ed. Z. Griliches. Chicago: University of Chicago Press.

Schmookler, Jacob. 1966. *Invention and Economic Growth*. Cambridge, Mass.: Harvard University Press.

Schumpeter, Joseph. 1939. *Business Cycles*. New York: Harper and Row.

Shapiro, Carl. 1983. "Premiums for High Quality Products as Returns to Reputations." *Quarterly Journal of Economics* 98(4):659–680.

Small, Kenneth A., and Harvey S. Rosen. 1981. "Applied Welfare Economics with Discrete Choice Models." *Econometrica* 49(1):105–130.

Spence, Michael A. 1973. "Price Quality, and Quantity Interdependencies." Center for Research in Economic Growth. Stanford, Calif.: Stanford University, Memorandum #161. Unpublished.

——— 1975. "Monopoly, Quality, and Regulation." *The Bell Journal of Economics* 6(2):417–429.

——— 1984. "Cost Reduction, Competition, and Industry Performance." *Econometrica* 52(1):101–121.

Technological Forecasting and Social Change. 1985. Complete May issue 27(2/3).

Trajtenberg, Manuel. 1979. "Quantity Is All Very Well But Two Fiddles Don't Make a Stradivarius: Aspects of Consumer Demand for Characteristics." Jerusalem: The Maurice Falk Institute for Economic Research in Israel, Discussion Paper No. 1008.

——— 1983. "Dynamics and Welfare Analysis of Product Innovations." Ph.D. diss. Cambridge, Mass.: Harvard University.

——— 1984. "The Use of Multivariate Regression Analysis in Contrast-Detail Studies of CT Scanners." *Medical Physics* 11(4):456–464.

Trajtenberg, Manuel, and Shlomo Yitzhaki. 1989. "The Diffusion of Innovations: A Methodological Reappraisal." *The Journal of Business and Economic Statistics* 7(1):35–47.

Triplett, Jack E. 1975. "The Measurement of Inflation: A Survey of Research on the Accuracy of Price Indexes." In *Analysis of Inflation*, ed. P. H. Earl. Lexington, Mass.: Lexington Books.

von Wëizsacker, Carl C. 1971. "Notes on Endogenous Change of Tastes." *Journal of Economic Theory* 3(4):345–372.

Willig, R. D. 1978. "Incremental Consumer's Surplus and Hedonic Price Adjustment." *Journal of Economic Theory* 17(2):227–253.

Wolinsky, Asher. 1983. "Prices as Signals of Product Quality." *Review of Economic Studies* 50(4):647–658.

Index